Art and Social T

Art and Social Theory

Sociological Arguments in Aesthetics

AUSTIN HARRINGTON

polity

First published in 2004 by Polity Press Ltd.

Polity Press
65 Bridge Street
Cambridge CB2 1UR, UK

Polity Press
350 Main Street
Malden, MA 02148, USA

A catalogue record for this book is available from the British Library.

Library of Congress Cataloging-in-Publication Data

Harrington, Austin, 1970–
    Art and social theory : sociological arguments in
    aesthetics / Austin Harrington.
        p. cm.
    Includes bibliographical references and index.
    ISBN 0-7456-3038-3 (hb : alk. paper) – ISBN 0-7456-3039-1
    (pb : alk. paper)
    1. Arts and society.   2. Arts – Philosophy.   I. Title.

    NX180.S6H324 2004
    306.4′7–dc21   2003013220

Typeset in 10.5 on 12pt Plantin
by Graphicraft Limited, Hong Kong
Printed and bound in Great Britain by
TJ International, Padstow, Cornwall

For further information on Polity, visit our website: www.polity.co.uk

Contents

Contents

Contents

Illustrations

Acknowledgements

I am very grateful to two anonymous referees for Polity Press who read an earlier version of the text of this book. Their comments were enormously useful in helping me improve the argument of the book. I also thank John Thompson, Carolyn Twigg, Rachel Kerr and Ann Bone at Polity Press. I am grateful for conversations with Hans-Peter Müller, Alan Scott and Richard A. Peterson, and I particularly thank Richard A. Peterson for some generous bibliographical recommendations.

I wrote parts of this book while I held research fellowships from the Leverhulme Trust and the European University Institute between August 2001 and June 2003. The book is not a product of the projects for which I officially held these fellowships but I would like to thank the Leverhulme Trust and the European University Institute for the opportunity to devote a part of my free research time to work on the book. I also thank the staff of the Internationales Forschungszentrum Kulturwissenschaften in Vienna for use of facilities while I held the position of research associate there in 2001–2.

Introduction

Sociological studies of the arts today are a broad and burgeoning field. They include approaches in art history and criticism, in cultural sociology and anthropology, in film and media studies and musicology, as well as in literary theory and criticism and philosophical aesthetics. This book addresses some of the most central debates of social theorists and sociologists about the place of the arts in society and the sociological significance of aesthetics. Among the leading topics of our discussion will be questions such as the following. What is art, from the point of view of social analysis? Can art be defined? How do we know whether or not something is art? Does art consist in universally recognizable qualities, or is art simply what different cultural institutions declare to be art? How are decisions about what counts as art influenced by social power? Can we speak of geniuses and masterpieces, or are these patriarchal constructions? How is art funded, produced and consumed? What is art's relation to religion, myth, politics, morality and ideology? What is it to judge a work of art as 'beautiful' or 'good'? How are tastes in art differentiated by social class, status and education? Can art bring about a better society? How does art relate to entertainment and popular culture? How is art transformed under modernity – and 'postmodernity'?

We will need to bear in mind a few preliminary considerations before beginning our substantive responses to these questions in chapter 1.

We must first emphasize that in selecting 'art' as our central subject of discussion, this book makes no a priori discrimination in favour of what is called 'fine art' or 'high culture' above what is variously called 'popular culture', 'low culture' or 'mass culture'.

The book supposes that what is called 'art' must be interrogated in the context of the much wider social domain known as 'culture'. But the book argues that prosecuting this interrogation is not itself prejudiced by the book's practical concentration on the thematic of 'art'. The book cannot address all sociological studies of culture in general.

Second, we must emphasize that in speaking of 'art' in the singular, the book makes no assumptions about a unitary singular *concept* of art. We will argue that a unified singular *concept* of art cannot be defined. Many commentators today understandably prefer to speak of 'the arts' in the plural rather than of 'art' in the singular. However, we will argue that it is still possible and legitimate to think of art *in a generic sense*. We will argue that it is still legitimate to speak of 'art' in ordinary language as making up a grammatically coherent linguistic *genus*. Clearly there are many different arts forms that make up this genus. There are the visual arts of painting, drawing, sculpture, photography and architecture; there are the performing arts of music, drama and dance; and there are the literary arts of poetry, prose and criticism; and there are combinations of these arts such as opera and film – to name only some of the most historically established forms. All of these forms generate their own sets of aesthetic questions, and all of them have attracted around them their own specialized bodies of criticism and theory. But we will argue that these forms are still capable of being thought about in a generic sense. Although most of our empirical analyses will be based on visual art forms, and to a certain extent on literary art forms, we will seek to show how sociological understanding of art in general is possible.

Third, in speaking of 'sociological studies of the arts', the book will prefer to avoid reference to any such thing as '*the* sociology of art'. Most commentators today tend not to use this locution because it suggests the notion of a single domain of disciplinary authority over sociological understandings of art. Today there exists a plurality of approaches to studying art 'sociologically', as much within the institution of sociology as within other disciplines such as art history, literary studies and cultural studies. All subsequent references to 'sociology of the arts' or 'sociology of art' will therefore occur in this book *without* the definite article.

But we will also prefer to avoid speaking of '*the* sociology of art' for a further, related reason. A central conviction of this book is that the grammatical construction denoted by the genitive '*of*' in 'sociology of art' gives excessive semantic prominence to the idea of art as an *object* for social science. We will argue that this genitive construction gives too much prominence to the idea of art as an object over which sociology exercises its independent scientific authority. In place of this genitive construction, we will prefer to use a more conjunctive construction. We will prefer to speak of art *and* social theory. To speak of art *and* social theory is to give support to the idea that art and social theory form *equal partners in a joint-venture of cognition of the world*. This is to say several things.

First it is to say that art is not understood properly when it is explained wholly and exclusively in terms of social conventions, social institutions and social power relations. We will describe any approach that attempts to explain art wholly and exclusively in terms of social conventions, institutions and power relations as guilty of methodological reductionism and methodological imperialism. To reject reductionism and imperialism in sociology of the arts is to insist that all explanations of the actions and experiences of producers and spectators of art must, in principle, be capable of recognition by these actors as valid interpretations of their own actions and experiences. To borrow a phrase of Max Weber's, all explanations in sociology of the arts must be 'meaningfully adequate' (*sinnadäquat*) to the lived experience of the individuals whose engagements with art are in question (Weber 1978: 20). Reductionist and imperialist approaches disregard the authority of producers and spectators of art over meaningful accounts of their own actions and experiences. They reduce participants' reports about their own actions and experiences to statements about them to which the participants could never conceivably give their assent, even when the participants are imagined as capable of entering on a process of theoretical self-reflection and theoretical dialogue with their sociological interpreters.

More radically, to speak of art and social theory as equal partners is to say that art represents a source of existential social knowledge that is of its own worth and is not inferior to the knowledge of social science. It is to say that there are certain things that art can tell us about society that social science cannot tell us; and further that there are certain *ways* in which art can tell us about things in society that a social-scientific way of telling us about these things cannot replicate and cannot claim to supersede. Novels, plays, films, paintings and drawings tell us different things about social life from the things a piece of sociological research can tell us about social life, and to the extent that they tell us these different things, they tell us *more things*. To be sure, novels, plays, films, paintings and drawings can be deceptive. They may not 'tell the truth', in any ordinary sense of truth as correspondence-to-the-facts. They are often referred to as works of 'fiction'. But works of art can be illuminating in their deception. They can be enlightening in their fictivity; and they can tell a truth that is of a different order from the truth of correspondence-to-the-facts. The knowledge they can convey about society is no substitute for the methodical knowledge of social science; but neither is it inferior or subordinate to the latter. Works of art should not therefore be viewed as telling us things about society always only in a documentary way, as confirmations of some more scientifically definable set of facts. The knowledge art can impart to us about the meaning of our lives in society is *sui generis*.

Further, to speak of art and social theory as equal partners is to say that art's reserves of knowledge for life in society should be taken into consideration by social scientists in the respects in which they relate their disciplinary projects to disciplinary projects in humanities disciplines. In this book, we will define social theory as that agency of reflection which relates sociology as a social science discipline to art history, literary criticism and philosophy as humanities disciplines. We will argue that social theory mediates between social-scientific methods of *value-distanciation* and humanistic practices of critical *value-appraisal* and *value-affirmation*. We will argue that social theory informs ways in which valuations of works of art are made in humanities disciplines by supplying observations about empirical processes of value-construction in real social contexts of cultural and historical life. Social theory refers valuations of works of art to social facts about different changing contexts of social institutions, social conventions, social perception and social power. But we will argue that social theory cannot *derive* valuations of works of art from social facts. Social theory cannot itself generate aesthetic judgements about works of art. Social theory can analyse and interpret value but it cannot itself ground value.

To say that social theory mediates between value-distanciation and value-affirmation is to assert two things. On the one hand, it is to assert that strict value-neutrality, or 'value-freedom', is not an option for sociology of the arts. Sociology of the arts must engage with questions of aesthetic value in works of art. In particular, sociology of the arts must engage with the ways in which received ideas of aesthetic value in art are contested by critics who invoke political values of equality of representation for particular producers of culture whose productions have not historically enjoyed legitimation as 'art'. This includes members of society who have suffered exclusion and marginalization in history on account of their

subordinate class positions, their gender (women) and their ethnicity (non-western cultures). On the other hand, to say that social
theory mediates between value-distanciation and value-affirmation
is to assert that sociology of the arts remains still able, entitled, and
intellectually obliged, to distanciate itself from acts of normative
advocacy about art. Sociology of the arts should neither reduce
questions of aesthetic value to questions of social fact, nor wholly
assimilate questions of aesthetic value to questions of political value.
Sociology of the arts can and should treat works of art in a way that
(1) takes seriously the possibility of their intrinsic aesthetic value, while
(2) recognizing political values of democracy of access to cultural
production and cultural valuation, but at the same time (3) seeks to
gain a scientific distance from both aesthetic and political valuation
by insisting on an intellectual ethic of clear distinction between
empirical modes of discourse on the one hand and normative modes
of discourse on the other hand.

We will base our arguments for this injunction on qualified adher-
ence to Max Weber's principle of 'freedom from value-judgement'
in social research. As is well known, Max Weber (1949) held that
while all social-scientific investigation is value-relevant (*wertbezogen*)
and driven in its selection of subject-matter by 'value-ideas', the
practice of research should aim at abstaining from value-judgements.
Weber acknowledged that in reality researchers almost never
genuinely succeed in abstaining from value-judgements. However,
Weber insisted that researchers should nonetheless always *orient*
themselves towards abstaining from value-judgements and towards
making every effort to disentangle those parts of their investigation
that proceed by empirical explanation from those parts that proceed
by normative advocacy. In this book, we will follow Weber's
intellectual ethic of clear distinction between empirical discourse on
the one hand and normative discourse on the other hand. However,
we will not give *unconditional* endorsement to Weber's principle of
orientation towards abstention from value-judgement. Rather, we
will argue that value-judgements should be allowed to come into
play in sociology of the arts and *can* be allowed to do so in a way
that does not jeopardize scientific impartiality. We will argue that
it is possible and necessary to mediate value-distanciation with value-
affirmation in sociology of the arts critically and fruitfully. We will
seek to show how, even against a sociological background of profound contrasts and often conflicts of value-orientation in different
societies and cultures, value-judgements about works of art can have
intersubjectively generalizable defensibility.

Finally we will argue that aesthetic frames of perception carry key implications for the practice of sociological writing. We will argue that artistic communication not only represents a fertile thematic subject of sociological inquiry. We will argue that it also describes some important dimensions of the very practice of sociological writing and reasoning. This significance has already been demonstrated for other disciplines such as history, ethnography and anthropology, by scholars such as Paul Ricoeur (1985–8), Clifford Geertz (1973) and Hayden White (1975); and it has always been a central consideration for classical figures in sociology and social theory such as Georg Simmel, Walter Benjamin, Siegfried Kracauer and Theodor Adorno, as well as for contemporary figures such as Fredric Jameson and for historians of sociology such as Robert Nisbet (1976) and Wolf Lepenies (1988). All these figures show how aesthetic frames of perception enter into textual aspects of metaphor, analogy and vignette; into sensuous media of data analysis such as visual images and life-story narratives; and into conceptions of theatrical qualities in social action. We will not be able to demonstrate this significance in full in the present book. Full demonstration would demand an entire additional volume devoted to questions of methodological self-understanding in sociology. However, we will make a fundamental presupposition of the salience of aesthetics for practices of sociological writing. We will argue that this salience is essential to any understanding of the arts that seeks to avoid treating works of art purely as objects for social science.

Outline of chapters

Chapter 1 introduces a variety of conceptions and philosophies of art relevant to sociological understanding of the arts. We begin with some long-standing metaphysical conceptions of art revolving around ideas of beauty, 'imitation of nature' and 'aesthetic experience'. Then we set out the broad spectrum of sociological approaches to art. These include historicist and humanistic conceptions of art history; Marxist social history of art; cultural studies, cultural materialism and postmodernism; institutional theories of art in analytical philosophy; anthropological studies of art; and empirical ethnographic studies of arts institutions.

Chapter 2 focuses on questions of political struggle over definitions of value in art history. We begin by establishing why strict value-neutrality is not an option in sociology of the arts. Then we move to a range of dilemmas that arise once some constitutive role of value-judgements is admitted in sociology of the arts. We set out the shortcomings of traditional liberal-humanistic conceptions of aesthetic value as these have been exposed by socialist, feminist and postcolonial critics. We conclude with some preliminary remarks on the scope and limits of consensus in aesthetic appraisal.

Chapter 3 examines theories of the determination of art forms and contents by socioeconomic structures. We consider Marxist theories of the 'reflection' of social class relations in works of art, as well as other, non-Marxist theories of evolutionary correspondence between social structure and artistic form. We conclude with an overview of the history of arts patronage, arts markets and arts funding in western society from the Middle Ages to the present day.

Chapter 4 examines theories of arts consumption in society in relation to ideas of the autonomy of aesthetic value and the autonomy of art. We begin by setting out Immanuel Kant's eighteenth-century philosophical conception of the transcendental validity of aesthetic judgement. Then we introduce a range of criticisms of the conception from the standpoint of empirical sociological analysis. We focus on the work of Pierre Bourdieu on art and 'cultural capital'. We also discuss the work of some contemporary American sociologists on taste and social class. We conclude with some further remarks on the scope and limits of consensus in aesthetic appraisal.

Chapter 5 addresses the ways in which post-Kantian German idealist philosophies of art have been deployed by social theorists in the tradition of Marxian critical theory. We address the thematic of ideology and utopia in art in relation to questions of myth and religion and in relation to concepts of illusion, enlightenment and sublimation in art. We discuss the significance of the visions of J. C. F. Schiller, Arthur Schopenhauer, G. W. F. Hegel, Richard Wagner, Friedrich Nietzsche and Sigmund Freud for theorists such as Ernst Bloch, György Lukács and Herbert Marcuse.

Chapter 6 continues the investigations of chapter 5 with a more specific focus on the concepts of modernity and modernism in art. We examine the work of the five most influential representatives of a 'modernist' canon in twentieth-century social theory of the arts. These are: Max Weber, Georg Simmel, Walter Benjamin, Siegfried Kracauer and Theodor Adorno. We examine these theorists' writings in relation to concepts of modernization, rationalization, aestheticization, 'mass culture' and the 'culture industry'. We conclude with a critical assessment of the work of the Frankfurt School.

Chapter 7 assesses the relevance of postmodernism to sociological understanding of the arts. We discuss the origins of debates about postmodernism in the writings of several twentieth-century philosophers and critics of the arts. These include Martin Heidegger, Hans-Georg Gadamer, Jürgen Habermas, Georges Bataille, Michel Foucault, Jacques Derrida and Gilles Deleuze. We then turn to the ways in which postmodernist motifs in late twentieth-century art and cultural discourse are theorized and evaluated in the writings of Arthur Danto, Jean-François Lyotard, Jean Baudrillard, Fredric Jameson, Niklas Luhmann and others. We conclude with an assessment of the significance of capitalistic globalization for the future of artistic life.

1

Conceptions and Approaches

'Sociology and art make an odd couple,' writes Pierre Bourdieu (1980: 207). Art tends to rebel against scientific images of the world, while sociology tends to thrive on demystifying the enchanting in social life. Art tends to revolt against materialistic explanations of life, while sociology tends to exult in exposing the singular and unique as socially constructed and socially reproduced.

We begin our exploration of this 'odd couple' here by first briefly reviewing some of the most long-standing conceptions of art in western thought which precede the emergence of self-consciously sociological and sociohistorical conceptions of art in the late nineteenth and twentieth centuries. We will describe these long-standing conceptions of art in the most general terms as 'metaphysical conceptions'. We will define metaphysical conceptions of art as conceptions that think of art in terms of certain timeless norms of communication valid for all history and all societies. We begin by discussing three such types of conception here: conceptions that think of art in terms of an essence of 'beauty'; conceptions that think of art in terms of an essence of naturalistic representation, founded on 'imitation of nature'; and conceptions that think of art in terms of an essence of 'aesthetic experience'. Then we turn to the variety of ways in which sociological thinking challenges these conceptions.

Metaphysical conceptions of art

Beauty

Metaphysical conceptions of beauty in western thought about art can be traced to the legacy of the ideas of the ancient Greek philosopher

Plato. In *The Republic* (written in *c.*360 BC), Plato held that if art was to contribute to the goodness of the commonwealth, it was essential that art elevated the minds of the people to the eternal beauty of the cosmos, alongside the eternal truth sought by philosophers, and the eternal justice sought by statesmen and lawgivers. Plato wrote in a context in which the word for 'art' in ancient Greek essentially meant 'craft' or 'skill' (*techně*). It did not possess the additional connotation of creative expression 'for its own sake' carried by the word today. Painters and sculptors in ancient Greece consequently carried low social status; they were viewed as craftsmen on the same level as carpenters or shoemakers. Plato thus held a low estimation of the role of artists in society. Plato viewed artists as dealing essentially in the mere appearances of things, not in the true nature of the world. Plato insisted that if artists and their works were to have a rightful place in society, they had to encourage people to transcend their finite earthly condition and aspire to knowledge of the unchanging order of the cosmos.

In the Italian Renaissance of the fifteenth and sixteenth centuries, Platonic ideas of beauty were associated with classical Greek principles of right measure, proportion and perspective in painting and sculpture. In the Baroque period of the sixteenth and seventeenth centuries, Greek principles of drawing and composition became institutionalized in the foundation of royal academies of art which taught a hierarchy of painterly forms. Historical, mythological and biblical scenes were regarded as the most noble of images, while portraiture and landscape occupied a lower place in the hierarchy, and 'realistic' scenes of ordinary people going about their daily life were viewed as beyond the pale of acceptable representation. The concept of beauty promulgated in the Renaissance and the Baroque academies thus remained highly idealized and prescriptive in character. It rested on a Platonic understanding of beauty as something eternal, absolute and transcendent, and as inhering in some basic cosmological content. This stands at odds with more modern understandings of beauty as being not absolute but *relative* to changing historical contexts of perception, and as existing only 'in the eye of the beholder' in some important general sense, not 'in itself'.

The imitation of nature

A second long-standing conception of art in western thought concerns ideas of the 'imitation of nature'. In both pagan and Christian cosmologies, art was thought to attain beauty by virtue of its imitation of the original beauty of nature. Nature was held up as the image of perfection; and art was seen as having the goal of imitating this perfection. In Greek thought, this is known as the doctrine of mimesis. Aristotle, in his treatise on theatre, *The Poetics* (written in *c.*350 BC), taught that

> Epic poetry and tragedy, also comedy . . . and most of the music performed on the flute and the lyre are all, in a collective sense, imitations (*mimesis*). . . . Just as certain persons, by rule of art or mere practice, make likenesses of various objects by imitating them in colours and forms, and others again imitate by means of the voice, so these arts . . . imitate by means of rhythm, language and melody. . . . [F]rom childhood it is instinctive in human beings to imitate, and man differs from the other animals as the most imitative of all and getting his first lessons by imitation, and by instinct also all human beings take pleasure in imitations. (Aristotle 1982: 45–7)

In the Renaissance, the most famous analogue of Aristotle's doctrine is Hamlet's speech in the play within a play that Hamlet stages in order to shame his uncle into confessing the murder of his father. Shakespeare's hero counsels his actors to be true to their parts, not to over-act, not to be false:

> Suit the action to the word, the word to the action; with this special observance, that you o'erstep not the modesty of nature; for anything so o'erdone is from the purpose of playing, whose end, both at the first and now, was and is, to hold, as 'twere, the mirror up to nature. (*Hamlet*, III. ii. 18–23)

Ideas of mimesis in art are often closely linked to concepts of naturalistic 'verisimilitude' in painting, where pictures are seen as having the goal of producing *copies* of reality, or *likenesses* between images and the objects they are held to 'represent'. This doctrine exercised considerable influence in the Renaissance period. It rested on the prestige of a story in Plato's *Republic* about a Greek painter Zeuxis who once painted a picture of some grapes so life-like that birds flew down to peck at it. The story encapsulates the attractions of the so-called *trompe l'oeil* effect that 'fools the eye' into mistaking an image for the real thing. The effect is often to be found in Renaissance and Baroque frescos containing scenes that appear to continue the space of the viewer so that the viewer is invited to walk into the scene, and most graphically in seventeenth-century Dutch still life paintings of opulent food on tables. In contemporary art-historical terminology, this doctrine is often referred to as 'illusionism'.

It should be clear that illusionism in painting is impossible to fulfil if it is interpreted in any literal sense. No picture can ever be said to be an entirely neutral reproduction of its object. The eye of the artist does not behave like the shutter of a camera – where camera shutters are thought of as purely physical mechanisms, without emotions and preconceptions. In their very framing and selection of objects of representation, artists always produce an interpretation of reality, which reflects something of themselves and their world. In *Art and Illusion*, Ernst Gombrich (1960) shows how while many western artists since the Renaissance can be seen as perfecting a technique of naturalistic perspective, this development always took the form of a discontinuous sequence. Artists always worked within prior frameworks of style and never gradually advanced to some 'innocent eye', free of social conventions. Thus it is misleading to think of perspective and recessive shading in painting as being more 'faithful to nature' than more schematic and 'flatter' languages of representation, such as those characteristic of medieval art and some non-western art. As Nelson Goodman (1976) demonstrates, perspective is a more rationalized method of representation than symbolic figuration, but it is not 'truer to nature' in any absolute sense.

We may observe that Platonic ideas of beauty and Aristotelian ideas of mimesis are not generally self-reflective conceptions of art. Just as ideas of beauty change over time, so different cultures construct different ideas of nature that reflect changing frameworks of perception. Ideas of nature and of the world 'in itself' are themselves artifice, constructed in the image of artistic change through history.

In the eighteenth century, much of the metaphysical contents of these earlier doctrines began to recede in the face of growing historical awareness and a gradual shift of attention towards subjective 'sensibilities' for perceiving things as beautiful. It was this shift that led to the rise of the idea of a science of aesthetics in the European Enlightenment, to which we now turn.

Aesthetic experience

Deriving from the Greek word for 'perception' – *aisthesis* – aesthetics refers to the study of *pleasure in perception*. Although some of its meanings have changed since its first appearance in eighteenth-century Enlightenment thought, aesthetics remains the key term today for that branch of philosophical inquiry that is concerned with the grounds for experiences of pleasure in sensory objects. In particular, aesthetics refers to the grounds for intersubjectively valid *judgements of taste* about sensory objects. Aesthetics is concerned in principle with judgements of taste about sensory objects of any kind, whether or not made by human hands. However, it is most often concerned with judgements of taste about those particular products of human agency known as 'works of art'.

The first significant occurrence of the term 'aesthetics' is to be found in the title of a treatise published in 1750 by the Prussian rationalist philosopher Alexander Baumgarten. Baumgarten defined beauty as the sensation of pleasure accruing from arrangements of forms in consonance with reason and logic. A second landmark was an essay published in 1746 by the French writer Charles Batteux, titled *Les beaux arts réduits à un même principe*. Batteux argued that a common principle could be discerned among all the fine art forms of painting, sculpture, poetry, music and dance. Batteux's text finally brought to an end the ancient association of artists with mostly practical skills and crafts. It inaugurated the idea of what Kristeller (1970) calls 'the modern system of the arts': the idea of a pantheon of art forms, all capable of realization and contemplation for their own sake, without regard to practical purpose or utility.

The idea that a work of art was to be savoured and contemplated was something new and specific to the secularizing spirit of Enlightenment Europe. The birth of aesthetics went together with a spirit of sceptical inquiry in relation to received understandings of the common good, as defined by the church and the Bible. In England and Scotland, this took the form of empirical psychological theories of morality, represented by a preoccupation with pity, sympathy and sensibility. In France it took the form of critical essays and pamphlets on progress, despotism, civilization and education, such as in the moral criticism of Jean-Jacques Rousseau and in the writings of the many authors of the French *encyclopédie*. However, the most systematic expression of the standpoint of aesthetic analysis comes to us from the Prussian Enlightenment philosopher Immanuel Kant, in the last of his three philosophical treatises, *The Critique of Judgement*, published in 1790.

One of the striking facts about Kant's text is that it makes relatively little mention of works of art as such. The first part of the text, titled 'Analytic of Beauty', is mostly concerned with the subjective act of perceiving something as beautiful, not with any particular sphere or substance in which beauty might be said to inhere. Kant made clear that in affirming a judgement of taste, the judging person makes no strict claim to state *what* the object is, in the sense of a scientific statement about its properties or causes, nor to state how 'worthy' or how 'useful' the object is, in the sense of a judgement of its moral integrity or a judgement of its practical utility. The person simply makes a claim for the pleasure it evokes on 'disinterested contemplation'. In this sense Kant established that aesthetic judgements possess an *autonomous character*. In his previous treatise, *The Critique of Practical Reason* (of 1788), Kant had sought to propound a non-theological account of man's grounds for refraining from actions that harm the well-being of others. In his first treatise, *The Critique of Pure Reason* (of 1781), he had sought to propound a non-dogmatic account of man's grounds for knowledge of experience. Thus in his third and final treatise, Kant completed his secular redefinition of the traditional contents of western philosophy in terms of the three autonomous domains of science, morality and aesthetics.

In the nineteenth century, ideas of the autonomy of aesthetic judgements soon became linked to the idea of the autonomy of art itself. Art was seen as resting on a self-evident value of its own. Among the German idealist and early romantic thinkers, art was held up as communicating a special kind of understanding of the world, equal to that of religion and philosophy. G. W. F. Hegel placed art alongside religion and philosophy as three forms of access to ultimate truth that he termed 'absolute spirit'. Later in the nineteenth century, some writers saw art as constituting a last remaining source of spiritual salvation for a society corrupted by industry, materialism and scientific rationalism. Art was seen as holding out possibilities of transcendence and mythical self-understanding for a society that had lost faith in the traditional institutions of religion. This outlook is often known as 'art for art's sake', after the French nineteenth-century slogan, *l'art pour l'art*.

Ideas of 'art for art's sake' represent the high-water mark of metaphysical conceptions of art. They are increasingly disputed in the nineteenth century by different currents of thought that seek to place ordinary craft skills on an equal footing with the fine arts. Some nineteenth-century currents of thought seek to establish a firmer connection between art and morality and different national traditions of culture, and they seek to understand art in a more comparative historical light, based on scholarly study of different civilizations and peoples and their different worldviews. These currents of thought lay the foundations for a more sociohistorical way of thinking about art. As early as the eighteenth century, writers such as Montesquieu, Dénis Diderot and Giambattista Vico wrote of the influence of climate, milieu and social order on historical traditions of art. In the nineteenth century, the utopian socialist thinker Pierre-Joseph Proudhon wrote of artists such as Jacques-Louis David and Gustave Courbet as spokesmen of the 'spirit of the age'. Similarly, Madame de Staël and the positivist historian Hyppolite Taine both wrote at length of geography, climate and 'race' as cardinal influences on historical schools and styles of art (Rifkin 1992). The nineteenth century also saw an increasing pre-occupation with artistic activities in 'primitive' societies. These had been brought to attention by a steady influx of exotic artefacts in western museums of archaeology and anthropology, plundered and trafficked across the seas by colonial travellers and merchants.

We may say that all these developments and currents of thought inaugurate a recognizably new way of thinking about art based on dissatisfaction with metaphysical conceptions of art. Late nineteenth-century historical consciousness ushers in a distinctively modern way of thinking about art that avoids attempting to define art in terms of norms and essences of beauty valid for all time and all societies. It is to this distinctively modern, sociological way of thinking about art that we now turn.

Sociological conceptions of art

Although it is possible to discern a few disparate strands of a sociological and sociohistorical way of thinking about art in the eighteenth and nineteenth centuries, it is only from the early twentieth century that we can speak of an institutionalized body of sociological studies of art. We will introduce six principal schools of approach here: first, humanistic historicist approaches in early twentieth-century art history; second, Marxist social history of art; third, cultural studies, cultural materialism and postmodernism; fourth, institutional theories of art in analytical philosophy; fifth, anthropological studies of art in indigenous societies; and sixth, empirical studies of contemporary arts institutions.

Humanistic art history

Humanistic historicist approaches to art history refer primarily to a succession of influential German scholars active in the early decades of the twentieth century. These scholars are today seen as founding

figures in the discipline of art history. They include the names of
Aby Warburg, Heinrich Wölfflin, Alois Riegl, Karl Schnaase, Adolf
von Hildebrandt, Erwin Panofsky, Ernst Cassirer and Edgar Wind.
The German art scholars developed methods of pictorial analysis
oriented to evaluating formal compositional structures in works of
art. They saw impartial historical understanding as contributing to
the enrichment of the human personality. They saw art as occupying a central place in the 'human studies', then known in German as
the *Geisteswissenschaften* or 'sciences of spirit', after the philosopher
Wilhelm Dilthey. They set about demonstrating the methodological
integrity of art history in relation to established disciplines such as
philology, archaeology, economy and the natural sciences. Wölfflin
(1950) held that paintings could be studied in terms of definite
types of form and style. He proposed that paintings could be analysed both in terms of their regional historical milieux and in terms
of formal polarities between linear form and painterly form, flatness
and depth, and 'closed' (schematic) versus 'open' (illusionistic) form.
Panofsky (1955) argued that pictorial analysis involved study of
'iconology' and 'iconography', based on close acquaintance with
literary, biblical and mythological sources. Panofsky saw pictorial
analysis as involving skills of deciphering symbolic systems in works
of art, such as St Peter and his keys, St Sebastian and his arrows,
Orpheus and his lyre, and so on.

It should be noted that the German art scholars were not exclusively
concerned with painting and sculpture. They saw art as emerging
from the entire material culture of historical life, in pottery, tapestry
and architecture and the like; and they developed a rigorous methodology of formal analysis balanced with historical contextualization
that emphasized cooperation between visual analysis and other disciplines of the human studies, such as anthropology and linguistics.
Ernst Cassirer in particular linked art history to the more general
study of symbols, language, myth, religion, science and philosophy.
In his *The Philosophy of Symbolic Forms* (1953) Cassirer argued that
symbols structure and synthesize human beings' way of experienc-
ing the world. Cassirer elaborated Immanuel Kant's conception of
the dependence of human knowledge and experience of the world
on concepts and categories supplied by the human mind. Cassirer
affirmed that to study art history was to study one of the manifold
respects in which human beings evolve ways of organizing their
experience under constructions of the imagination, from the mythological belief-systems of archaic peoples to the abstract systems of
modern logic, arithmetic, algebra and mathematics.

In chapter 2 we will discuss some criticisms of the German humanistic scholars revolving around claims that their underlying cultural values led them to take an unjustifiably eurocentric and patriarchal view of the relevant constituents of 'art'.

Marxist social history of art

Marxist social history and sociology of art refers to a range of scholars active from around the middle decades of the twentieth century. These scholars sought to tie the study of works of art and artists' lives to analysis of economic modes of material production and social class structures. Most of these scholars draw on concepts in Marxist historical theory, either directly or indirectly. They include historians such as Meyer Schapiro (1973), Arnold Hauser (1951), Frederick Antal (1948), Pierre Francastel (1956, 1970), Francis Klingender (1968), Jean Duvignaud (1972), Max Raphael (1968), Lucien Goldmann (1970) and others. Alongside these, we must also mention a wide variety of twentieth-century Marxist philosophers and critics of the arts. These range from Russian and Soviet figures such as Plekhanov and Trotsky to western European critics such as Jean-Paul Sartre, György Lukács, Walter Benjamin, Ernst Bloch, Bertholt Brecht and Siegfried Kracauer. They also include the members of the Frankfurt School of social research, chiefly Theodor Adorno, Max Horkheimer, Herbert Marcuse and Leo Löwenthal. They include numerous French intellectuals associated with the movements of surrealism and situationism such as André Breton, Georges Bataille and Cornelius Castoriadis; and they include more recent historians and theorists such as John Berger (1972), T. J. Clark (1973, 1985) and Fredric Jameson (1984).

All these writers have propounded principles of materialist analysis that have since become more or less standard in sociological studies of the arts. They include the proposition that artists are not solitary individuals endowed with unique creative gifts but members of definite collectivities; that works of art are funded and purchased by social agents and institutions by payments in money or in kind; that works of art depend on material and technological media of production that presuppose social systems of labour; that works of art 'reflect' or 'encode' the social structures of their time in their aesthetic forms and contents; and that works of art carry values that are not necessarily valid for all time and may only be valid for particular social groups who 'consume' them in specific social settings.

These writers' contributions raise the question of the extent to which Marx's own writings provide grounds for a specifically Marxist approach to sociological studies of the arts. We will attempt a brief provisional response to this question here.

We should note first that Marx himself wrote little of any great note on individual works of art. Among Marx's few comments on works of art are some remarks on Eugène Sue's *The Mysteries of Paris*, a popular novel of the 1840s; some remarks on a play by Ferdinand Lassalle, leader of the German Social Democratic Party in the 1870s; some references to Shakespeare and Honoré de Balzac; and some unfinished notes on ancient Greek art and culture (Marx and Engels 1976). However, other passages of Marx's writings addressing questions of value, labour and sensuous well-being – notably in the *Grundrisse, Theories of Surplus Value* and the *Economic and Philosophic Manuscripts of 1844* – contain ideas which have provided a point of departure for much twentieth-century Marxist aesthetic theory. A preliminary summary of these ideas here will serve as a guide to our discussions later.

The most central proposition of classical Marxist thinking about art is that a society's ability to produce works of fine art is a privilege of its ruling classes. Peasants, serfs and factory workers are not in a position to produce works of fine art because they lack the time, leisure, material resources and advantages of technical know-how to do so. It is most obviously a privilege of the aristocracy because landowners are relieved of the necessity to earn a living. It is also a privilege of the middle classes because merchants, industrialists and employees of skilled professions are only compelled to sell the products of their labour, not their labour-power itself. Therefore they possess a degree of free time to acquire the means of producing art, such as materials, instruments and access to technical training and education.

A second central proposition of classical Marxist thinking about art is that in so far as exploited classes in society supply ruling classes with the necessities of life, the ability of the ruling classes to produce works of art presupposes an extraction of value from the life possibilities of the exploited classes. Value in art for the enjoyment of a few rests on an extraction of value from the material livelihood of the great mass in society. The existence of the Egyptian pyramids is founded on the labour of thousands of slaves. The existence of palaces and castles is founded on the labour of thousands of serfs. The ability of sons of industrialists to write love poetry, play the piano and paint pictures of Venus is founded on the labour of thousands of workers in the factories. In a capitalist society, fine art is the spiritualized form of a quantity of extra labour-power and extra labour-time which has been extracted from the life horizons of the proletariat and converted into capital.

A third proposition in classical Marxist thinking is that works of art reflect the social class relations from which they derive in their aesthetic forms and contents. Visual and narrative contents reflect the interests of the ruling classes in maintaining their position of domination. They transmit the ideology of the ruling classes. However, they do not do so in a direct way. They do so only in an indirect way, by acts of intellectual mystification. Pre-communist art makes actually existing conditions of social order appear natural, eternal and unchangeable. Pre-communist art is in this respect comparable to religion, theology and metaphysical philosophy.

A fourth proposition in classical Marxist thinking is that pre-communist art is valuable for contemporary society only in so far as it is related to revolutionary struggle. Marx argued that ancient Greek art is meaningful to the present in so far as it reveals stages in the historical development of the human species towards commun-ism. Proletarians can appreciate ancient Greek and high bourgeois art up to the point that they see dramatized in it the logic of class conflict and hence the early makings of their own historical predica-ment. Therefore pre-communist art still contains a potential moment of truth. But this potential moment of truth awaits redemption through revolutionary praxis.

We will be concerned at several places in this book with the ways in which twentieth-century theorists have criticized and qualified the more reductive tendencies of classical Marxist thinking about art. In chapter 3 we will assess Marxist theories of the determination of art by socioeconomic structures. In chapter 4 we discuss Marxist accounts of the thesis of 'aesthetic autonomy'. In chapter 5 we examine Marxist theories of ideology and utopia in art; and in chapters 6 and 7 we discuss Marxist positions in debates about modernity, modernism and postmodernism.

Cultural studies, cultural materialism and postmodernism

The variety of approaches associated with 'cultural studies' refers to the work of critics and theorists who have built on Marxist thinking but have sought to refine and combine Marxist ideas with other

theoretical sources. These include psychoanalysis, structural linguistics and semiotics, deconstruction, discourse analysis, poststructuralist criticism and feminist and postcolonial criticism. The broad
unity of these approaches can be summed up in the concept of
'cultural materialism' – a term first coined by Raymond Williams
(1981). Unlike Marx's historical materialism, cultural materialism
does not hold class struggle to be the only and ultimate source of
conditioning power over cultural life. Cultural materialism emphasizes
other sites of struggle for recognition in culture bearing on issues of
gender, ethnicity and sexuality. Cultural materialism consequently
recommends a more attenuated concept of ideology than that
deployed in classical Marxist analysis. It does not directly associate
ideology with 'false consciousness'. It rejects orthodox Marxist conceptions of cultural 'superstructures' determined by an economic
'base'; and it does not directly reduce cultural and aesthetic value to
labour value. Drawing on figureheads such as Antonio Gramsci,
Mikhail Bakhtin and Roland Barthes, many cultural studies writers
argue for concepts of 'hegemony' in culture that articulate relations
of subordination and exclusion while at the same time mediating
elements of dissent and contestation. Cultural forms are seen as
transmitting power from some groups in society over others without
necessarily revealing any single originating source of domination.

The rise of cultural studies occurred at a time when many university departments began to incorporate more explicitly political and
theoretical approaches to the humanities than in earlier decades of
the twentieth century. In the 1970s and 1980s teaching and research
programmes began to explore issues such as the exclusion of women
painters from traditional narratives of art history; the role of
museums, galleries and academies in constructions of national canons
and representations of other peoples; and the relationship of fine art
forms to commercial art, advertising, fashion, industrial design and
popular culture in the broadest sense. In Britain this was known as
the 'New Art History' (Borzello and Rees 1986). In literary studies,
influential movements have included the 'New Historicism' in
Renaissance studies, which emphasized literary writers' involvements
in negotiations with political and ecclesiastical authorities (Greenblatt
and Gallagher 2000). Many critics have thematized issues of sexual
politics and issues of national, ethnic and postcolonial identity
(Dollimore and Sinfield 1985; Eagleton 1983). These interventions
have been decisive in extending cultural analysis to include film,
TV, video and the mass media, and lifestyle and consumption choices
in general. They have placed fine art among the general 'signifying

practices' of society. Poetry is set alongside pulp fiction; painting alongside commercial photography; the string quartet alongside the folk singer and the rock video, and so on. It is in this sense that writers such as Stuart Hall (1980) and Michel de Certeau (1984) speak of popular culture as an activity of reading and assemblage, or *bricolage*, as much as one of consumption. Popular culture is seen not in terms of passive ingestion of ready-made symbols but in terms of a texture of everyday creativity.

A further aspect of the range of approaches encompassed under cultural studies is a certain association with 'postmodernism'. Postmodernism is a diffuse term which is by no means affirmed in any unequivocal way by cultural studies writers. However, it has some uses in designating a broad attitude of epistemological pluralism in contemporary cultural and political discourse. Postmodernism in social theory is associated with Jean-François Lyotard's (1984b: xxiv) conception of 'incredulity toward meta-narratives'. Postmodernism in art theory is associated with the dissolution of ideas of internal progressive development in artistic language. It is associated with the disappearance of any single dominant centre of artistic innovation since the 1970s. It is associated with a discrediting of prejudices in favour of 'depth', 'purity' and 'authenticity' in art over against surface, play, eclecticism and hybridization between genres, forms and materials. It is associated with the dissolution of binary oppositions between 'high culture' and 'low culture' and a blurring of art's boundaries into popular culture and the mass media.

Postmodernism first became current as a term in the 1970s when it was used to denote a new playful attitude in forms of architectural construction. Thereafter it spread rapidly to become a general concept of social science discourse in the 1980s. It is analysed in the commentaries of numerous critics such as Arthur Danto (1997), Andreas Huyssen (1986), Rosalind Krauss (1985), Hal Foster (1985), Fredric Jameson (1984, 1991) and David Harvey (1990). These commentaries challenge the discriminations of earlier twentieth-century social and aesthetic theorists in favour of autonomous fine art above 'kitsch' and 'mass culture'. They show how postmodernism signifies a break not only with metaphysical conceptions of art but also with eminently 'modernist' conceptions of normative sociohistorical development in art.

In chapter 7 we will argue that postmodernism should not be treated as a set of indisputable facts about the fate of contemporary culture. But we will emphasize that postmodernism enjoys real existence in late twentieth-century aesthetic culture and therefore that its claims should be taken seriously. Elements of postmodernist thinking underpin each of the remaining three schools of approach to which we now turn.

Institutional theories of art in analytical philosophy

'Institutional theories of art' comprise a set of contributions by scholars trained not primarily as sociologists or as art historians but as philosophers. They are associated with writers in the tradition of Anglo-American analytical philosophy since the 1950s. The two most notable representatives of an institutional theory of art in this tradition are Arthur Danto and George Dickie. Other representatives of the tradition more generally include Richard Wollheim, Mary Mothersill, Stanley Cavell, Oswald Hanfling and B. R. Tilghman.

Many analytical philosophers of the arts take their point of departure from Ludwig Wittgenstein's analyses of ordinary language in his late philosophical writings of the 1930s to 1940s. Analytical philosophers invoke Wittgenstein's insights to show how the central problem in metaphysical conceptions of art lies in their attempt to define a *singular concept* of art. They show how standard logical procedures for defining concepts by stipulating 'necessary and sufficient conditions' are of little use in the case of 'art'. 'Necessary conditions' refer to properties that objects must possess in order to be examples of a concept X. Sufficient conditions refer to properties that make objects examples of X but need not be the only properties that make objects examples of X. If X is taken as a place-holder for 'art', it appears that metaphysical conceptions of art specify properties which satisfy only sufficient conditions for making objects examples of 'art', not *necessary* conditions for making them examples of 'art'. Properties of 'possessing beauty', 'imitating nature', 'creating a likeness' and 'giving pleasure to the eye' appear to suffice for making objects examples of 'art', but do not appear to be necessary for making them examples of 'art'. On the one hand, many other objects and entities also possess these properties but are not usually regarded as works of art. We may think of human faces, passport photos, motorcars. On the other hand, works of art need not possess beauty in any essential sense; they might look grotesque, bleak or horrifying. Nor need they imitate or resemble anything; they could be abstract or expressionist. Nor need they give pleasure to the eye; they could be painful and discomfiting to look at (Hanfling 1992).

In place of this enterprise of conceptual definition of art, some analytical philosophers propose grammatical analysis of ordinary uses of the word 'art' in terms of what Wittgenstein called their 'family resemblance' to one another. Although Wittgenstein did not himself write about 'art' in this way, he pointed to uses of the word 'game' in ordinary language. Most speakers of language know how to use the word 'game' quite routinely, even though the word is very hard to define as a concept. Thus these writers suggest that just as Wittgenstein (1953: 67) showed how games are linked together only by 'a complicated network of similarities overlapping and criss-crossing', so referents of the word 'art' lack any essential conceptual connection to one another but are nevertheless routinely understood by ordinary speakers of language.

Other philosophers, however, have argued that this suggestion is not without certain problems. For whereas the boundaries of the word 'game' are relatively taken for granted in social practice, the boundaries of the word 'art' are continually being extended and contested over time. Therefore it is not enough to assume that any competent speaker of language will routinely recognize referents of the word 'art'. Some people – most notably art critics and artists – may be more likely to see art in things in which other people may be more likely to see only bicycle saddles or sewing machines. Therefore it is necessary to analyse art not only in terms of uses of language but also in terms of changing contexts of institutional authority over uses of language. These considerations provide the starting-point for Danto's and Dickie's institutional theory.

Danto (1964) and Dickie (1974) propose that what distinguishes art from non-art is not anything that can be observed with the naked eye. Danto and Dickie argue that works of art are not distinguishable by any particular quality of material appearance. They are distinguishable solely by the decision of a certain social institution to *confer status* on them. This institution is called the 'art world'. The art world consists of artists, critics, curators, sponsors, agents, dealers, collectors. Only this institution can discriminate between two physically identical objects and determine that one of them is a work of art and the other not a work of art; for example, a brick or a beer can in a gallery as against a brick or a beer can at a building site. Dickie takes the action of the Dada artist Marcel Duchamp on presenting a men's urinal to the Museum of Modern Art in New York in the 1920s, titled *Fountain* (see illustration 1). Duchamp's work was physically indistinguishable from an ordinary men's urinal in a cloakroom. Duchamp procured his object 'ready-made',

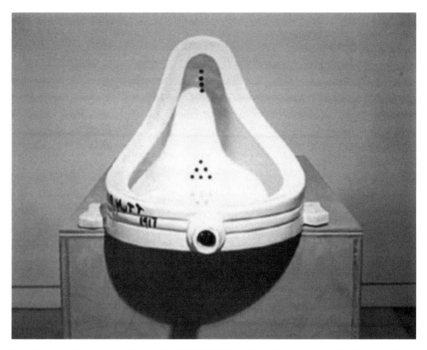

1   Marcel Duchamp, *Fountain*, 1917/1964. Glazed ceramic with black paint, 38.1 × 48.9 × 62.55 cm. Museum of Modern Art, San Francisco. Purchased through a gift of Phyllis Wattis. © Succession Marcel Duchamp/ADAGP, Paris and DACS, London 2003

mass-produced in a ceramics factory; and it was (eventually) accepted by the gallery as art. Similarly, Danto takes the case of Andy Warhol's *Brillo Boxes* from 1964, consisting of plywood replicas of the famous cardboard cartons of soap scourers. Danto also observes that towards the end of the nineteenth century many western cities began to display objects in art galleries previously housed in museums of archaeology and anthropology. Danto argues that only a change of perception driven by actions of institutional authorities can explain this sudden creation of works of art out of objects hitherto constituted as non-art artefacts. Danto and Dickie conclude that art objects do not exist in the art gallery because they are art before they enter the gallery; they exist as art objects because they exist in the gallery, and because they are admitted to the gallery by authorities. In Dickie's words: 'A work of art in the classificatory sense is (1) an artefact (2) a set of the aspects of which has had conferred upon it the status of candidate for appreciation by some person or persons acting on behalf of a certain social institution (the artworld)' (Dickie 1974: 34).

Dickie emphasizes that not anything can be a work of art if anyone says it is. Dickie acknowledges that simply saying something can indeed make something the case in the world. In 'speech-acts' such as 'I promise' or 'I apologize', the speaker does not merely describe a state of affairs in the world; the speaker creates that state of affairs in the act of uttering these words. In this sense the speech-act of declaring something a work of art can have a 'performative' effect that creates the fact of its own declaration – like the agreement of certain associations of people to accept certain pieces of paper as money. But Dickie stresses that in order for this performative effect to be socially valid, the speaker must hold a certain institutional authority and must make the declaration in an institutionally recognized setting. When a priest baptizes a child, the priest's utterance creates the social fact of the child's baptism, but only a priest can perform this act, and if anyone else uttered the priest's words, no such fact would be created. Thus those conferring status on objects must enjoy a certain social authority for the conferral to succeed.

In chapter 2 we will discuss some objections to Danto's and Dickie's theory. We will criticize their thesis that objects exist as art if, *and only if*, some formal art institution declares them to be art. However, we must acknowledge some insights in the general claim of their work that objects do not necessarily exist as art if their original makers and recipients possess no idea of them as 'art', or as candidates for 'art'. For example, African tribal dance masks are not necessarily art if the African tribespeople who made them do not, or did not, have some idea of them as 'art'. At the very least, they are not necessarily art in a traditional western metaphysical sense of 'art'. This observation is particularly emphasized by anthropological studies of art in indigenous societies, to which we now turn.

Anthropological studies of art

Anthropological studies of art in indigenous societies further help us see the extent to which western metaphysical conceptions of art and beauty reflect specific intellectual developments of their time and milieux and do not necessarily possess transcultural validity. They further help dissolve assumptions first entertained in eighteenth-century Europe about a transcendental realm of experience called 'art', set apart from the rest of life. Anthropological studies typically concentrate on the place of the things, actions and experiences called 'art' within total cultural systems, alongside other social activities such as hunting, agriculture, eating, festival, play, trade, war, dance, worship and ritual. Classical studies in this vein include work by Franz Boas (1955) and Alfred Louis Kroeber (1957) on the material culture of the North American native peoples, as well as work by Claude Lévi-Strauss on symbolic kinship relations among South American Amazonian tribes.

Typical objects of anthropological analyses of art are designs and decorative patterns carved on tools and utensils, embroidery on clothing, body painting, masks and staffs, stone arrangements, cave paintings, and images on shields and weapons. These are typically seen as elements within communication systems revolving around signs and symbols of group territory, group totems and group clan and kin relations; or they are seen as elements within purposive action systems oriented to magic and sorcery. Much anthropological research focuses on close interactions between imitation, illustration and ornamentation and beliefs in spirits and cultic practices.

We will not be able to discuss all the many examples of anthropological studies here (see Coote and Shelton 1992). In the following we will briefly review the work of two representative authors: Clifford Geertz and Alfred Gell.

In his essay 'Art as a Cultural System' (1983) Clifford Geertz sets out a number of problems with mid twentieth-century structural-functionalist approaches to anthropological research on art. Geertz argues that structural-functionalist approaches to anthropology rest on some implicitly ethnocentric assumptions. They tend to assume that activities such as dancing, singing, weaving, pottery and horticulture carry no intrinsically 'artistic' meanings for the actors themselves. They explain such activities solely in terms of certain structural functions, such as functions of 'group socialization' and 'group differentiation'. Geertz criticizes these approaches by arguing that while no indigenous societies possess ideas of art directly comparable to western metaphysical ideas of art, it is not the case that such societies possess no ideas of artistic expression whatsoever. Geertz comments on the Yoruba tribe of Nigerian Africa who attach special significance to lines and linearity. The Yoruba carve lines in wood sculpture and paint lines on their faces. The Yoruba word for 'line' is the same as the Yoruba word for 'civilization'. The Yoruba mark 'civilization' by tracks slashed in the forest and boundaries incised in the earth. Similarly, Geertz discusses the Abelam tribe of New Guinea who paint much of their houses and clothing in coloured oval shapes. The Abelam see these oval shapes as representations of the bellies of pregnant women. The Abelam believe that as men are born of women, so women created the vegetation that men eat, and further that women first encountered the spirit beings, which men turned into sculptures. Geertz argues that inasmuch as line carvings for the Yoruba enact their idea of civilization and oval paintings for the Abelam enact their idea of the womb of nature, they enact these ideas *immediately*. They are not merely functional outcomes of a system of social imperatives – to do, say, with forest clearance or sexual reproduction. In Geertz's words:

> the central connection between art and collective life does not lie on ... an instrumental plane, it lies on a semiotic one. ... [T]he Yoruba's line arrangements do not ... celebrate social structure or forward useful doctrines. They materialize a way of experiencing, bring a particular cast of mind out into the world, where men can look at it. (1983: 99)

Alfred Gell pursues a different but complementary approach influenced by studies of animistic belief-systems in tribal societies. In *Art and Agency* (1998) Gell proposes that art objects compose a socially constructed category of special objects endowed with magical or quasi-magical status. In both indigenous and developed western societies art objects are believed to possess special kinds of causal powers that mimic the causal powers of human persons. Gell proposes that art objects are objects that are experienced as carrying derivative causal agency with respect to their producers, their recipients and their subjects of presentation. They are objects from which members of social groups infer or 'abduct' certain originating processes, for which these objects are thought to stand as signs or 'indexes' and as transmitters of further effects. Thus the cartoon caricature transmits agency from the artist who produced it to the person it ridicules. The voodoo doll is experienced as exerting agency over the real person it is held to embody. The sacred stone or piece of sacred wood or surrealist 'found object' compels the artist to display it or craft it in a particular way. The sacred stone or piece of sacred wood or surrealist 'found object' also moves its intended recipients into states of awe and veneration. Art objects also transmit agency from the recipients for whom they are made to the artists who make them. A patron may oblige a painter to represent the patron in the painting. In many portrait images, both the intended recipient and the intended subjects of the images imprint themselves in the forms of the canvas. Gell concedes that none of these cases are comparable to first-order intentional action by persons. They are derivative cases of agency, and they all depend on the mediating causal agency of the artist. However, Gell insists that they are still genuine cases of agency and are not irrational reifications.

Gell's proposal goes some way towards showing how anthropological ideas of art in terms of a socially generated category of magical or quasi-magical objects applies to modern western contexts of art as much as to indigenous contexts. This ethnographic way of thinking is explicitly pursued by many contemporary empirical sociologists of western arts institutions, to whose work we turn finally.

Empirical sociology of contemporary arts institutions

Empirical sociology of arts institutions refers to a type of research dating from around the 1960s and 1970s onwards by scholars trained primarily as social scientists. It is based on quantitative and qualitative analyses of arts markets, arts employment structures, arts administration, specialist arts networks and arts consumption patterns. This research differs from Marxist social history of art in that it is more consistently value-distanciating in its methods. It is more consistently oriented to abstention from value-judgement, and it usually eschews questions of aesthetic evaluation. It also differs from cultural materialist approaches by scholars trained primarily in humanities disciplines in that it focuses less on aesthetic contents in works of art and more on behavioural and institutional practices of public arts reception. The research may be seen in terms of a variety of projects of empirical application of the institutional theories of Danto and Dickie. It is represented mostly by a network of researchers from the US and a network of researchers from France. Both networks show affinities with social constructionist approaches to the study of science, such as in the work of Bruno Latour and the Edinburgh school of the sociology of science. The American network has strong connections with traditions of ethnomethodology and participant observation. It is particularly represented by the work of Howard Becker (1982). The French network has similarly strong ties to sociological ethnography, in the tradition of the journal founded by Émile Durkheim, the *Années Sociologiques*. It is particularly represented by the work of Pierre Bourdieu. A brief overview of the work of the main contributors here will serve to make these orientations clear.

In his book *Art Worlds* (1982), Howard Becker makes use of Danto's and Dickie's institutional theory and symbolic interactionist sociological theory to develop a value-neutral account of the place of the arts in society. Becker argues that art is less a history of outstanding creations by visionary individuals than a social configuration of practices guided by social conventions. Works of art are products of cooperative activity between networks of actors; and artists are only one type of actor within these networks. The networks include other actors such as dealers, agents, patrons, critics, curators, publishers and promoters. Becker notes the vast army of personnel required to script, direct, produce, edit and distribute films; the equally vast membership of ballet and theatre companies and classical orchestras; and the wide range of technicians, assistants, engineers, printers, editors and suppliers of equipment and materials who support painters, sculptors, photographers, writers, musicians and singers. Becker argues that these actors' activities are not secondary or exterior to the work of artists. Artists should be seen as conditioned in their actions by at least four main sets of social relations: by shared conventions and norms of art worlds; by material media and technologies of production; by patrons, sponsors and art markets; and by public tastes and public channels of reception in general. Becker contends that once these circumstances are identified, sociologists are equipped to explain why artists produce particular works in particular ways at particular times and places, and why they come to prominence at particular times and places. Sociologists help us to see how artists' reputations are made less by any gifts of 'genius' than by such unspectacular contingencies as shifts and fashions in the distribution of patronage and publicity. According to Becker:

> Art worlds consist of all the people whose activities are necessary to the production of the characteristic works which that world, and perhaps others as well, define as art. Members of art worlds coordinate the activities by which work is produced by referring to a body of conventional understandings embodied in common practice and in frequently used artefacts. The same people often cooperate repeatedly, even routinely, in similar ways to produce similar works, so that we can think of an art world as an established network of cooperative links among participants.... Works of art, from this point of view, are not the products of individual makers, 'artists' who possess a rare and special gift. They are, rather, joint products of all

the people who cooperate via an art world's characteristic conventions to bring works like that into existence. (Becker 1982: 34–5)

Becker's work stands behind a number of recent American cultural sociologists concerned with social relations in the organization of artistic work; with social relations in the construction of art genres and classifications; and with class and status differences in distinctions between 'high' and 'low' culture and in public arts consumption in general. Particular studies have concentrated on interactions between galleries, collectors, dealers and auction houses in the shaping of market demands and market prices for particular artists and art styles and movements, as well as on arts funding policies and arts education policies, and on the impact of processes of institutional professionalization, bureaucratization and commercialization on arts workers. These include studies by Blau (1989), Crane (1987), DiMaggio (1982, 1987), Dubin (1987), P. P. Clark (1987), Gans (1999), Griswold (1986), Halle (1993), Larson (1993), Levine (1988), Peterson (1986, 1997), White and White (1965) and Zolberg (1990). We will discuss some of these studies at length in chapters 3 and 4.

The French school consists of similar empirical studies of arts administration and status and prestige distribution in social classifications of cultural goods. Particular studies have concentrated on relations between art and money in the rise of commercial art markets since the nineteenth century and their impact on the celebrity of artists and art works, as well as on genre choices by artists in terms of career prospects. The French sociologists show how arts markets and patronage systems function as variables of the field of cultural production, constituting and differentiating the field's codes and delimiting the direction of artistic creativity. They show how artists shape and supply niches in cultural markets in response to changing patterns of audience expectation. The research is comparable to some extent to the French *Annales* school of historians in its use of quantitative frames of analysis, but it also has roots in a French anthropological tradition reaching back to the work of Marcel Mauss on gift exchange. More recently, it has developed in conjunction with analysis of competing 'discourses of justification' in social valuations of symbolic goods, such as in the work of Luc Boltanski and Laurent Thévenot (1991). At the centre of this research stands the figure of Pierre Bourdieu, whose work we discuss at length in chapter 4. But it is also represented by other important studies by Chiapello (1998), Heinrich (1998), Menger (1983), Menger and

Ginsburgh (1996), Moulin (1986, 1987), Hennion (1993) and Bourdieu and Passeron (1979).

The French and American sociologists bring to fulfilment the concerns of earlier generations of social historians of art with a non-metaphysical and non-ethnocentric understanding of art in society. They develop empirical research programmes consonant with the concerns of cultural studies writers, with institutional theories of art in analytical philosophy, and with the stock of concepts in anthropological studies of art. In later chapters we will explore both the strengths and some limitations of this work in relation to questions of aesthetic meaning and value in works of art.

Conclusion

We have introduced a range of approaches to sociological under-standing of the arts that pose challenges to long-standing metaphysical conceptions of art. These challenges reveal the shortcomings of metaphysical ideas that seek to define art in terms of one-sided prescriptive norms and essences. Metaphysical conceptions rest on attempts to define art in terms of sets of criteria that cannot be satisfied in sociohistorical reality without rather distorting and exclusionary consequences. In contrast, sociological approaches generally possess a stronger sense of the material preconditions, historical flux and cultural diversity of discourses, practices and institutions of art. We should, however, stress that it would be wrong to conclude that metaphysical conceptions lack relevance to contemporary under-standings of art, or that ideas of beauty, mimesis and aesthetic experience are meaningless ways of appreciating and thinking about art. Metaphysical conceptions are not inferior to sociological conceptions in any ultimate sense. They are simply different conceptions, which emerge from different historical universes of thought. In later parts of this book, we will argue that sociology of the arts is most informative for experience when it seeks to reconstruct the best insights of metaphysical conceptions concerning value and meaning in art at the same time as renouncing their more essentializing prescriptions in these regards. In the next chapter we discuss some first steps towards this position by investigating some essentially contested dimensions of *value* and *valuation* in art in relation to questions of politics and aesthetics.

2

Aesthetic Value and Political Value

We have reviewed a number of sociological approaches that challenge long-standing metaphysical conceptions of art by reference to changing sociocultural institutions of art. We now examine some implications of these challenges for questions of value and valuation in art. We begin by showing why a problem of value exists in sociology of the arts and why the problem cannot be wholly side-stepped in favour of 'value-free science'. This involves first pinpointing some limitations with George Dickie's and Arthur Danto's institutional theory of art, as well as some problems with Howard Becker's ethnographic approach. We will argue that the accounts of each of these writers represent overly stringent examples of projects of value-neutrality in sociology of the arts. Then we address a range of issues that arise once some constitutive place of valuation in art is openly accorded to sociology of the arts. These have to do first with the shortcomings of liberal-humanistic conceptions of 'timeless greatness' in fine art, and then with ways in which such conceptions are contested in the name of political values of equality of representation for marginalized social agents in cultural history, most notably in the work of socialist critics, feminist critics and postcolonial critics of art. We conclude with a preliminary assessment of the scope and limits of consensus in aesthetic appraisal.

Value-relevance and value-neutrality

We have said that sociological conceptions of art, unlike metaphysical conceptions, generally avoid making prescriptive value-laden

judgements about art. However, we must now attach certain qualifications to this assertion.

We stated in our introduction that Max Weber's conception of
'value-relevance' in sociological research holds particular importance
for sociology of the arts. Weber (1949) maintained that all researchers
should seek to refrain from value-judgements in their empirical
inquiries and not take advantage of the scientific prestige of their
occupation in order to propagate partisan normative agendas through
their work. However, Weber also accepted that in practice researchers
very often fail to refrain from value-judgements. Further, Weber
affirmed that no sociological research can be coherently thought of
as fundamentally 'value-free' because he argued that it is the existence
of values and 'value-ideas' in the minds of researchers which first
makes sociohistorical reality meaningful to researchers and first
conditions their selection of the very aspects of reality they hold to
be relevant to investigation.

Weber's conclusion holds special significance for sociological
studies of the arts because uses of the word 'art' in ordinary language
appear to be very deeply value-laden. Let us consider in this
instance the difference between two exemplary cases of ordinary
linguistic usage. A person who tastes the contents of a jar of edible
white crystals and declares 'That is sugar!' makes a statement of
fact. The person describes or identifies a state of affairs (the person
identifies, say, that the crystals are not salt). A person, on the other
hand, who looks at a picture on the wall and declares 'That is art!',
or 'That is a work of art!', makes more than merely a statement of
fact. The person expresses an evaluation. The person does not merely
describe what is on the wall; the person simultaneously expresses
approval of what is on the wall, at least implicitly. One might object
that this is not necessarily the case. One might argue that the person
who looks at the picture on the wall and calls its 'art' merely classifies
the picture as being an object of a certain type, without necessarily
expressing approval. This would appear to constitute a purely
classificatory, value-neutral use of the word 'art'. It would appear to
explain how there can be many references in ordinary language to
undistinguished creative productions by amateurs and by children
under the name of 'art'. This is the use of the word that many
empirical sociologists have sought to make central to their research
on grounds of cultural impartiality. However, it can be argued that
very strict scientific treatments of uses of the word 'art' are, nevertheless, limited and not entirely coherent in their operation, because
they try to extract from ordinary language only those dimensions of

uses of words that are factual and descriptive and artificially try to separate these dimensions from the words' broader context of value-relevance in lived experience.

We will now demonstrate the limitations of strict scientific analyses of 'art' by discussing several difficulties with two representative cases of a value-neutral attempt at understanding art: first some difficulties with Danto's and Dickie's institutional theory of art, and second some difficulties with Becker's empirical application of the theory.

A first difficulty with Danto's and Dickie's institutional theory concerns its proposition that works of art *must* have had conferred on them the status of art by some authoritative institution. What are we to say of works that have had no such treatment, such as pictures or poems that have not been exhibited or published, or of works deriving from a time or place in which no institution of art existed or exists in any formally developed sense? Must such works always receive status from an institution to exist as works of art, and must their creators always produce them with the intention of winning such status? Dickie's argument works well with the case of dadaist ready-mades in the twentieth century, but it does not account so well for a whole range of artefacts unlikely to have been produced with any conscious thought of enfranchisement by a formal institution. Danto contends that a society cannot produce objects of art unless and until it has a conception of art, where possession of a conception of art depends on the social existence of an 'art world'. Thus prehistoric cave paintings in Danto's view were not art until a century ago when western society began to develop a consciousness of them as art. It would, he says, 'never have occurred to the painters of Lascaux that they were producing *art* on those walls' (1964: 581). But does it follow from this that they were *not* producing art on those walls? Can we not still speak of recognizing art in them today? As Hanfling (1992: 26) points out, it seems reasonable to say that we do recognize the Lascaux paintings for what they are: they *are* works of art, and do not acquire this character only by some modern institution's act of designating them as art.

A second difficulty arises when we consider whether conferral of status by an institution *suffices* for things to be works of art. Is it really the case that just because something is on show in a gallery, it must be art? Do not ordinary spectators have a need (and perhaps a 'right') to form a decision for themselves about whether it is art, and whether it is 'good enough' to be art? Hanfling (1992: 29) raises the question of whether an object's being declared art is more like a child being baptized 'John' by a priest or more like a ball being declared 'out' by the umpire in a game of tennis. If it is more like a child being baptized 'John', then someone who goes to an art gallery and disagrees that something in it is art would be like someone denying that a person called John is called John. On the other hand, if it is more like an umpire declaring the ball 'out', the sceptical spectator would have to be taken more seriously because just as a tennis spectator can question whether the umpire's decision is fair by reference to the actual physical position of the ball, so the art spectator could point to some relevant feature of the object that exists independently of the institution's declaration. The difficulty with the institutional theory is that it views art as mostly analogous to the baptism case rather than to the tennis case. It assumes the truth of whether something is or is not art to be entirely determined by the institutional setting.

This particularly becomes a problem when we investigate Dickie's concept of 'appreciation'. Normally one would expect the word 'appreciation' to mean some disposition of approval resulting from a process of consideration. Therefore one would expect the phrase '*candidate* for appreciation' to refer to something that awaits or solicits approval, with the possibility of its *not* gaining approval, just as a candidate for an examination may or may not pass. But then Dickie's talk of 'candidate for appreciation' would seem redundant because *ex hypothesi* the whole question of whether something is to be 'appreciated' has already been answered in favour of a 'yes'. It certainly looks as though the institutional theory needs some conception of appreciation in order not to appear arbitrary. Yet it cannot coherently accommodate this conception because appreciation implies independent processes of aesthetic valuation by ordinary spectators based on what they see, feel and sensuously experience in the work. Pursued to its logical conclusion, Dickie's argument is unable to account for the abilities of art world personnel to justify their decision to confer status on objects *even to themselves*, because, *ex hypothesi*, art world personnel cannot have a reason to regard an object as art unless the object has already had art status conferred on it previously. No object could ever become art if this were the case. We must therefore conclude that objects do not become works of art solely by the *fiat* of a formal art institution. As Wollheim (1980) points out, conferring art status on something implies making a judgement by reference to reasons capable of backing up the judgement; and offering reasons for a judgement involves referring to qualities, aspects or features of perception in the object which any ordinary spectators could, in principle, see for themselves and come to a view about.

In truth, there are many ways in which we can demonstrate that actual decisions by art worlds are not arbitrary. Duchamp's ready-mades and Warhol's Brillo boxes were, and are, recognizable and appreciable as works of art because they are visually thought-provoking and illuminating; because they make use of a sensuous medium in a spatial setting to communicate an idea (about 'civiliza-tion', 'culture', the 'consumer society', and so on) that could not have been communicated in any other way, such as in a newspaper article or an academic book, with the same interesting aesthetic effect. For these reasons, they remain, in principle, open to appre-ciation by any ordinary member of the public, not only to expert institutional authorities. However, the problem with Dickie's and Danto's theory is that it tends not to make this public basis of appreciation explicable. It makes it appear as though the art world's decisions were merely those of an insider coterie. Danto and Dickie do not give a perspicuous account of how curatorial decisions to purchase and display works respond to art journalism and criticism, and of how this criticism responds in turn to general appreciation based on direct value-relevant experience of the works in question. In their attempt to elaborate a purely value-neutral conception of art, they misconstrue the basis of lived value-relevance that first makes art meaningful to ordinary spectators and that is the only ultimate source of normative authority from which institutional authorities derive their social credibility.

Similar difficulties arise with Becker's ethnographic approach. Becker is certainly right to point out that virtually all artists rely on a variety of supporting personnel whose actions play a significant part in the constitution of artists' works. He is also right to point out the sociological peculiarity of the codes of etiquette that regulate conduct in art world milieux. One thinks of vernissages, premières, prize ceremonies, and the like. But we must question the relevance of these facts to the specific reasons for which artists win acclaim for their work. If theatre lighting engineers are to be recognized as contributing to the merit of performances, are we to say the same of the stage hands – and the catering services for actors behind the scenes? And if it is significant to say that art worlds comprise systems of in-group behavioural codes, can we not say exactly the same of other institutional worlds – such as prisons, psychiatric hospitals, gambling syndicates, Freemasons' lodges, drug rings? What is there that is specific to *art* worlds in this assertion?

Further, if it is the case that works of art are understood socio-logically when various material, institutional and financial circum-stances are adduced that led to their production at definite times and places, in what sense are they understood specifically as works of *art*, rather than as works of some other content of production – such as plastic boxes, contraception pills, mobile phones? It appears that Becker's arguments tell us nothing very relevant either to *aesthetic contents* in works of art or to *aesthetic norms* guiding artists' engagements with these contents. Aesthetic contents are not reducible to material media of works of art. Aesthetic contents are what makes it meaningful for Duchamp's *Fountain* to exist in the exhibition space of the gallery rather than in the men's toilets of the gallery. Aesthetic norms, similarly, are not reducible to social conventions. Aesthetic norms refer to the internal reasons artists have for accepting, modifying or transforming previous styles and idioms of invention. They are of a different order both from wider social mores and from the institutional structures that shape artists' careers.

Becker overlooks these distinctions in his attempt to account for the genesis of artistic value by stating that artists' 'mutual apprecia-tion of the conventions they share, and the support they mutually afford one another, convince them that what they are doing is worth doing', and therefore 'if artists act under the definition of "art", their interaction convinces them that what they produce are valid works of art' (1982: 39). Becker's reasoning in this statement is circular. Becker effectively states that some works are good because some people talk themselves into believing they are good. This rather behaviouristic way of proceeding vitiates Becker's attempt to draw a cogent link between artists' reputations and contexts of historical accident and contingency. Certainly it is informative to point out the 'accident' that the music of J. S. Bach was not recognized as profound in his day. But should we also say that when it *was* recog-nized as impressive, sixty years after his death, this too was an 'accident'? Why should we not say that by the later date, public consciousness had corrected its earlier opinion and come to a more reasonable estimation? Are changes and revisions in aesthetic judgement only to be deemed changes of fashion? We would not normally think of the making and unmaking of scientists' reputa-tions in this way. Nor would we normally think of changes and revisions to judgements in courts of law in this way. So why should we think of the making and unmaking of artists' reputations any differently? Contingent shifts of institutional favour, patronage and fashion are, to be sure, important in art history, just as they are in the history of science. But they are not *all* the story.

The aforegoing objections to Danto, Dickie and Becker underscore some limits around attempts to construct strictly value-neutral analyses of art. These objections should certainly not be seen as demonstrating that such analyses possess no empirical utility. Approaches such as Danto's, Dickie's and Becker's and other approaches in empirical sociology of arts institutions illuminate a multitude of ways in which artistic practices relate to social conventions and social codes of interaction. But the problems we have highlighted indicate that if sociology of the arts is truly to be 'meaningfully adequate' to its subject, it must involve some evaluative engagement with the normative contents of its subject. Sociology of the arts must be capable of giving some cogent account of the experienced value-qualities that make it meaningful for objects to be recognized and appreciated as art. This is not to say that researchers' every single act of empirical observation immediately commits them to affirming a value-judgement about the objects of their analyses. And it is certainly not to say that it is not feasible and desirable for researchers to seek to separate descriptive components of their discourse from normative components of their discourse, as Weber enjoins. But it is to say that, at some stage or other, researchers cannot abjure their intellectual responsibility to declare to the reader the relation of the empirical objects of their research to the informing values and valuations that motivate them to select these components, and to give an account of how these informing values and valuations address questions of value relevant to the objects themselves.

A new set of problems now opens up at this juncture. If it is accepted that value-freedom is not an option in sociology of the arts, new difficulties arise. If it is granted that sociological analysis requires critical engagement with values, researchers have to address the question of what these values are, and whose values they are. If spectators of art express their appreciation of works of art by praising them as 'good' (or their non-appreciation of works of art by criticizing them as 'bad'), researchers have to ask: Who are these spectators, and do their judgements speak for everyone? Are values in art to be seen as holding for everyone and for all time, or only for certain groups of people at particular times in history? Is value in art to be seen as objective and universal? Is it possible to speak of 'great' art? If so, what might such 'greatness' mean? What is to be said of the voices of relatively powerless social agents in history who have not traditionally enjoyed a claim over definitions of such 'great-ness', such as the voices of subordinate social classes, and women, and non-western peoples?

The complexity of these issues makes it understandable that many sociologists have sought to store questions of value in art in a strategic 'black box'. But the challenge remains to address these questions. In the following, we will proceed first by setting out a number of objections to traditional liberal-humanistic conceptions of timeless greatness in art. Then we set out the main arguments about value in art advanced within three standpoints of politically engaged criticism: socialist criticism, feminist criticism and postcolonial criticism.

Liberal-humanistic art scholarship

Liberal-humanistic conceptions of value in art are associated with the outlook of the founding figures in art history from the early twentieth century. They are associated with the German art scholars to whom we referred in chapter 1: Heinrich Wölfflin, Aby Warburg, Erwin Panofsky, Alois Riegl and others. They are also associated with similar founding figures in the discipline of English literary criticism, including F. R. Leavis, I. E. Richards and the Victorian critic Matthew Arnold, who famously spoke of 'Culture' as 'the best that has been thought and said in the world', in his influential pamphlet from 1869, *Culture and Anarchy*.

All these authors – the German scholars in particular – took a view of life rooted in the values of the classical Greek and Roman civilizations and the European Enlightenment. They saw art history as forming an integral part in the education and spiritual cultivation or *Bildung* of the university graduate, in the spirit of Renaissance humanism. They pointed to Renaissance figures such as Alberti, Leonardo, Michelangelo and Dürer as paragons of 'universal men', steeped equally in the arts and the sciences. The most celebrated statement of this worldview is Jakob Burckhardt's *Civilisation of the Renaissance in Italy* (of 1860), which spoke of the creative genius of the Italian people in an age that recognized free inquiry and free self-expression of the individual. Panofsky echoed Burckhardt's worldview in his definition of humanism as 'not so much a move-ment as an attitude which can be defined as the conviction of the dignity of man, based on both the insistence on human values (rationality and freedom) and the acceptance of human limitations (fallibility and frailty): from this two postulates result – responsibility and tolerance' (Panofsky 1955: 24). These convictions have led many humanistic art scholars to speak of certain works of art and literature as 'masterpieces', created by artists of 'genius' who speak for the universal values of humanity. Probably the most widely read example of humanistic art scholarship is Ernst Gombrich's *The Story of Art*, first published in 1950.

Taken as a whole, and at the risk of some elision of differences between actual individual scholars, we may enumerate at least four main sets of problems with liberal-humanistic conceptions of value in art.

First, humanistic scholarship tends to be highly selective in its assumptions about which kinds of cultural objects contain value, and it tends not to account for this selectivity in a transparent way. Its preferred cultural objects are invariably the work of men, most often from a white European background, and most often from the more privileged social classes; and usually the objects are self-contained works of 'fine' or 'high' art preserved in a definite material medium, rather than popular practices or ways of life.

Second, humanistic scholarship invariably thinks in terms of exclusive canons of influence and stylistic descendancy. A canon takes the form of a singe line or arrow of development over time, represented by beacon-like individuals. We may think of the Italian canon of Renaissance painters narrated in Giorgio Vasari's *Lives of the Artists* (of 1550), passing from Giotto to Masaccio to Botticelli and then on to the high Renaissance masters of Leonardo, Michelangelo and Raphael. Similarly we may think of the canon of nineteenth-century English novelists celebrated in F. R. Leavis's *The Great Tradition* (of 1948), passing from Jane Austen to George Eliot, Henry James and Joseph Conrad. The concept of the canon is biblical and ecclesiastical in origin, deriving from the Greek word for 'rule' or 'standard', *kanon*. It was originally used to denote the legitimate non-apocryphal books of the Bible, and then was also used to denote the appointment of saints by the Roman Catholic Church, as in the 'canonization' of saints. Thus the idea of a canon in literary and art history carries the connotation of a sacred sequence, based on a succession of 'founding fathers', a holy parade of the saints of art through history. It is an exclusionary, patriarchal construction of thought.

Third, humanistic scholarship approaches its objects predominantly from the standpoint of formal aesthetic evaluation, at the expense of aspects of social, economic and political context. It tends to privilege questions of such kinds as: How does Raphael's coloration of the face of the Virgin contribute to her aspect of purity? Or, how does Shakespeare's metaphor of the summer's day enliven the rhetoric of courtship in sonnet number 18? Or, how does Picasso's use of line enhance the appearance of monumentality in his neoclassical paintings? If it asks questions about socioeconomic or political context, it tends to view these only as auxiliary subordinate questions. It tends to regard formal evaluation as the principal and authentic task of criticism, relative to which all other angles of analysis are extraneous or appropriate only to some other discipline. While it often does consider elements of material culture, it mostly only considers these elements from the standpoint of formal aesthetic qualities of design, rather than from the standpoint of their technological context of production and social function. Thus its conception of the material relations of culture tends not to be particularly sociologically developed.

Fourth, humanistic scholarship tends not to consider ways in which the prestigious value it awards to certain cultural objects relates to conditions of power and hegemony in society. It tends not to consider the ways in which this prestigious value might be contested by particular groups in society, or reinterpreted and recombined by these groups with different cultural meanings in different practices of reception and appropriation. It tends to take meaning and value in cultural objects as invariant for different groups in society. It therefore tends to overlook or underestimate the respects in which prestigious cultural objects depend on relations of domination and dissent in society. It assumes value in works of art to be self-evident and everlasting, irrespective of past changes and all possible future changes in social structure; and it focuses on cultural forms more or less exclusively from the point of view of their existence as self-subsistent works, not from the point of view of their consumption by social audiences or from the point of view of the contribution of these audiences to the construction of their significance.

These four sets of objections to humanistic thinking summarize many of the arguments of recent cultural-materialist writers about social and political constructions of aesthetic value. We will reappraise these objections at the end of this chapter in our general assessment of the scope and limits of consensus in aesthetic appraisal. But we will now turn to the ways in which these objections are developed specifically by socialist art critics of the 1960s and 1970s, concentrating in particular on the work of two British authors, John Berger and Janet Wolff.

Socialist criticism

Originally based on a TV series for the BBC, John Berger's influential book *Ways of Seeing* (1972) is conceived in a spirit of polemical critique of the cultural establishment. Berger begins with some comments on two group portraits of public benefactors by the seventeenth-century Dutch painter Frans Hals. Berger here attacks the mystifying tendencies of humanistic scholars who gloss over the political intentions and real material conditions of poverty of the artist. Berger argues that it is misleading to speak of Hals's 'vivid characterisations', or of his 'close view of life's vital forces' or his 'harmonious fusions' of colour. Instead, Berger argues that Hals has deliberately rendered his sitters in sanctimonious poses as an expression of his own powerless and impoverished position in society. Berger argues that with the rise of oil painting in the seventeenth century, typically in the form of smaller sized works that could be more easily transported, and typically in a variety of genres such as landscape, domestic interior, still life and portraiture, painting attested to the increasing effects of capitalism on social relations. Berger argues that this was especially the case at centres of trade such as Amsterdam and London. Berger argues that oil painting enabled some artists to depict in highly sensuous detailed and tactile terms precisely what art collectors wished to possess and to see represented as a sum of possessions.

Berger also argues for this position through a discussion of a landscape painting by Gainsborough from 1750, depicting a landowner with his wife standing in the foreground, *Mr and Mrs Andrews*. Berger argues that Gainsborough's painting cannot be understood in terms of a notion of 'man in harmony with nature'. It can only be understood as an image of the pride of a member of the eighteenth-century propertied English ruling classes. Berger argues that humanistic scholarship ignores these issues by venerating the uniqueness of original 'great paintings' in pseudo-religious terms. Humanistic scholarship mystifies sociohistorical realities in an attempt to confer legitimacy on a legacy of domination and subordination. It effectively champions the interests and identities of elite oligarchies in the name of a spurious national cultural past. Berger declares: 'In the end, the art of the past is being mystified because a privileged minority is striving to invent a history which can retrospectively justify the role of the ruling classes, and such a justification can no longer make sense in modern terms.' Therefore we must choose 'between a total approach to art which attempts to relate it to every aspect of experience and the esoteric approach of a few specialised experts who are the clerks of the nostalgia of a ruling class in decline' (1972: 11, 32).

In a similar spirit, Janet Wolff (1981) sets out to demonstrate that works of art do not arise from divine inspiration to individuals of innate genius. Wolff argues that the concept of 'creativity' must be replaced by that of 'production', and further that artistic work should not be seen as essentially different from other kinds of work. Wolff singles out several factors for analysis: relations to technologies and media of production; social systems of production, involving supporting personnel; training and schooling of artists; patronage sources and markets, and sponsoring institutions. Wolff proposes that social analysis requires concentrating first on empirical facts about relationships between socioeconomic structure and artistic agency, and then on assessing the extent to which these relationships give grounds for deeming works of art to be enacting 'ideology'. To say that a work of art enacts ideology is to say that the social interests that govern its patronage and reception and that thereby shape its contents of expression are the interests of dominant classes in society. However, Wolff counsels against reductive theories of ideology in art. Ideological elements in a work of art must be seen as 'mediated by the existing aesthetic codes and conventions in which it is constructed' and must not be seen as 'simply reflected in art, not only because it is mediated by a variety of complex social processes, but also because it is transformed by the modes of representation in which it is produced'. But she insists that liberal-humanistic ideas of artistic creativity are not valid objections to the concept of ideology in art. 'Insofar as people, including artists, are socially and historically located, and are members of particular social groups, then their thought, including their artistic ideas, is ideological.' Analysis of ideology in art is essential, so long as it does not 'crudely overlook the complexities of specific groups and individuals' often contradictory positions within them' (1981: 66, 70).

Wolff's contribution for the most part avoids what many commentators have seen as a difficulty with John Berger's work. In a way that is typical of some mid-century Marxist historians of art, Berger takes a political, socio-critical approach to art history but still takes for granted the greatness of a certain select canon of artists. Berger does not show how the socialist considerations he advances might suggest different constructions of the canon involving agents who are not necessarily all white European men. Berger places himself in the rather inconsistent position of asserting both that all artists' works are conditioned by political interests of power and that some select artists such as Hals and Rembrandt rise above this conditioning and achieve greatness. Wolff, on the other hand, generally produces a better attempt at marrying materialist analysis with aesthetic evaluation and distinguishing between them. In a later text, Wolff (1993) counsels against doctrinaire Marxist approaches that try to clothe particular normative positions on aesthetic value and political value in the guise of impartial socioeconomic analysis. Wolff argues that aesthetic value retains a degree of specificity in relation to political value and should not be conflated with the latter. While some humanistic authors tend to draw reactionary conclusions from this specificity, seeing no relevance for sociological arguments except as an invasion of 'political correctness', some Marxist approaches pre-judge works of art according to a predefined scheme of political history. Such approaches effectively assimilate aesthetic evaluation to a deterministic philosophy of history based on a putative 'science of ideology' – such as in the work of the French structuralist Marxist, Louis Althusser.

The problems Wolff identifies in these observations are complex ones to which we will return in later chapters, and also at the end of this chapter. We turn now to a second body of objections to humanistic scholarship: to feminist criticism.

Feminist criticism

Feminist criticism in art history is represented by a wide range of critics, notably Chadwick (1990), Nochlin (1989), Pollock (1988, 1999), J. Rose (1986), Mulvey (1989) and many others. We can say there are fundamentally two angles from which feminist critics examine women's involvement in art: from the angle of women's passive appearance as objects of representation by male artists, and from the angle of women's role as active producers of art. We treat these two aspects in turn.

Until the twentieth century, it would seem that women have appeared in art history far more in the role of passive objects of art than they have as active producers of art; at least, that is, on the assumption of a restrictive definition of 'art' limited to prestigious genres such as oil painting, portraiture, history painting and mythological painting. In a vast quantity of representations traditionally defined as 'art', women scarcely figure in art otherwise than as objects of a male gaze, as objects of spectacle and curiosity, or as symbols of male material wealth and social prestige. Humanistic discourses of the timeless dignity of the female nude, of feminine 'grace' and 'beauty', ignore the ways in which men have historically been able to define themselves in relation to objects that are external to them and over which they exercise power, whereas women in traditional domestic settings have only been able to define themselves by their own appearance and demeanour. These circumstances help explain why countless traditional art images depict women in ways that fixate on their visual presence, and seldom investigate their actions or thoughts as independent rational agents. Often these images portray women in ways that border on the pornographic, and at the same time invoke hypocritical notions of virtue and vice, chastity and modesty, sin and desire – most primordially in representations of the story of Adam and Eve. Among the most typical are those revolving around allegories of vanity where women are depicted as gazing at themselves in mirrors while revealing their faces and bodies for delectation by male spectators (see illustration 2).

From around the nineteenth century, it is possible to speak of certain changes in these patriarchal relations. In the nineteenth century, realist and impressionist male painters such as Courbet, Manet and Renoir painted images of women and men in society that probed conventional codes of comportment between the sexes. One of the most discussed examples of this is Manet's *Olympia* (of 1864), a painting of a prostitute reclining in a pose that strikingly recalls traditional representations of the goddess Venus. The reclining woman has a defiant manner which repels the curious male viewer and dramatically deflates discourses of female virtue and grace by associating divinity with the profane and the execrated. Many feminist critics have also argued that even within contexts of conventional social order, representations of women and men can be ambiguous in ways that unconsciously or unintentionally undermine dominant sexual stereotypes. Some feminist writers have made qualified use of Jacques Lacan's psychoanalytic notion of woman as the sex of 'otherness' and 'absence' which reappears in the societal imaginary as the site of semiotic plenitude, as the excessive and uncontrollable which subverts stable categories of identity. In this sense, many feminist critics have analysed representational schemes of sexuality by showing how these schemes both encode social regimes of control and surveillance and are at the same time fallible and contradictory. One case of this is male artists' preoccupation with muscularity, valour and manliness veering over into homoerotic

2 **Hans Memling,** *Vanity, c.1485.* Musée des Beaux Arts, Strasbourg

passion – perhaps most famously in the sculpture and frescos of Michelangelo.

Turning now to the aspect of women as active producers of art, many feminist critics have addressed the question of why apparently so few women feature in the history of 'great artists' (Nochlin 1989). Feminist critics have proposed several types of response to this question: responses bearing firstly on the reasons for women's historical debarment from access to the spaces of formal art worlds, and secondly on constructions of 'greatness'.

The reasons for women's historical exclusion from formal art worlds include women's confinement to domestic roles across all social classes; their restriction to manual labour and child-rearing in the lower classes and to entertainment functions in the upper strata; their lack of access to education and training, except in respect of certain prescribed activities such as piano-playing, embroidery or book illustration; lack of the basic prerequisites of money to buy materials, and access to a personal space such as a studio. In addition, there are the taboos responsible for women's exclusion from life-drawing classes in the academies and from literary and artistic clubs and intellectual networks, as well as social expectations of humility, virtue and service. These taboos operate at the expense of opportunities for independent creative and intellectual development, except perhaps in the form of largely private confessional activities such as diary-keeping and letter-writing.

It is well known that until the late nineteenth century very few women writers were able to secure publication contracts unless they adopted male pseudonyms. As for women painters, almost all before the nineteenth century were daughters of some already established master, or closely sponsored by some dominant male artist. Very few women are known to have been able to make their names independently of some form of patriarchal endorsement. In sixteenth-century Italy Marietta Robusti was promoted by her father Tintoretto, and in seventeenth-century Holland Judith Leyster was promoted by her teacher Frans Hals. In both these cases, paintings by the two women have been repeatedly misattributed to their male tutors. This has also been the case for two eighteenth-century women painters, Constance Charpentier and Adélaïde Labille-Guiard, who were pupils of Jacques-Louis David. Such misattributions indicate a deep structural bias in the way women's involvements in art have been traditionally recorded. Women artists have been described as being only 'in the school of', 'in the style of' or 'under the influence of' some apparently more important male artist.

It should be noted that women painters have also been subject to severe social constraints relating to the forms and contents in which they were permitted to work. Women were not permitted to work on projects larger than relatively small-scale oil or watercolour paintings. They were debarred from prestigious commissions such as frescos, sculpture or church panel painting; and they were strongly discouraged from producing images that did not demonstrate their 'feminine' virtues of modesty, diligence and composure. Although some women were able to elude or subvert these norms and stigmas in subtle ways, the majority of women painters were socially constrained to depict women in poses and occupations acceptable to men: for example domestic interiors showing women engaged in knitting and housework, or receiving guests, or praying, writing and reading letters, or being courted for marriage.

These considerations have led feminist critics to challenge traditional conceptions of art history, as much at the level of concepts and categories of art as at the level of socioeconomic conditions and institutional contexts of production. They have shown how canons and traditions of art have themselves been determined by patriarchal structures of institutional power. They have highlighted the ways in which decisions to select works by male artists for presentation in galleries and then for reproduction and discussion in catalogues and academic books and education programmes have themselves been influenced by male appointments, gentlemen's clubs and old-boys' networks in the management structures of arts institutions and offices of state. They have shown that women's subordination in historical cultural valuation follows the same pattern as women's subordination in the political, legal and economic structures of society. In challenging this subordination, feminist critics have sought to generate alternative concepts and categories of analysis capable of bringing into focus a wide range of once virtually anonymous creative women individuals. These include not only oil painters but also manuscript illustrators and decorators, printers, embroiderers, tapestry makers, clothiers, lace-makers, and a plethora of women involved in craft, horticulture, furnishing and design of various kinds. This has involved rejecting the denigration of predicates traditionally attached to femininity such as 'decorative' and 'miniature', and other gendered inflections of language. Feminist critics have argued that instead of accepting an already fixed bench-line of male artists and tagging on to this bench-line a list of extra, more or less 'exceptional' women's names, art history should radically revise the vocabulary in which analysis and evaluation is carried out. They have highlighted the historical reality of lack of opportunity for women artists but have also drawn attention to hitherto occluded dimensions of creative agency for women in the production of culture – beyond traditional conceptions of the boundaries of 'art'.

A similar revisionary approach occurs in postcolonial criticism, to which we now turn.

Postcolonial criticism

By addressing issues of ethnicity alongside issues of class and gender, postcolonial art criticism injects a further dimension of reflexivity into the critique of liberal humanism. Postcolonial criticism sets out from similar premises to anthropological studies of art: it pinpoints the limited relevance of western ideas of beauty and aesthetics to indigenous societies. However, it does not restrict itself to scientific value-neutrality. It interrogates western discourses from the aspect of their ethnocentric worldview of other cultures and from the aspect of their relationship of colonial power over these cultures. Like feminist criticism, postcolonial criticism aims to be a critique of exclusionary structures of cultural valuation. We may examine it both from the angle of colonized cultures as objects of western representations, and from the angle of colonized cultures as artistic agencies in their own right.

From the first angle, many postcolonial critics have commented on visual logics of mystification and obfuscation of 'other', 'native', 'primitive' and 'oriental' cultures in western art. They have highlighted the way in which western symbols of 'man' in general invariably depict white Caucasians, endowed with a range of attributes of strength, courage, reason, cunning and invention, in contrast to the 'brutality' of 'darker races'. Christian religious, historical and mythological paintings of scenes from the Bible, or from Greek mythology, or from ancient history, invariably depict Christ and the Old Testament prophets and the Greco-Roman heroes as white men. Darker skinned peoples are consigned to the role of marginal background figures, nomads or enemies. In a large swathe of European artistic imagery, the Orient stands for despotism against enlightenment, decadence against civilization, sensualism against reason (Said 1978). In some cases this imagery is romanticized, as in Eugène Delacroix's early nineteenth-century images of dashing Arab travellers on horseback, or it is sentimentalized in discourses of innocence and the 'noble savage' (Hiller 1991). In late nineteenth- and early twentieth-century European modernist art, preoccupation with the primitive, the irrational and the instinctual suggests possibilities of spiritual healing from the ills of western modernity, such as in Gauguin's images of Arcadian tribespeople from the South Sea islands, or it suggests fear of violence and fateful anxiety, such as in Picasso's cubist painting, *Les Demoiselles d'Avignon* (of 1907) depicting African prostitutes as emblems of dark urban conflictual forces (see illustration 3).

Several postcolonial critics have made use of André Malraux's reference to modern culture as a *musée imaginaire* of objectifications

3   Pablo Picasso, *Les Demoiselles d'Avignon*, 1907. Museum of Modern Art, New York © 2003, digital image The Museum of Modern Art, New York/SCALA, Florence. © DACS/Succession Picasso 2003

of the past. Writing in France in the 1950s, Malraux meant the way in which modern western societies turn the life practices, belief-systems and structures of vision of past historical worlds into objects of curiosity, petrifying and disconnecting them from one another in their living relations of meaning (Malraux 1967). Modern society reacts to the traditions of its past and 'other cultures' by laying them out on a surface before the gaze of the spectator. This occurs literally in the glass cabinets of the museum, on the walls of the gallery, on the pages of the illustrated catalogue, on the tourist balcony or viewing prospect. More metaphorically, it occurs in the mind of the collector, the antiquarian, the scholar and, not least, the colonial traveller. Flattened out in this way, artefacts of the past and other cultures tend to become interchangeable, like simple combinatory elements in the museum of our imagination.

Postcolonial critics emphasize that colonized cultures should be understood from the angle of their own artistic agency. They examine the ways in which native art produced before colonization has become appropriated by colonizers and the ways in which colonized peoples have reacted to this colonization. They have underlined the ways in which religious artefacts in the Christian West have been singled out for deep spiritual appraisal, whereas religious artefacts from other world cultures have been apprehended mostly only with the eye of anthropological curiosity. They have drawn attention to the ransacking of ancient African, Asian and American holy shrines and settlements for objects of display in western museums or for private delectation in the mansions of wealthy aristocrats. In this sense they show how the exotic objects plundered by adventurers and trafficked across the seas by merchants form an integral part of the culture of western antiquarian connoisseurship. It is this legacy of violence that motivates postcolonial writers and artists to voice the experiences of colonized peoples through their work. Representatives of colonized peoples have sought to speak on a universal stage: to have their works displayed in the historic galleries of the West and their writings published in the West; and to write and create in the national languages of the West – the languages of their colonizers – while at the same time speaking from the position of 'others' and 'outsiders' and articulating their marginalized and injured identities. However, their work is frequently seen by western publics as being only of particularistic interest, segregated from the implied greater universality of the western mainstream. Postcolonial works of art and literature raise a claim to intrinsic intellectual and aesthetic universality. They are often motivated by protest and insistence on recognition for legacies of injustice. But in this very insistence, they call out for specific aesthetic and intellectual engagement, on the same universal stage as the hegemonic cultures of the West (Price 1989).

Sociology, politics and aesthetics

We have discussed three sets of politically engaged art criticism revolving around the three inequality dimensions of class, gender and ethnicity. We will now propose some provisional conclusions on the scope for political contestation of constructions of aesthetic value in art history.

We began this chapter by arguing that sociological understanding of the arts requires more than strictly value-neutral analysis if it is genuinely to be 'meaningfully adequate' to its subject. We have argued that achieving meaning-adequacy requires engagement with questions of aesthetic content and value in works of art. Yet we have also seen the complexity of the issues that arise when such engagement is attempted. Socialist critics interrogate aesthetic value from the standpoint of class struggle in art history. Feminist critics reveal women's exclusion from patriarchal institutions of art history. Postcolonial critics uncover dimensions of violence against subaltern peoples in western art history. These three types of intervention raise important questions about the scope and limits of consensus in aesthetic appraisal. They raise the question of how much agreement can be reached about value in art history if all such value is understood from politically antagonistic points of view.

It seems likely that socialist, feminist and postcolonial critics could come to agreement about the mutually reinforcing significance of class, gender and ethnicity as dimensions of hegemony and domination. The more difficult question is whether politically engaged art critics could come to agreement with liberal-humanistic critics who tend to insist strongly on the distinctness of aesthetic evaluation from questions of politics. We have argued that it is wrong to separate aesthetic evaluation from questions of politics. But we now need to establish the precise sense of this non-separateness. If questions of aesthetic value are not separate from questions of politics, are they indistinguishable from one another? Are no distinctions permissible between aesthetic evaluation and political advocacy?

We will argue in this book that if aesthetic valuation were indistinguishable from political valuation, the rational motive for politically engaged critics to think politically about art would dissolve entirely. If questions of aesthetic value were reducible to issues of cultural hegemony, there would be no reason for political critique of art in particular. There would be no basis for agreement about aesthetic value, nor even for disagreement about aesthetic value in the light of questions of politics. We will therefore argue that while liberal-humanistic scholarship's typical lack of sociopolitical reflexivity needs to be exposed and challenged, its emphasis on the specificity of questions of aesthetic value need not be seen as necessarily problematic and need not be seen as necessarily incompatible with more politically engaged art criticism. The fact that some groups in society have historically enjoyed greater power to make their per-spectives on aesthetic value dominate over other groups' perspectives does not entail that works of art cannot be shown to possess aesthetic value in themselves. It does not entail that all historically received valuations of works of art are nothing but reflections of the power of the most dominant agents in history. It does not entail that the arguments put forward by a white upper-class man for the aesthetic value of a particular work could never conceivably be endorsed by a black working-class woman, and it does not entail that the arguments put forward by a black working-class woman for the aesthetic value of another work could never conceivably be endorsed by a white upper-class man. Questions of social power are relevant to questions of aesthetic value; but questions of aesthetic value are not reducible to questions of social power. To deny this would be to adopt a position of *relativism* in aesthetic appraisal, which has self-contradictory consequences.

In chapter 4 we discuss further aspects of the problem of relativism in aesthetic appraisal with reference to sociological criticisms of Kantian philosophical aesthetics. In the following we introduce a few preliminary considerations.

A first consideration is that it is important not to criticize liberal-humanistic scholarship in an undifferentiated manner. The concept of a liberal-humanistic stance in art criticism is an ideal-typical construction which has been employed here deliberately in order to highlight particular aspects of a mode of art scholarship. In real-ity, however, some individual representatives of liberal-humanistic scholarship are more variegated in their outlook than we have been able to present them here. It should not be thought that all liberal-humanistic scholars are as averse to direct politicizations of art history as the most patriarchal-chauvinistic representatives of art criticism in Victorian England, nineteenth-century Prussia or nineteenth-century France. Some liberal-humanistic scholars are more reflexive about their values than others; and not all scholars have been resistant to sociological analysis of value-orientation in art history. For example, Panofsky's and Cassirer's writings are rich in insights into socially constructed value-systems and symbol systems in history that anticipate more recent structuralist and poststructuralist accounts of cultural meaning.

A second central consideration is that it is important not to impugn humanistic scholars' emphasis on the specificity of aesthetics wholly and exclusively on grounds of their defective sociopolitical reflexivity. It certainly should not be thought that the intellectual integrity of humanistic scholarship falls by the political insensitivities of its rhetorical constructions alone. The characteristic appearance in humanistic scholarship of words such as 'genius', 'masterpiece' and 'mastery' need not be seen as inherently objectionable. These words occur just as much in the language of ordinary spectators of art, and they do so because they are linguistically rich ways of expressing appreciation, wonder and admiration. It is possible to distinguish ideological contents of traditional rhetoric in art history from the basic senses of merit, quality, distinction and accomplishment to which this rhetoric attempts to make reference. There is no a priori reason why more reconstructed uses of these predicates should not be possible and legitimate, on the understanding that *any* subject positions can be bearers of them – women, children and non-western peoples as much as white European males.

It is worth underlining in this connection that for Kant and the German idealist philosophers – whose ideas influenced humanistic traditions in art scholarship – 'genius' carried a carefully defined meaning. It was not an obscurantist term. It meant the ability to see a rule where all rules have been surpassed, to create a law in that which is beyond law, to bring forth a new genus, to originate. Sociological reflection certainly shows that structures of social and economic inequality and power have been such that predominantly only white European men have been in a historical position to enjoy this accolade. But as a normative epithet, 'genius' is not reducible to these social facts. Expressions of appreciation by reference to 'greatness' and 'genius' are compatible with sociological understanding and are open to reflexive self-criticism in the light of sociological understanding. It is, in principle, no less, and no more, legitimate to speak of greatness in art produced by marginalized women and non-western artists than it is to speak of greatness in art produced by privileged male European artists.

These considerations suggest a need for some distinctions between different modes of operation in sociohistorical studies of the arts. There would appear to be three distinct modes: (1) value-distanciating sociological analysis; (2) value-affirming aesthetic appraisal; and (3) value-affirming political advocacy. These modes need to be seen as both analytically distinct from one another and practically dependent on one another. Value-distanciating sociological analysis seeks to determine empirical diversity of value-orientation among actual groups of appraisers. Value-affirming aesthetic appraisal seeks to determine aesthetic value in works of art themselves. Value-affirming political advocacy seeks to inform aesthetic appraisal with reference to different relations of power between groups of appraisers.

We may say that the problem with humanistic scholarship is not the mere fact that it sees aesthetic appraisal as distinct from the other two modes of operation. This distinction is legitimate and necessary. Rather, the problem with humanistic scholarship is that it has practically privileged aesthetic appraisal at the expense of the other two modes of operation. Conversely, we can say that the problem with excessively scientific projects of value-neutrality in sociology of the arts is not that they seek to refrain from value prejudice. This abstention is legitimate and necessary. Rather, the problem with excessively scientific projects of value-neutrality is that they practise value-distanciation to the neglect of critical value-affirmation in aesthetics and politics. Finally, we can say that the problem with politically engaged art criticism is not that it seeks to introduce political self-awareness into aesthetic appraisal. This undertaking is legitimate and necessary. Rather, the problem with politically engaged art criticism is that it practises political advocacy sometimes at the expense of aesthetic appraisal and sometimes at the expense of sociological impartiality.

We may say that no one of the three modes ought to usurp the operation of the other two. Political advocacy ought not to masquerade as impartial social science or as aesthetic appraisal. But aesthetic appraisal ought not to see itself as exempt from sociological and political self-reflection. And social science ought not to see itself as indifferent to questions of political and aesthetic value.

Several recent contributors have proposed similar recommendations to these. Boudon (1999) has underscored the dangers of reacting against Platonic conceptions of transcendent validity in aesthetic value by recourse to forms of sociological conventionalism which reduce values to pure contingencies of social organization. Heywood (1997) demonstrates that social science has no absolute authority over the meaning of artistic action. Zolberg (1990) argues for forms of critical cooperation between humanistic concerns for aesthetic value and social-scientific analysis of art in terms of institutional structures. Heinrich (1998) has examined ways in which artistic values inform languages of sociological inquiry, even as sociologists try to analyse different 'orders of justification' about value in cultural goods. Wolff (1993) proposes that while there can be no such thing as a pure aesthetic attitude, free from social and political interests and other normative attitudes, aesthetic understanding remains a specific mode of engagement in a phenomenologically significant sense.

We will return to all of these propositions at greater length at later stages of this book.

Conclusion

We have seen that questions of demarcation between art and non-art are not only questions of semantic fact. They are also questions of lived valuation. The question of whether a particular object is to be accounted a work of art is not only a question about whether the object corresponds to a particular description of a cultural category of objects. It is also a question about whether the object is *good enough* to be accounted art. 'Art' is an intrinsically value-laden word in ordinary language, and this intrinsic value-ladenness does not entirely disappear when 'art' is treated social-scientifically. Up to a point – but only up to a point – social science is capable of treating 'art' value-neutrally. Social science is capable of analysing 'art' as a socially constructed category of cultural objects. But social science has limited 'meaningful adequacy' to art if it does not also engage with questions of aesthetic content and value in works of art. This raises a number of issues about appropriate modes of engagement with questions of value in sociology of the arts. Liberal-humanistic art scholarship typically isolates aesthetic evaluation from questions of politics and sociology. Socialist, feminist and postcolonial critics challenge this isolation. They contest received assumptions of the timeless greatness of canonical works of art by pointing to social facts about logics of power and exclusion in cultural valuation. Sociology of the arts needs to find ways of mediating these socio-political considerations with practices of aesthetic appraisal. Aesthetic appraisal needs to be seen not only as a battleground of social identities competing for voice. It also needs to be seen as an effort at discerning features of perceptual experience in particular objects capable of supporting claims for their universal worth.

In the next chapter we step back from questions of value temporarily in order to look more closely at the bearing of socioeconomic structures on artistic production. In chapter 4 we return to questions of value.

3

Production and Socioeconomic Structure

Empirical sociological studies of the arts generally proceed from two basic standpoints of analysis: from the standpoint of arts *production* in society, and from the standpoint of arts *reception* or *consumption* in society. In this chapter we proceed from the standpoint of production. In chapter 4 we proceed from the standpoint of consumption.

In this chapter we address a range of questions about how socioeconomic structures shape artists' creative decisions and condition the aesthetic contents and forms of their works. We begin by outlining a number of problems with generalizing theories of socioeconomic determination in art that try to assert regular relationships between socioeconomic structures and artistic forms. We first highlight these problems in classical Marxist accounts of the determination of artistic forms by social class relations. Then we turn to the work of three twentieth-century authors who assert various kinds of evolutionary correlation between changes in social structure and changes in artistic form. These are Pitirim Sorokin, Arnold Hauser and Robert Witkin. We conclude by discussing some more historically specific cases of socioeconomic determination in relation to changing historical types of arts patronage, arts markets and arts funding, from the Renaissance in Europe and the early modern period to the present day.

Art and social class structure: Marxist theories

We have referred to some difficulties with classical Marxist sociology of art. We now take a closer look at these difficulties by concentrating on the scope and limits of classical Marxist accounts of the determination of artistic forms and contents by social class struggles.

Writing at the turn of the nineteenth century, the Russian Marxist critic G. V. Plekhanov argued that literary criticism had the task of translating apparently psychological relationships between characters in novels and dramas into their underlying corresponding social class relationships. Plekhanov saw criticism as translating psychological notions in literary narrative into what he called their 'sociological equivalent'. Thus Plekhanov (1953) argued that in seventeenth-century classical French drama, the prestige of tragedy above farce was be explained in terms of ideologies of moral nobility among the French courtly aristocracy. Plekhanov argued that this order of prestige then reversed in the eighteenth century with the rise of the middle classes and the emergence of a new genre of 'sentimental comedy' that no longer portrayed the hero as a 'superior being' but as an idealized man of the emerging 'middle estate'. Similarly, Leo Löwenthal (1957), an associate of the Frankfurt School, interpreted the plays of the seventeenth-century French dramatist Racine in terms of clashes between the middle classes and the absolute monarchy. He saw this as reflected in an emergent bourgeois of ideology of individual freedom in Racine. Writing in the 1960s, the French Marxist critic Lucien Goldmann defended a similar interpretation of Racine. Drawing on French structuralist theory, Goldmann (1964, 1970) saw Racine's dramas as enacting the collective 'group worldview' of the seventeenth-century French *noblesse de robe*. The *noblesse de robe* were a newly formed stratum of lawyers and administrators appointed by the monarchy but originating mostly from the middle classes. They tended to affiliate with the Jansenist faction in French Catholicism which emphasized intense religious austerity and personal self-scrutiny. Goldmann argued that Racine's tragic themes of moral misfortune and moral uncertainty expressed feelings of social and political frustration and isolation on the part of this upper middle-class stratum in seventeenth-century French society (Swingewood 1986).

We can say that the most general defect of each of these cases is their rather mechanical notion of artistic forms as 'reflections' of the class structures of their time. To say that works of art 'reflect' class structure is to deploy a mirror metaphor. Works of art are said to reflect class relations like a mirror which distorts these relations in the consciousness of the participants but reflects them transparently in the consciousness of Marxist observers. This notion owes much to Marx's analogy of a 'hidden chamber' or 'camera obscura' which receives impressions from the external world in an inverted form (Marx and Engels 1965: 47). Dominant class ideologies are said to turn the world upside down. They make what is transitory and contingent appear eternal, unchangeable and natural. Revolutionary critique reverses this inversion and returns the world to its true social condition. We may say that this conception suffers from at least three problems.

A first defect of classical Marxist thinking about art is its insensitivity towards relatively autonomous logics of formal development in aesthetic codes, norms and styles of art. Works of art enact relatively autonomous systems of signification which originate in contexts of social interaction and organization but do not reproduce these contexts by any relationship of direct resemblance or imitation. Works of art do not *copy* social relationships. They *encode* social relationships in formal relationships between their constituent marks, signs, lines, shapes, colours, sounds. Many contemporary literary critics and theorists develop the insights of the pioneer of French structural linguistics, Ferdinand de Saussure, who showed in his *Course in General Linguistics* (of 1916) how the strings of dashes and twirls that make up letters of words and the vocal sounds that constitute spoken utterances of these words need in no way resemble the objects for which they are held to stand by associations of users of language. According to Saussure, words, sentences, texts and all other meaningful objects acquire meaning primarily, if not solely, through differential relationships of interaction between their component sensory elements, not by any naturalistic relation of depiction or imitation. In this sense we can say that social relationships are not impressed in works of art and literature like footprints in sand or faces in masks of plaster. They are encoded in works of art in relatively autonomous systems of semiotic signification.

This insight is particularly developed by the Russian literary critic and theorist Mikhail Bakhtin. In his numerous studies of European literature and popular culture, Bakhtin demonstrates that writers can belong to, and speak on behalf of, particular social milieux and at the same time enact pluralities of social voices very different from their own. Bakhtin (1996) shows how writers can operate in a diversity of 'speech genres' expressive of different social worlds. In this sense Bakhtin shows how writers are not *caused* by their social relations of upbringing to write in any particular way. Writers and artists are not caused to produce in any way that might conceivably be compared to stimulus–response reactions in an organism in relation to its environment. Bakhtin (1968) shows how the medieval French poet Rabelais articulated the entire oral culture of folk comedy and burlesque in medieval French peasant society, even though Rabelais himself belonged to a tiny Latin-speaking elite. Similarly, Bakhtin (1981) shows how the nineteenth-century Russian novelist Dostoevsky stages an entire panoply of social voices in the form of a 'dialogic imagination' that cannot be seen as foregrounding any particular social class position over another, whether orthodox Christian, Russian nationalist, landed conservative or liberal-utilitarian. Bakhtin thus shows how social relations in textual meaning systems stand in relative independence from the social relations of their authors.

A second defect of classical Marxist thinking is its tendency to neglect ways in which cultural and artistic forms themselves contribute to the shaping of structures of socioeconomic life. Cultural studies critics such as Raymond Williams and Stuart Hall emphasize that socioeconomic practices can differ according to the ways in which religious, ethnic, regional and national identities are shaped and sustained by artists, poets and charismatic folk figures (Williams 1981; Hall 1980). Economic action is itself structured around what Castoriadis (1987) has called the 'social imaginary', based on nexuses of norms, values and beliefs expressed in cultural tradition, folklore, legend and mythology. Art and culture feed back into the constitution of society in a diversity of ways. This should not be seen as occurring only by social reproduction of an all-determining economic 'base' through cultural 'superstructures'. It occurs through the mediation of symbolic systems that convert creativity in cultural life into creativity in social action (Joas 1996). Williams speaks of societies in this sense as 'expressive totalities' in which structures of economic production are as much expressions of cultural ideas as determinants of these ideas.

A third defect of classical Marxist thinking is its tendency to take an invidious view of creative agency in individual artists. Classical Marxist thinking certainly concedes a degree of agency to artists in so far as it sees all individuals as free to initiate courses of action within definite structural contexts. As Marx famously wrote, human beings 'make history but not in circumstances of their own choosing' (1972: 15). However, classical Marxist thinking tends to think of these structural contexts predominantly in terms of limiting constraints on artistic agency. It tends not to see material and economic structures as in any way enabling of artistic agency and creativity or as in any sense constitutive of this agency and creativity. It tends not to acknowledge respects in which structural and agential dimensions of social processes form a 'duality' of mutually implicated 'conditions' and 'outcomes' of action, in the sense in which this duality is theorized in the work of writers such as Giddens (1984) and Bourdieu (1990). The chief reason for this is that classical Marxist thinking asserts a normative claim for the ultimate dependence of freedom of individuals on abolition of class structures. This normative claim is eminently open to debate as a position in political philosophy. However, it is not compatible in any immediate way with value-distanciating sociological research.

We may illustrate this problem with some historical case examples. In the fifteenth, sixteenth and seventeenth centuries, the cities of Florence, Venice, Rome, Bruges, Antwerp and Amsterdam were all centres of thriving economic trade. This thriving economic trade both depended on, and further intensified these cities' political and ecclesiastical power over their surrounding territorial networks. Thus these cities are cases of centres of eminently structural socioeconomic power. But these cities are recognized today as among the foremost generators of the artistic and intellectual creativity of the European Renaissance. They are the cities that produced Dante, Michelangelo, Leonardo, Canaletto, Rubens, Rembrandt. It is not meaningful to think of these artists as being denied possibilities of creative freedom they might otherwise have enjoyed had they not lived under an obligation to satisfy the political and economic interests of their paymasters. Fifteenth-century Florence's competition for the dome of its cathedral and for a new statue of David provided the occasion and motivating impulse for the architecture and sculpture of Brunelleschi and Michelangelo, not a reduction of their creative horizons. Similarly, commerce in seventeenth-century Amsterdam provided the stimulus for creativity in seventeenth-century Dutch genre painting, not a limitation of it. In these respects we can say that economic conditions do not constrain artistic possibilities in the sense of curtailing or emasculating them. In these respects economic conditions enable artistic creativity.

One might, however, object that while economic conditions *in general* do not curtail and emasculate artistic possibilities, capitalist economic conditions *in particular* do curtail and emasculate them. One might argue that capitalist economic conditions compel artists to satisfy the demands of market-places which select only those products capable of sustaining systematic profit for agents who invest capital in them by sponsoring or contracting their producers. We will address this important argument in Marxist theory in chapters 5 and 6. However, we must note that the argument remains essentially normative in character and is not immediately compatible with a value-distanciating understanding of structure and agency in sociology of the arts.

Classical Marxist theories are not the only theories that seek to establish law-like relationships between socioeconomic structures and artistic forms. Some earlier examples are to be found in nineteenth-century positivistic conceptions of the regular influence of types of climate, ecology and geography on art, such as in Madame de Stäel's *De la littérature considerée dans ses rapports avec les institutions sociales* (of 1800) and Hyppolite Taine's *Philosophy of Art* (of 1879). Another example is to be found in the work of the early twentieth-century German art historian Wilhelm Worringer (1953). Worringer proposed that archaic societies tend to produce abstract schematic art, reflective of a fear of natural forces. In contrast, modern societies tend to produce realist-naturalistic art, reflective of a position of control over nature and subsequently of a search for 'empathy' with nature. These speculations are rather problematic examples of attempts to link types of artistic language to types of social structure under a single explanatory principle. We now turn to the work of three authors who propound more sophisticated conceptions of correspondence between artistic change and social change but whose work also reveals difficulties of various kinds. These are Pitirim Sorokin, Arnold Hauser and Robert Witkin.

Art and social evolution: Pitirim Sorokin, Arnold Hauser and Robert Witkin

Pitirim Sorokin emigrated from Russia to the US, where he founded the department of sociology at Harvard University in 1930. Sorokin taught in the tradition of British and American evolutionary social thought. In his monumental work, *Social and Cultural Dynamics*, first published between 1937 and 1941, Sorokin sought to provide empirical evidence for a set of systematic correlations between types of social-economic structure on the one hand and types of art, science, religion, government and warfare on the other hand. Sorokin argued that tribal stages of social organization correlate with what he called 'ideational art', where flat schematic forms function as emblems of ideas of a shared spiritual order. In contrast, technologically and economically advanced stages of organization correlate with what he called 'sensate art', where naturalistic forms respond directly to sense impressions. Sorokin argued that 'sensate art' replaced 'ideational art' around the time of the Renaissance in response to evolutionary changes in social structures. However, Sorokin also spoke of 'mixed styles' of art, involving elements of both sensate and ideational art, in various periods both before and after this time. He also spoke of an 'idealistic' art in classical Greece and the late Middle Ages, involving a harmonization of spiritual ideas with sensate visuality.

There are several problems with this thesis. Although Sorokin based his thesis on a great number of images, charts and diagrams of empirical data, he pressed these data into an overarching schema. This schema is laden with unacknowledged value-judgements about the 'decadent' character of sensate art, the 'primitive' character of ideational art and the 'perfect' character of idealistic art. Further, Sorokin's two master concepts of sensate and ideational art are mostly only classificatory concepts that sort artistic forms into types. They are not explanatory concepts that establish concrete causal relationships between socioeconomic conditions and artistic forms in particular periods. Sorokin's conception of a single line of evolutionary development in art and social structure thus lacks justification. It remains a speculative metaphysical thesis, masquerading as empirically established science.

A more illuminating approach is taken by Arnold Hauser in his *The Social History of Art*, published in 1951. Hauser begins with the earliest art of Paleolithic cave painting. He surveys all the civilizations of the ancient Mediterranean and medieval Europe, before finally reaching what he calls the 'film age' of the twentieth century. Hauser's account is influenced by a rather doctrinaire Marxism, but it remains of considerable interest to contemporary scholars.

The theoretical centrepiece of Hauser's work is a systematic correlation he draws between two basic types of social structure and two basic types of artistic style: (1) between hieratic, aristocratic and authoritarian societies and a type of art that is characteristically flat, symbolic, formalized, abstract and concerned with spiritual beings; and (2) between individualistic, mercantile, bourgeois societies and a type of art that is characteristically naturalistic and realistic, employing perspective and concerned with everyday material life.

By the flat symbolic form, Hauser means a style of representation found in art of the Christian Middle Ages, in the art of the Byzantine empire and the Greek-Russian Orthodox Church, among the ancient Egyptians and Assyrians, and among numerous tribal societies. It is exemplified in Bonaventura Berlinghieri's *Madonna and Child with Saints and Crucifixion* from the 1230s (see illustration 4, especially the right-hand panel). In this style, human and animal

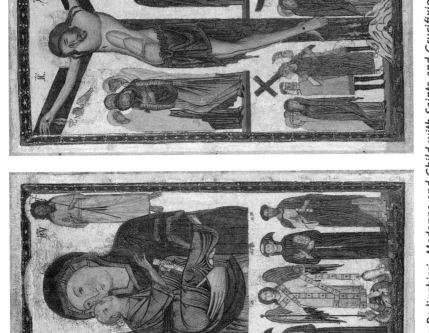

4 Bonaventura Berlinghieri, *Madonna and Child with Saints and Crucifixion*, 1260–70. Galleria degli Uffizi, Florence, photo SCALA

figures, images of plants and other objects are always in a two-dimensional, non-perspectival form. They usually float against a flat background; lack obvious physical connection to one another; and are often in inconsistent relative sizes and proportions. They give an impression of something close to writing or pictorial communication; and most often they possess a spiritual or supernatural reference. Hauser argues that such art is necessarily of this form because it is born of a type of social organization that is (1) communal and cohesive, and therefore encouraging of uniform, non-deviant forms of expression; (2) hieratic and authoritarian, and therefore encouraging of images of an eternal and unchangeable order; (3) anchored in religious tradition, and therefore discouraging of preoccupation with worldly goods; (4) mainly agrarian rather than urban, and therefore encouraging images of nature and the supernatural, rather than of human achievements.

By the realist naturalistic form, Hauser means styles of representation found in art of the ancient Greeks and Romans, in the Renaissance, in seventeenth- and eighteenth-century neoclassicism, and in realist and naturalist movements of the nineteenth century. It is exemplified in Piero della Francesca's *The Flagellation*, of 1455 (see illustration 5). In this style, all figures, objects and spaces are represented in perspective, in three-dimensional recession, in consistent relative proportions and consistent lighting and shading, in variegated colour, and with subject-matter modelled on real-life situations. Hauser argues that such art is necessarily of this form because it is born of a type of social organization that is (1) egalitarian and proto-democratic and therefore not deferent to tradition and authority; (2) individualizing and individualistic, and therefore encouraging of initiative, inquiry and experimentation; and (3) urban and mercantile, and therefore encouraging of preoccupation with human labour and worldly affairs.

Hauser's reflections are considerably richer than Sorokin's speculative conjecture. They strike a chord with some central themes of classical sociological writing concerning transitions from 'communal' to 'societal' forms of association (Tönnies) and from 'mechanical' to 'organic' solidarity (Durkheim), through more complex systems of division of labour, through erosions of customary ties to tradition and the rise of scientific attitudes to the world (Weber). However, there are problems with Hauser's thesis.

The first and most obvious difficulty is the sheer weight of empirical counterevidence to Hauser's statements. Hauser's abstract schematic style need not only be found among hieratic social orders.

5   Piero della Francesca, *The Flagellation*, c.1455. Galleria Nazionale delle Marche, Urbino, photo SCALA

It is also to be found in the art of highly individualist societies, such as in the modernist avant-garde of the twentieth century. Conversely, Hauser's naturalistic style need not only be found in bourgeois individualizing societies. It is also to be found in collectivist, communal societies. For example, it is to be seen – either partially or completely – in cave painting, in some Egyptian and sub-Saharan

African art, and in some Indian art. Although Hauser gives explanations for these counterexamples, there are too many counterexamples to make his thesis plausible. In a great many of his cases, it is possible to find both styles combined in the same art. For example, the Egyptians tended to depict plants and animals in naturalistic form, while reserving schematic forms for human figures. Cave painting in Europe and Africa alternated over time between naturalistic and schematic modes. Much late medieval and early Renaissance painting incorporates both modes; for example in two-dimensional halos around three-dimensional angels and saints. Further, it is not clear that Italian Renaissance society was unequivocally 'bourgeois' at the time in which naturalistic styles began to emerge. Nor is it clear that realist art has always and only emerged in towns. And nor is it clear that ancient Greece and Rome were more egalitarian-democratic than aristocratic-authoritarian in their social structure.

In essence, we can say that the problem with Hauser's thesis is that it attempts to explain artistic styles by means of a 'covering-law model' of historical explanation. (The term 'covering-law model' derives from the writings of C. G. Hempel and Karl Popper on scientific explanation in the 1950s.) Covering-law models of explanation seek to subsume individual cases under a general law of cause–effect relationships. They take the form: 'Whenever condition C, event E.' Similarly, Hauser's thesis takes the form: 'Whenever social structure S, artistic form F.' The problem with covering-law models of explanation is that they cannot be applied informatively to events in human history. Events in human history do not repeat themselves in any intelligible sense. They are not comparable to events in physical and biological processes. Events in human history do not admit of prediction; and therefore they cannot be subsumed under general causal laws. Thus Hauser's thesis is problematic because it attempts to subsume events in art history under a general law of causation. His cases do not satisfy the general explanatory principle under which he attempts to subsume them. If they satisfy his explanatory principle at all, they do so only at an abstract level, not at a concrete level relevant to particular historical contexts. This is demonstrated by Wollheim (1970), among others.

A more promising approach is taken by Robert Witkin (1995). Witkin seeks to salvage the best general insights of Hauser's thesis while rejecting its problematic features. Witkin seeks to show how 'principles of social organization are made visible in art styles' in such a way that a work of art 'can be seen as ordering its relations in a way that simulates the manner in which a given society orders its relations'. This 'simulating' of social relations takes place through a work's 'means of symbolling significant values', an important function of which is 'to incorporate the code, the principles governing the ordering of experience, which are at the heart of the social system in which it is grounded' (1995: 12, 30). Witkin proposes that works of art enact typical kinds of 'presentational code'. These 'presentational codes' articulate shared 'perceptual systems' specific to broad phases of sociohistorical evolution. Witkin proposes that 'perceptual systems' acquire increasing cognitive abstraction and cognitive reflexivity as structures of social integration and social interaction become more complex.

Witkin distinguishes three main types of presentational code in western art: codes that 'invoke' meaning, codes that 'evoke' meaning and codes that 'provoke' meaning. Witkin associates 'invocative codes' with archaic art from the ancient civilizations of the Mediterranean up to the Christian Middle Ages. They invoke meaning from a pre-given social authority that is external to the object; for example, an inscrutable Egyptian statue or a Byzantine icon. 'Evocative codes' arise with the emergence of realist-naturalistic art in the Renaissance. They evoke meaning by relating sense impressions from the external world to the perspectives of individual perceivers; for example, in anatomical drawing by Leonardo and Dürer. 'Provocative codes' emerge with modernist art from the late nineteenth century. They provoke meaning by deliberate self-reference, by a lifting out and reinsertion of signifiers in the form of irony, parody and quotation; for example, in Dada, surrealism and expressionism.

Witkin supports this analysis with a number of case examples from the work of the early twentieth-century German art scholars. These include studies of differences between ancient pagan temples, built essentially to be seen from outside as an open exterior space, and Gothic cathedrals of the Christian Middle Ages, designed essentially as an interior space of communality (Karl Schnaase). Witkin proposes that a transition here occurs from a social order in which interior and exterior space are more or less co-extensive to a social order in which interior and exterior are more or less differentiated from one another. Witkin also discusses some differences between the solid impassive character of archaic art forms, which occupy a 'haptic' space, discontinuous with the spectator, in contrast to a more modern 'optical' art space, which invites spectators into its total artistic effect; for example, in impressionist painting (Alois Riegl). Similarly he discusses some ways in which figures in classical Greek friezes tend only to coexist with one another or only to relate to one another through a single exchanged gesture (such as a lunge of the sword), in contrast to more modern paintings of battle scenes where figures interact with one another more fully in a rhythmic totality (William Ivins).

Witkin argues that these cases illustrate sociologically significant stages of evolutionary development in artistic form. Artistic forms become more reflexive and more differentiated with respect to subjective and objective references as social structures become more complex. At the level of cognitive structures of perception, artistic forms correlate first with what the Swiss social psychologist Jean Piaget calls primary 'contact relations' with objects. Piaget held that children first learn words and names through immediate physical contact with their referents. They tend to understand names for things as materially embedded in those things. Piaget held that this then gives way to more developed mental operations where children understand words as abstractly representing objects. Finally there is a stage of purely formal operations where children understand functions of analogy and metaphor. They recognize signifiers as separable from their usual significations. Witkin argues that comparable cognitive developments in artistic presentational codes correlate with broad changes in social structure. Invocative art codes correlate with what Durkheim called 'mechanical' structures of social integration, where social relations have a mostly co-actional character. Evocative art codes correlate with what Durkheim called 'organic' structures of social integration, where social relations have a more fully interactional character. Provocative art codes correlate with highly differentiated, sometimes anomic structures of integration, where social relations are more intra-actional in character, express-ive of reflexive personal identity projects. Provocative codes and intra-actional social relations are the paradigmatic components of modernist art of the nineteenth and twentieth centuries.

Witkin's thesis is a more compelling evolutionary theory of art than Sorokin's or Hauser's. It avoids Hauser's problem of explaining art styles by subsuming them under potentially predictive laws of causation. In Witkin's picture, art history is not theoretically repeatable or reversible. Sequences of artistic change correspond to historically specific contexts of social evolution. However, Witkin's thesis still raises problems of its own. It is a reworking of a story first told by the German art scholars of the early twentieth century, who in turn looked back to German idealist philosophy of the early nineteenth century, most notably to Hegel's theory of mediation between 'subject' and 'object' in art history. (We discuss Hegel's philosophy of art at length in chapter 5.) Witkin seeks to translate the frameworks of German idealist philosophy and early twentieth-century German art scholarship into a social-scientific framework of empirically falsifiable propositions, based on sociological and social-psychological concepts drawn from the work of Durkheim, Piaget and G. H. Mead. However, it is not clear how far he succeeds in this enterprise. Like the German scholars, Witkin asserts a unilinear conception of development where 'archaic' art forms are assumed to lead in one direction only: towards the stage of development reached by modern European art. We may say that his thesis stretches to the limit the feasibility of an evolutionary theory which supports empirical research without lapsing into metaphysical ethnocentrism. It is in this respect comparable to the evolutionary theories of Talcott Parsons and Jürgen Habermas in their attempts to propound accounts of normative social integration through 'cultural systems' and 'communicative processes', while walking a tightrope between empirically falsifiable 'grand theory', on one side of the precipice, and speculative metaphysics, on the other side.

We may conclude that while comparative trans-historical generalizations are possible, desirable and necessary in sociology of the arts, these generalizations need to be capable of verification against individual cases and contexts of art. To speak with Max Weber (1949), sociology has an orientation towards showing how general explanatory constructs contribute to our understanding of individual cultural phenomena. Sociological explanation involves a work of constructing types of articulation between the general and the particular. It is a search for 'affinities' or exemplary constellations of interaction between individually significant historical moments. We can say that the best kinds of explanation in sociology of the arts are those that achieve what Weber called the highest degree of adequacy between the form to be explained and the structure doing the explaining. The most adequate explanations are those that show that only these two moments of the explanation can be paired with each other and only in this way. They show what is culturally unique and significant in the relationship.

With these points in mind, we will now take a look at some more historically specific cases of socioeconomic determination in art. We will propose a typology of three main regimes of economic support for the arts in western art history: (1) a regime of private patronage by the church, the monarchy and the nobility, lasting from the Middle Ages until around the end of the eighteenth century; (2) a regime of free sale of works of art on an open market, beginning in different European countries in the seventeenth, eighteenth and nineteenth centuries; (3) and a regime of state subsidies for the arts, in combination with charitable philanthropy and commercial sponsorship, beginning in the twentieth century. We illustrate this typology with some notable case studies by arts historians.

Patronage: the church, the monarchy and the nobility

Until around the late eighteenth century, most painters, sculptors, architects and composers in Europe produced their works according to commission by private patrons. These would be representatives of the church and the papacy in various cities and regions, such as bishops, or they would be representatives of the monarch, emperor or head of a principality, or men of the nobility in the service of the royal court, as governors of territories or mayors of cities. Poets and dramatists would be less dependent on patronage because books could be printed, distributed and sold by more independent market mechanisms, while playwrights often found employment in the many travelling companies of actors performing as freelance popular entertainers, although some poets and dramatists still remained closely attached to the royal courts. Later in the period, patrons of the arts would not only be members of the historic landed aristocracy; they would increasingly be merchants or sons of merchants aspiring to the grace of the aristocracy through investment in land, property and art for display in their own estates, or through public charitable benefactions.

Under this regime of patronage, most artists lived in close dependence on a small number of politically powerful individuals. Often artists would be contracted for several months or years at a time, and often their projects would be physically attached to the property of the patron, as with a chapel fresco or altarpiece or palace interior. We may think of Michelangelo's frescos for the papacy in the Sistine Chapel. Frequently artists would reside on the estate of the patron, where they would have the status of servants. This was typically the case for composers. We may think of Rameau at the court of Louis XIV, Haydn at the court of Count Esterházy, or J. S. Bach as resident choirmaster at the state chapel of Leipzig. Under this regime, artists rarely created works prior to the commissions of their patrons. They would not usually conceive and execute a work first and then search for a client. Although artists in the Renaissance were seen as no longer belonging to the 'mechanical

arts' but to the more prestigious 'liberal arts', on a par with philosophy and theology, they still remained essentially craftsmen. Their
way of life was to produce work on demand. The idea of artistic
labour as a personal quest for perfection in particular objects without immediate thought to buyers or clients did not arrive until the
nineteenth century.

We may say that the structures of power to which artists were
answerable under the patronage system were of a kind that Weber
describes in terms of 'traditional domination' (1978: 226–40).
Patronage descended from political and ecclesiastical elites endowed
with sacred or quasi-sacred authority, most notably in the person of
the king, the emperor or the pope. Domination was not of a formal-
legal or modern bureaucratic nature: it consisted of informal codes
of honour, tradition, loyalty and faith in a higher moral order. It is
possible to discern some effects of these relationships in the characteristically hierarchical organization of content in medieval art,
and in Renaissance and Baroque art. Art of these periods tends to
demonstrate a hierarchical schema of moral orders vested in revered
institutions and individuals. It characteristically displays scenes
and figures symbolic of virtue, heroism, sovereignty and charismatic
leadership, or symbolic of justice, forgiveness and salvation. We see
this most spectacularly in Baroque ceiling frescos of heaven ascending
upwards to God, in battle scenes depicting the moment of triumph,
or the moment of adversity which tests the courage of the group,
or moments of charity and magnanimity, or in biblical narrations of
sin and damnation associated with the low, dark, small or earth-like;
for example, in the bottom or marginal parts of a painted panel,
or placed at the beginning of a narration, then to be succeeded by
paradise at the end of a long epic journey, such as in Dante's *Divine
Comedy*.

Michael Baxandall's study, *Painting and Experience in Fifteenth
Century Italy*, illustrates these structures particularly clearly. Baxandall
writes that fifteenth-century paintings were 'the deposit of a social
relationship' (1972: 1–2). They can be seen today as 'fossils of
economic life'. Baxandall shows this through the way Renaissance
painters produced works on a bespoke basis, tailor-made to the
demands of a client. The client's precise wishes and specifications
would be laid out in a legal agreement with a date for completion.
Typically, clients would specify distinct material properties, such as
that the baby Christ be haloed in a distinct quantity of gold leaf or
that the Madonna's clothing be painted in a distinct pigment of
blue. The artist's funds would be reckoned according to these

distinct requirements. If the patron was not satisfied, the artist would be left in considerable financial insecurity. Art would be commissioned for displays of conspicuous largesse designed to impress service and loyalty to the prince or bishop, or to show civic devotion to the patron's home city. Baxandall also shows how many Italian Renaissance art patrons were merchants or merchant clients of the aristocracy preoccupied with calculating and sizing up quantities. Baxandall argues that this preoccupation appears in the notably geometrical organization of Italian Renaissance paintings. We see this, for example, in Piero della Francesca's very mathematically organized *The Flagellation* (illustration 5 above) (see also Ginsburg 1985).

Fifteenth-century Italian merchants were unique in their intense loyalty to the municipal and ecclesiastical authorities of their home city-state. Later, however, in the second half of the eighteenth century, in many parts of Europe, royal, municipal and ecclesiastical authorities no longer exercised the same dominant influence over organized cultural life. They came to be replaced partly by a new order of sale of works of art on a more or less open market, without secure guarantees of buyers and sponsors. This affected the livelihood of artists in dramatic, often traumatic ways. We see this most revealingly in a study of Mozart by Norbert Elias (1993) who shows how Mozart's economic misfortunes arose from his attempt to break away from the system of low status in-house subservience to royal courts in favour of a position of freelance self-employment, yet before any alternative market system had fully arrived. Humiliated at the royal courts and frustrated by the knowledge of his celebrity among wider public circles, Mozart sought to arrange his own public concerts and recitals. This appeared viable by comparison with other professions in eighteenth-century middle-class Vienna. However, Mozart failed in this enterprise because a market-led system of anonymous public consumption of music had yet to fully establish itself. Similarly, Tia DeNora (1995) shows how Beethoven stood on the fault-lines between a not yet defunct patronage system and an emergent but not yet fully established market system. DeNora argues that Beethoven resolved this dilemma through a strategy of careful cooperation with a stratum of the upper aristocracy in Vienna. This upper aristocratic stratum staged ostensibly public but in practice highly exclusive concerts devoted to a form of advanced classical music that demonstrated their discerning taste – in distinction to the lower aristocratic strata and the middle classes. In these respects both Mozart and Beethoven represent artists caught in the transition between two regimes of economic support of the arts: an older regime of private patronage and a new but not yet hegemonic order of sale on an open market.

Arts markets in early modern Europe

The new order has its roots as far back as the early seventeenth century. However, it affects different art forms at different speeds in different countries and regions. Northern European countries are the first to experience the new formation. In contrast, southern Catholic Europe and those parts of central and eastern Europe under the control of the Hapsburg empire remain under the patronage system for much longer. After literature and poetry, which had long been part of the book trade, painting is the next art form to experience the new order. In contrast, music is the last to move over due to the high financial risks of expenses to be laid out for large numbers of players without a guaranteed audience, especially, for example, in the case of opera.

We may say that whereas artists under the patronage system are bound to their paymasters by a feudal tie of personal obligation, artists under the market system are formally free to sell the products of their labour as they themselves determine. Artists are not dependent on the whims and idiosyncrasies of any particular client. They are dependent only on purchase of their works by a more or less anonymous public. This brings about a stronger division between artists' personal and professional relationships. Artists develop a stronger distinction between the private and public sides of their personalities. They separate more clearly that which pertains to their 'inner' creative selves from that which pertains to their 'outer' mundane means of subsistence. But artists remain considerably less financially secure than under the patronage system because they can no longer rely on any continuous client relationship.

The market system is to be glimpsed most clearly in seventeenth-century Dutch oil painting. Seventeenth-century Holland saw an efflorescence of artists painting relatively small-sized, easily transportable canvases for sale to merchants operating through the trading ports of Amsterdam and Rotterdam. John Berger comments that material objects in seventeenth-century Dutch oil painting appear with a kind of fleshy materiality, rendered in clearly defined contours and rich colours. Oil painting, Berger writes, 'did to appearances what capital did to social relations'. Painting 'had to be able to demonstrate the desirability of what money could buy. And the visual desirability of what can be bought lies in its tangibility, in how it will reward the touch, the hand, of the owner' (1972: 87, 90). We can say that seventeenth-century Dutch painting demonstrates some characteristic features of an advanced capitalist economy, marked by high degrees of specialization in the division of labour. Painters would specialize in a particular genre such as landscape, domestic interior, still life or portraiture; and merchants and agents would specialize in trading in any one of these genres. Although much portraiture still remained dependent on commission – the artist often being commissioned to paint group portraits of town councillors, lawyers, business families and other notables – some artists painted portraits of undistinguished individuals as aesthetic objects in their own right. Dutch painters thus worked on a more or less freelance basis, adapting their output to fluctuating market demands.

It can be argued that much seventeenth-century Dutch painting evinces a proto-democratic ethos in the organization of its component features. Although much of it is imbued with a strict sense of the authority of the civic patriarchs, it is not common to see a strongly hierarchical ranking of some figures higher up or further to the front of the canvas. There is a clear preponderance of secular subject-matter, rooted in everyday affairs of work, and this subject-matter is at the same time framed by a strong Calvinist ethos of thrift, frugality and abstention from wasteful pleasure (Schama 1987). As Weber shows in his famous study *The Protestant Ethic and the Spirit of Capitalism*, ascetic Calvinist ethics in Holland and England had an effect of legitimating preoccupation with worldly business, rather than of proscribing such preoccupation.

It is instructive to compare seventeenth-century Dutch art markets with the market for literary fiction in eighteenth-century England. Where seventeenth-century Dutch painters still supplied a relatively small mercantile elite, eighteenth-century English novelists supplied a broad tranche of the property-owning middle classes. This included not only families of extensive capital wealth but also families of relatively modest means; and it included both male and female readers. We can say that literature in eighteenth-century England became concerned for the first time with demonstrably bourgeois interests and experiences. In a study of the rise of the English novel, Ian Watt (1957) shows how a new market for literary fiction arose from a dramatic increase in the cheap availability and reduced printing costs of books, as well as from an increase of literacy among artisanal classes. Advanced conditions of trade in cosmopolitan urban centres such as London, Liverpool and Bristol went together with a burgeoning public interest in politics. Newspapers, coffee-houses, religious nonconformism and a spirit of scientific experimentation created the conditions for a new genre of writing to flourish which became popular with the middle classes. This new genre was the novel, and at its centre stood the figure of the ordinary individual. The individual in eighteenth-century English novels is faced with a problem of reconciling private feelings and personal interests and ambitions with public duties and social obligations. Watt argues that a new spirit of 'affective individualism' can be discerned in popular novels such as Daniel Defoe's *Robinson Crusoe*, Henry Fielding's *Tom Jones* and Samuel Richardson's two epistolary novels *Pamela* and *Clarissa*, addressed to female readers contemplating marriage. Bourgeois women and men could read these novels in private and empathize with their protagonists' psychological dilemmas, without betraying their emotions in public. To read a novel was a much more private experience than the act of attending a night at the theatre.

Watt (1996) also notes how the moral message in Defoe's *Crusoe* strikingly differs from the moral message in three of the most archetypal stories of errant individuals in the sixteenth and seventeenth centuries: whereas Faust, Don Juan and Don Quixote are all punished for their individualism – Faust for wanting to know too much, Don Juan for seducing too many women, Don Quixote for not conforming to daily normality – Crusoe's individualism is celebrated. In Defoe's novel, Crusoe's solitary quest for himself, for the meaning of his life and his relationship to God through uncompromising personal initiative, is no longer a crime against society. It is held up as an example for society to follow.

In nineteenth-century painting and literature, we can say that the relationship of the individual to society takes on much more variegated and complex aspects. Though still themselves mainly from middle-class backgrounds, many painters and writers become increasingly alienated from their class and its commercial and industrial values. A new note of scepticism and disillusionment can be discerned in their works that tells us much about the relation of culture and economy in the period. We see this in social realist painters such as Jean-François Millet and Gustave Courbet, and in the sharp social criticism of writers concerned with class, poverty, women, marriage and the family, such as Jane Austen, Stendhal, Honoré de Balzac, Gustave Flaubert, Charles Dickens, Georges Sand, George Eliot, Henrik Ibsen and Émile Zola. We see it also in more conservative writers preoccupied with nationhood, religion, faith and social harmony such as Matthew Arnold, Benjamin Disraeli, Alexander Pushkin, Leo Tolstoy and Fyodor Dostoevsky.

We will discuss further aspects of this atmosphere of anxiety and disenchantment in nineteenth-century art in chapter 5 in relation to links between art and the return of myth and religious identity in modern culture. But we will now turn to a third regime of economic support of the arts, marked by state subsidies in combination with philanthropy and commercial sponsorship in the twentieth century.

The state and the market in twentieth-century arts funding

In contrast to private patronage and free sale on open markets, this third regime is characterized by an attempt to place artists' material means of subsistence on a rational footing. It involves the planned establishment of arts institutions capable of rational administration.

The clearest example of an attempt at rationalizing artists' material means of subsistence is to be found in Soviet Russia after 1917. Soviet communism is the clearest case of a project of 'organized modernity', marked by an attempt to place all sectors of the social system under rational administration, including cultural and artistic life as well as economic and political life (Wagner 1994). The communist movements that swept through Europe after the First World War led to the idea that if artists could receive funding from the state, they would be liberated from the vagaries of the capitalist market-place. Artists would be able to work creatively without having to pander to market trends or to flatter corrupt princes and bishops. They could experiment as their consciences dictated, as authentic non-alienated members of society. This idea became a policy for Lenin's first commissar for culture in the 1920s, Lunacharsky. It is fair to say that for about eight years it was responsible for a remarkable wave of modernist experimentation in Soviet art; for example in the constructivist painting and sculpture of Kasimir Malevich, Vladimir Tatlin, Naum Gabo and El Lissitsky, in the theatre of Vladimir Mayakovsky, the film of Sergei Eisenstein and the music of Dmitri Shostakovich.

Very soon after Lenin's death, however, the reality of state support for the arts in Soviet Russia strikingly departed from official proclamations. Under Stalin, Soviet doctrine required that artists pursue their experimentations solely in their capacity as representatives of the proletarian masses. The state would support artists only in so far as artists looked to the state as the guardian of the people. All notes of purely personal subjective feeling, expressed through ambivalent or comic uses of formal invention, were soon denounced as reversions to 'decadence' and 'bourgeois formalism'. On pain of deportation, artists were forcibly compelled to create in the name of 'socialist realism'. In practice this meant propagandistic images of happy factory workers and farmers, and narrative stories of corrupt capitalists versus socialist revolutionaries, and the like.

In the postwar social-democratic states of western Europe, most sponsorship of the arts came from semi-autonomous state agencies administering funds from general taxation. This system reached its high point in the 1960s and 1970s, but is today much curtailed. In the US today, some arts funding derives from federal subsidies, notably from the National Endowment for the Arts founded in 1965. However, the greatest part of American arts funding has always depended on philanthropic endowments by entrepreneurs, such as the Rockefeller, Carnegie and Guggenheim foundations, as well as on a federal system of tax exemptions for business corporations in return for donations to cultural and educational institutions. In Europe since the 1980s, state funding of the arts has diminished as both centre-right and centre-left governments have sought to reduce general public expenditure. Consequently, artists and arts institutions in Europe since the 1980s have had to seek increasingly greater proportions of their income from commercial sponsorship and from charitable organizations.

At this juncture, it is important to observe a number of comparative distinctions. In chapter 7 we will discuss some ways in which neoliberal economic policies since the 1980s have affected, and in several respects arguably undermined, the welfare of contemporary arts institutions. However, at our present juncture, it should be noted that even during the time of greatest state support for the arts in the 1960s and 1970s, state subsidies and charitable benefactions have always remained in a significant relationship to free market environments. Public galleries and museums have always operated in close interaction with private commercial actors such as dealers, collectors, agents and auction houses; and galleries have always competed among themselves for public attendance on commercial, or commercially related, grounds.

In particular, many empirical studies indicate that public arts bodies have not generally been the first or strongest stimulant or sponsor of artistic creativity in the twentieth century (Crane 1987;

Moulin 1987; White and White 1965). The greatest impetuses to artistic creativity in the twentieth century appear to have come not from public funding commissions but from the actions of private collectors and dealers systematically collecting works by particular artists in particular genres. Thus Moulin (1987) shows in his study of French art markets since the 1880s how private collectors created market demands for particular artists and for particular styles and schools of art, to which public arts institutions subsequently responded by purchasing works from dealers and organizing retrospective exhibitions – but always only after the initiatives of the collectors. Moulin shows how the first movers in the development, diversification and public recognition of movements in painting in France were not academies, curators or critics but private commercial actors creating market prices for works by particular artists, and speculating on future rises in these prices with a view to future return sales to galleries. Moulin argues that public arts institutions in the twentieth century have acted mostly in a gatekeeping role, adding a stamp of public cultural legitimacy to prior mechanisms of selection that are significantly economic in character. Once artists have made their careers in mainly commercially driven market-places of cultural goods, public institutions help to stabilize their careers by conferring status on them.

Similarly, Crane (1987) shows how the leading art galleries of the 1950s in New York, notably the Museum of Modern Art and the Guggenheim Museum, were quick to acquire works of abstract expressionist art, and thereby sanctify this genre as part of a new canon of American modernism, but were slow to acquire works of Pop Art in the 1960s. In the 1960s, the New York galleries acted as gatekeepers for some sectors of the market for artistic goods but not for others. In the case of Pop Art, the initiative fell instead to galleries in more provincial American cities. Crane attributes this loss of initiative to strains of organizational expansion and bureaucratization among the New York galleries. Dubin (1987) also shows how federal funding for public arts projects and arts education in the US since the 1930s has never been entirely free from commercial pressures. Dubin investigates federal initiatives to widen public participation in artistic activities, through projects such as murals in underprivileged city neighbourhoods, sculpture in city parks and creative development projects at drug rehabilitation units and shelters for the homeless. However, he shows how these initiatives have been continually permeated by vested business interests tied to concerns for the public image of the city as an attractor of investment.

Dubin argues that these interests have acted as powerful regulators of the range of acceptable outlets of federal sponsorship of American public arts, if not as outright censors.

These studies indicate ways in which twentieth-century state support for the arts has been substantially moulded, framed and in some ways constrained by commercial interests. We may safely say that since the 1980s these commercial interests have gained markedly greater power over arts institutions as a result of reductions in public expenditure. However, we must also note some more cultural reasons for these developments that have to do with changes of attitude among artists. Before about the 1980s, many avant-garde artists tended to define their work in conscious opposition to the capitalist market-place. In some cases they would see themselves as openly defying capitalistic desires to possess, collect and accumulate rare material artefacts. This was the case, for example, with minimalist and conceptualist works of the early 1970s which often left little material trace of themselves. However, since this time, artists have become generally less hostile to commercial involvement in art and less trusting of state management of arts funds and state authority over cultural affairs in general (McGuigan 1996). There has been a perception that the postwar state arts agencies tended to favour projects with a demonstrable relation to national historical traditions with a classical humanistic pedigree, at the expense of ethnic diversity in art and at the expense of popular culture. Commercial agencies have been seen in contrast as in some ways more open-minded and egalitarian with respect to sponsorship decisions; and commercial agencies have in turn been eager for opportunities to demonstrate healthy public relations through sponsorship projects. This has created an environment in which artists have become increasingly self-conscious in their relations to sponsors, dealers and the media. They have become what DiMaggio (1982) and others have called 'cultural entrepreneurs' in media-saturated environments of niches of artistic invention. We will be concerned with further aspects of this condition in chapter 7.

Conclusion

We have discussed a number of theories and accounts of socio-economic determination in art. Classical Marxist accounts tend to presuppose excessively reductive theories of determination by social class structures. We have seen that social relations are not reflected or impressed in works of art by any direct causal mechanism. They are encoded in works of art through the agency of artists' creative imagination and through relatively autonomous aesthetic systems of signification. Some writers have proposed alternative general theories of structural determination in art, including Wilhelm Worringer, Pitirim Sorokin and Robert Witkin, and also Arnold Hauser (although Hauser's writing remains indebted to classical Marxist thinking). Problems arise with these theories, however, when they attempt to establish regular causal relationships between social change and artistic change, or when they assert totalizing evolutionary frameworks that either come close to or relapse into speculative metaphysics. These difficulties indicate that comparative historical generalizations about art and social structure need to be capable of case-by-case validation if they are to demonstrate genuine interpretive adequacy to what Max Weber called the historical 'individuality' of cultural phenomena. More historically particularizing approaches would suggest concentration on study of the sources of artists' means of material subsistence, through analysis of regimes of private patronage, regimes of free sale of art objects on open markets, and regimes of state subsidy, charitable philanthropy and commercial sponsorship of the arts.

4

Consumption and Aesthetic Autonomy

We have discussed various issues bearing on contexts of artistic production in society. We turn now to a further set of issues bearing on questions of artistic reception and consumption in society. We begin by examining the normative thesis that works of art can be, and ought to be, valued 'for their own sake', rather than for the sake of some ulterior interest or purpose, such as for entertainment or for a moral or political purpose of instruction and exhortation. In the history of western thought, this thesis is known as the thesis of 'aesthetic autonomy'. We first set out this thesis in the writings of its most influential eighteenth-century exponent, Immanuel Kant. Then we discuss a number of critical sociological observations about the thesis. These bear on contexts of ideas about art and aesthetics in eighteenth- and nineteenth-century European society and their relation to the consumption habits of the European middle classes and the aristocracy. Then we turn to some more contemporary observations about the thesis concerning structures of cultural and educational stratification in present-day society. We discuss these considerations primarily in the work of Pierre Bourdieu, as well as in the work of several contemporary American sociologists on socially differentiated 'taste cultures'. We conclude with a critical assessment of the sociology of taste in relation to the problem of aesthetic validity.

Kantian aesthetics

The thesis of aesthetic autonomy has its origins in eighteenth-century European culture. In the early eighteenth century, a number of English and Scottish scholars began to write about feelings of pity, sympathy and trust between human beings in terms of a 'moral sense'. The English and Scottish writers argued that this 'moral sense' could be observed empirically in human nature without need for appeal to biblical authority. They suggested that this moral sense also laid the basis for feelings of pleasure and displeasure in relation to fictional images and entities in art and poetry. Thus Lord Shaftesbury, in his *Characteristics of Men, Manners, Opinions and Times* (of 1711), wrote that human beings have a natural inclination to refrain from harmful action to others because they possess a reflex 'sensibility' that allows them to imagine what others' pain would be like if they were to experience it themselves. In Scotland, Francis Hutcheson, in his *An Inquiry into the Original of Ideas of Beauty and Virtue* (of 1725), extended these considerations to suggest that feelings of taste and distaste towards works of art derive from the way works of art imitate moral virtues and vices in the actions of real people. Adam Smith later wrote of a sensibility of the common good in his *Theory of Moral Sentiments* of 1759. Similarly, David Hume, in his essay, 'Of the Standard of Taste' (of 1757), sought to explain feelings of pleasure in works of art in terms of psychological laws of harmony and coherence in the perception of sensuous forms.

These writers demonstrate the emergence of a distinctive pre-occupation in eighteenth-century thought with the sensory grounds of moral and aesthetic experience. They saw judgements of taste in art as both analogous to moral conceptions of the right order of things and at the same time distinct from moral conceptions in so far as they referred only to sentiments of experience rather than to duties of conduct. It was this preoccupation which underpinned Immanuel Kant's undertaking in the last of his three philosophical treatises, *The Critique of Judgement*, published in 1790.

In the Introduction to his treatise, Kant declares that judgements of taste are formed from the 'free play' of the faculty of intellect with the faculty of perception. By this Kant means that when something is experienced as beautiful, the spectator has no interest strictly in knowing what that thing is. The spectator has no primary interest in identifying the object by finding a concept for it or giving it a definite description. Rather, the spectator is primarily oriented to perceiving the object in all the richness of its sensory form. The spectator does not classify the object as a member of a general class of objects. Rather, the spectator experiences the object as something uniquely particular which, through its particular sensory qualities, shows or presents something general. Kant calls this ability to see something general *in* something particular – as distinct from subsuming particular things *under* general concepts – man's Faculty of Judgement. Judgement in the broadest sense for Kant means the ability to reconcile knowledge with morality. It is the ability to understand intuitively how all that is known relates to all that is felt to be good (and evil) in the universe, in so far as the universe carries an end or 'telos'. Thus Kant's last *Critique* is not only concerned with beauty in nature and art. It is also concerned with man's ultimate grounds for hope in a meaningful cosmos, or what Kant called 'teleological judgement'. In a famous passage in the *Critique of Pure Reason* (B, para. 833), Kant summed up his philosophy as answering the following three guiding questions: What can I know? What should I do? What may I hope for?

In the first part of the text, titled 'Analytic of Beauty', Kant argues that aesthetic judgements neither communicate any information about the physical properties or causes of their object, nor express any judgement about the moral worth or practical utility of their object. They express purely the pleasure of the spectator on apprehending the object. In particular, Kant states that aesthetic judgements comprise four 'moments'. First, they are 'disinterested'. That is, they are not based on an interest in using the object for some ulterior purpose or for satisfying some ulterior need. They are based purely on a state of 'disinterested contemplation'. Second, they are 'necessary'. That is, they are laid down in the form of a challenge to others to accept the judgement, in an analogous (but not identical) manner to the way moral judgements are made. Third, they possess the 'form of finality'. That is, they view the object as an end in itself: not as having a purpose but as being its *own* purpose. Kant says that the object is experienced as being 'purposive without a purpose' (*zweckmäßig ohne Zweck*). Fourth, they are 'universal'. That is, they presuppose a universal capacity for common feeling that Kant calls human beings' 'sensus communis', which also forms the basis of morality.

In addition, Kant discusses another type of judgement relating to experiences of the 'sublime'. Kant's distinction between the beautiful and the sublime is central to several other eighteenth-century writers, including notably to Edmund Burke, in his *A Philosophical Enquiry into the Origin of our Ideas of the Sublime and the Beautiful* (of 1757). Kant defines the sublime as all that attests to the infinite power of reason in nature. The sublime is experienced at the sight of phenomena such as waterfalls, mountain ranges, sweeping cliffs and boundless oceans. Kant states that the sublime is an experience of reason's infinite overpowering of the senses, in distinction to beauty, which rests on an experience of harmonious consonance between reason and the senses.

Kant argues that judgements about beauty and the sublime always lay claim to universality. However, he adds that this claim to universality is not founded on a universal *concept* of the beautiful or the sublime. There are, he insists, no objective concepts, principles or formulae of beauty (or the sublime) – such as, say, a special colour, a magic musical chord, or a 'golden mean' of proportions of parts – which will always render any given object beautiful (or sublime). Every object of an aesthetic judgement is experienced as achieving beauty by its own unique means; and any particular quality that might be a reason for judging one object as, say, 'elegant' or 'graceful' might well be a reason for judging another object as, say, 'contrived' or 'meretricious'. A quality of pinkish red that might be a reason for praising one painter's representation of a sunset as 'subtle' and 'expressive' might equally be a reason for criticizing another's painter's representation of a sunset as 'overdone'. Nonetheless, Kant insists that the fact that there cannot be universally valid aesthetic concepts or principles does not mean there cannot be universally valid aesthetic *judgements*. Kant argues that aesthetic judgements not only involve an avowal by persons that they *like* the object in question, that the object is an object of pleasure to them. They also involve a commitment from these persons towards showing how the object could, and should, be an object of pleasure for everyone. Aesthetic judgements involve pointing to particular features in the object and showing, through critical communication, how these particular features contribute to the total aesthetic merit of the object; by showing, for example, how the colours and lines complement each other, or how the stages of the drama unfold in a tragic sequence, and so on.

This leads Kant to propose that aesthetic judgements are of a different order from purely corporeal tastes, such as tastes in food. Tastes in food are founded only on what Kant calls 'pleasures of sensation', not on what he calls 'pleasures of reflection' (1928: 166). Further, Kant proposes that precisely because such tastes are founded only on pleasures of sensation, it is not possible for people to *argue* for these tastes and come to *agreements* about these tastes. If one person has a taste only for white wine, and another person a taste only for red wine, there can be no argument between these two persons. According to the traditional Latin proverb: de gustibus non disputandum est. In contrast, works of art enable people to argue for their judgements and come to agreement over their judgements because works of art communicate contents of reflection. Works of art enable, and command, agreement about their value, because they please not merely by gratifying the senses but by imparting ethically significant 'aesthetic ideas' which, Kant says, 'induce much thought' (1928: 175). Therefore works of art command contemplation for their own sake. They do not serve to satisfy our bodily needs or appetites or to entertain us. Like other human beings to whom we owe unconditional respect, works of art command our whole and unconditional appreciation. Kant concludes by distinguishing between the 'agreeable arts' of amusement, which serve purposes of distraction and entertainment, and the 'fine arts', which are their own purpose:

> Agreeable arts are those which have mere enjoyment for their object. Such are all the charms that can gratify a dinner party: entertaining narrative, the art of starting the whole table in unrestrained and sprightly conversation, or with jest and laughter inducing a certain air of gaiety. Here, as the saying goes, there may be much loose talk over the glasses, without a person wishing to be brought to book for all he utters, because it is only given out for entertainment of the moment, and not as a lasting matter to be made the subject of reflection or repetition.
> [. . .]
> Fine art, on the other hand, is a mode of representation which is intrinsically final, and which, although devoid of an end, has the effect of advancing the culture of the mental powers in the interests of social communication.
> The universal communicability of a pleasure involves in its very concept that the pleasure is not one of enjoyment arising out of mere sensation, but must be one of reflection. Hence aesthetic art, as art which is beautiful, is one having for its standard the reflective judgement and not organic sensation. (1928: 165–6)

This thesis of aesthetic autonomy exemplifies Kant's conception of 'transcendental philosophy'. Kant's conception of philosophy is 'transcendental' in the sense that it regards judgements and statements in science, morality and aesthetics as staking a claim to a priori validity. Kant held that the logical validity of judgements and statements in science, morality and aesthetics is not conditional on facts about the empirical circumstances under which these judgements and statements are produced. In *The Critique of Judgement*

Kant was concerned more than anything else with the logical structure of judgements about art and beauty, not with any empirical historical circumstances under which objects of art and beauty come to be valued by society.

In contrast, numerous historians and sociologists have been concerned with the ways in which works of art come to be valued in different ways by different societies at different times and places. This has led to them to question many of the central tenets of Kantian thinking. It has led them to question the proposition that aesthetic judgements are produced under states of 'disinterested contemplation'; that art appreciation serves no ulterior interests or purposes; that judgements about art are capable of universal acceptance; and that 'fine arts' can be distinguished without prejudice from mere 'agreeable arts'. Instead, many historians and sociologists have argued that notions of aesthetic autonomy are a specific product of the leisurely ways of life of members of the aristocracy and the upper middle classes in eighteenth- and nineteenth-century Europe. They have argued that different classes and status groups in society possess habits of consumption of cultural goods at different times in history; and they have therefore argued that art appreciation *does* serve numerous ulterior interests and social purposes.

As an example of these interests and purposes, we may think of the multifarious functions of the opera house in nineteenth-century European high society for seeing and being seen by others, for displaying one's wealth and status according to one's place in the auditorium and for spying on others. Or we may think of piano music in the nineteenth century for the accoutrements of the aristocratic lady. Or we may think of the sentimental German *Lied* for courtship and fraternizing in the bourgeois German home. Or we may think of romantic film in the dimmed intimacy of the cinema for the stirring of companionate relationships. Or we may think of avant-garde art exhibitions in Paris or New York for displays of distinction by educated elites keen to mark the exclusivity of their group.

All these cases appear to indicate that arts consumption serves eminently social interests and functions by forging communities of taste and inculcating group identities. They appear to indicate that even after artistic activities acquire degrees of independence from services to the church and the royal courts in the early modern period, art today continues to serve purposes and interests that make it 'heteronomous', not 'autonomous', in society.

We now discuss some contexts of social history that suggest justification for these propositions. We begin with some reflections on leisure and connoisseurship in the eighteenth century, followed by some further reflections on fine arts consumption in nineteenth-century high society. We also develop some more normative considerations on the relation of aesthetic autonomy to moral and political movements.

Leisure, gentility and aesthetic autonomy

Ideas of aesthetic sensibility have their roots in codes of social behaviour in eighteenth-century civil society. To understand these roots, we need to consider the significance of an emergent culture of leisure, tourism, connoisseurship and gentility.

The eighteenth century in England and Scotland was the great age of the 'gentleman' (Abrams 1989). The two Italian words *gusto* and *virtuoso* had been imported into the English language in the seventeenth century and by the early 1700s had become staple emblems of the lifestyle of the propertied classes. Gentlemen had to be polite and polished in their demeanour, discerning and cultivated in their tastes. If they were to distinguish themselves from the 'vulgar' and from those of recently acquired wealth, they had to show no care for the utility of their possessions. They had to flaunt a life of disinterested display. The fashion was to collect and contemplate decorative objects such as vases, carpets, tapestries, silverware, embroidery and furniture. Often these would be exotic objects and antiquities purchased at the newly founded auction houses of Sotheby's (1740) and Christie's (1762). Sons of the English aristocracy would take a Grand Tour of continental Europe, lasting several months or years, with Italy and Rome as its chief destination. They would return from their tour owning and displaying in their estates the historic works of art they had learned to prize. They would discuss and read about the latest fashions in the newly founded magazines, notably Joseph Addison's *The Spectator*. Their wives likewise would cultivate a taste for *belles lettres*. Attendance at concerts and recitals was the vogue for members of the gentry in the towns. The same period also saw the foundation of numerous national galleries and museums throughout Europe, including the British Museum in 1759, the Vatican Museum in 1773 and the Uffizi gallery in Florence, many of them replete with artefacts brought back by merchant shipping companies active in the new trade routes to the east.

These circumstances provide a context for discourses of sensibility among writers such as Kant, Burke, Hutcheson and Shaftesbury. They show how an ethos of delectation of non-utilitarian objects could have emerged out of a culture of connoisseurship among the members of the burgeoning commercial classes, anxious to refine and naturalize their wealth in land and art. They suggest an explanation for ideas of aesthetic autonomy in terms of interests of the upper strata of society in displays of status and charity as signs of refinement, gentility, polish and distinction.

One of the first sociological thinkers to write about fine arts consumption in relation to specifically European social mores was Alexis de Tocqueville. In *Democracy in America* (of 1835), Tocqueville conjectured that fine arts institutions such as academies of painting and music were unlikely to flourish on American soil because fine arts institutions required stratified social structures characterized by strict status distinctions among its elite groups. America's fledgling democratic society possessed no such stratified structure. It had no historic aristocracy, nor any tradition of guild-like occupations for the training of artists under old masters. It was also marked by the intense moral austerity of Protestant Puritanism. Tocqueville argued that while America's egalitarian norms would encourage considerable upward social mobility, they would not necessarily prevent downward mobility as families made and broke their fortunes in the cycles of the young economy. He conjectured that this would result in a large but constantly changing market of buyers for cultural goods without long-standing knowledge of differences. Owners of cultural objects would be happy to maintain a contrived appearance, without great insistence on distinction.

Tocqueville tended to look at America with European preconceptions. He tended to regard the factors he saw as working against the existence of American fine arts institutions as barriers to quality and excellence in American cultural life. However, his general conception of reduced distinctions between 'high' and 'low' cultural traditions under egalitarian social norms is plausible. It has much to tell us about differences between Europe and America in the eighteenth and nineteenth centuries.

At the end of the nineteenth century, in 1899, Thorstein Veblen in Wisconsin in America published his *Theory of the Leisure Class*. An emigré from Norway, Veblen proposed that ideas of objects of art arise from a need of the leisured classes to display their wealth and position through acts of 'conspicuous consumption'. Veblen pointed out that a large number of the precious objects acquired by aristocracies are coveted not for their beauty 'as such' but for their rarity, ingenuity and novelty value. The hand-wrought solid silver spoon is more desirable than the machine-made spoon, not because it is intrinsically more beautiful but because it is costlier – and also because its additional heaviness makes it mechanically less useful for its ostensible purpose. Such objects become socially useful in their practical uselessness. Settled societies evolve 'pecuniary canons of taste' where those of greatest wealth compete with another for status and distinction through acts of wasteful expenditure that reveal their independence from material necessity. This gives rise to the peculiar logic of social emulation that is called fashion. Veblen proposed that works of art are no less subject to codes of fashion and prestige than dress, food, property and land. Works of art are one case of the lusting of the privileged in society for objects that are unmistakably expensive, unique, handmade and practically useless (Veblen 1994).

We have now discussed several sociological contexts for ideas of aesthetic autonomy in eighteenth- and nineteenth-century society. In the following we turn to some further reflections on moral and political movements of the period.

Throughout the nineteenth century, values of savouring artefacts for their own sake became increasingly reinforced by ideas of artistic creativity as an end in itself. In France, this doctrine of 'art for art's sake', or *l'art pour l'art*, was associated with poets and writers such as Théophile Gautier, Paul Verlaine, Arthur Rimbaud and Joris Huysmans. In Germany, after the turn of the century, it was associated with the salon around the cult poet Stefan George. Probably the most famous English manifesto of the ethos of art for art's sake is the collection of witty epigrams that make up Oscar Wilde's Preface to his novel *The Picture of Dorian Gray*, first published in 1890. Wilde begins with an affirmation of beauty as an end in itself:

> Those who find beautiful meanings in beautiful things are the cultivated. For these there is hope.
> They are the elect to whom beautiful things mean only Beauty.

Then comes a rejection of moral criticism:

> There is no such thing as a moral or an immoral book. Books are well written, or badly written. That is all.
> No artist has ethical sympathies. An ethical sympathy is an unpardonable mannerism of style.

Then the credo of art for art's sake:

> All Art is at once surface and symbol.
> Those who go beneath the surface do so at their peril.
> All art is quite useless.

Wilde's Preface can be understood as a sort of tongue-in-cheek defence of art for art's sake against its condemnation by conservative religious groups in the nineteenth century who excoriated what they saw as the 'decadence' of modern art. Wilde here ridicules the hypocrisy of the Victorian and Edwardian moralists who will eventually consign him to prison for his homosexuality. However, it is worth following the reasoning of these moralistic groups because their stance points to some further observations about aesthetic autonomy of a more normative character.

Writing between the 1850s and 1890s, John Ruskin (1991) maintained that all people were entitled to expect from the artist a passionate sense of moral dignity and sincerity. Art for Ruskin had to express the common faith of humankind. Art had to involve the whole human being in goodness and truth, not merely delight the spectator with aesthetic elegance. Similarly, in his *What is Art?* (of 1896), Leo Tolstoy in Russia averred that art was of no value for humankind unless it attested to the workings of God in creation. Tolstoy (1995) saw the very idea of the distinctness of beauty from goodness and truth as an abomination of Enlightenment man. Tolstoy maintained that art had once remained in touch with the common feelings of ordinary people. It had once enjoyed an organic place in society under the arms of the Christian church. But Tolstoy argued that art soon departed from these natural sources of goodness: since the Renaissance art had become a narcissistic product of high society in an age of irreligious decadence and complacency.

More politicized criticism in the nineteenth century came from socialist writers such as William Morris who spoke for the Arts and Crafts movement in England. Other similar movements spread throughout Europe, notably the Wiener Werkstätte group in Austria. In the twentieth century, more revolutionary criticism came from the Russian constructivists and the founding members of the German Bauhaus in the 1920s, headed by Walter Gropius. All these figures saw ideas of aesthetic autonomy as estranged from the ordinary lives of working men. They wanted to unite artistic expression with the plight of workers on factory production lines. We will explore many further aspects of these political critiques in chapter 5.

But we will pause here for a moment to dwell on the interventions of one of the most eloquent political critics of the period: the German dramatist and polemicist Bertholt Brecht.

Writing in Berlin in the 1920s and 1930s, Brecht instructs his readers about the political limits of aesthetics. In his poems, essays and trenchant dramas that deliberately employ what Brecht called an 'alienation effect' designed to disrupt the flow of action and bring the audience to its senses rather than allow it to lose itself in the action, Brecht shows how there can be no pure aesthetic attitude. In works such as *The Caucasian Chalk Circle, The Three Penny Opera* and perhaps above all *The Resistible Rise of Arturo Ui –* an allegory of the rise of Hitler – Brecht shows that audiences cannot choose whether or not to adopt a moral or political attitude to life. They can choose whether or not to adopt an aesthetic attitude to life, but they cannot choose whether or not to adopt a moral or political attitude – because they already *are* moral and political beings just in so far as they are members of society. Therefore lovers of art cannot allow art to become an absolute end in itself, like a kind of surrogate religion. If they do so, they evade their moral and political responsibilities to society. They make themselves complicit with the status quo in all its patent injustices (Brecht 1967).

Brecht's and other socialist writers' opposition to aesthetic autonomy are of a more political kind than the more distanced sociohistorical analyses of Tocqueville and Veblen. But these two kinds of considerations can be shown to dovetail with one another in important respects. They show us how aesthetic autonomy reflects both some complexes of *interests* of elite social classes and some typical *ideas* of these classes about the separateness of art from moral and political contestation.

This combination of analysis of interests and ideas is central to the work of several contemporary Marxist cultural historians of the nineteenth century. These historians relate aesthetic autonomy to the needs of the new bourgeois classes to articulate an independent value-system of their own, distinct from long-standing patrician chivalric values and from values of trust in the monarchy and the church. Terry Eagleton (1990) speaks in this sense of a new 'ideology of the aesthetic'. Eagleton argues that it was not inconsistent of nineteenth-century industrialists to believe themselves devoted to art for art's sake while relishing every opportunity to broker business deals and forge marriages in the intervals during performances at the theatre. They needed their investments and calculations to appear sanctified in the garb of some sublime idea. Eagleton speculates that aesthetic autonomy marks a transposition of the fascination of the seventeenth-century Baroque monarchies with absolute power into the private world of bourgeois households. Ideas of the transcendent glory of art provided edifying legitimation for humdrum chores of book-keeping and factory management. They suggested ways in which an increasingly isolated bourgeois class could patch up the holes and crevices opening up in a conflict-ridden society oriented to laissez-faire capitalism.

Marxist accounts of aesthetic autonomy such as Eagleton's need not necessarily be seen as reductive. In so far as they treat aesthetic autonomy as a system of ideas and not only as a configuration of behavioural codes, they hold open the possibility of a degree of independent normative validity in art with respect to social facts. They suggest ways of reconciling sociological analysis of cultural consumption habits with the idea of aesthetics as an autonomous 'value sphere' in modern society. This conception of aesthetics as an autonomous 'value sphere' is developed at length in the work of Max Weber with reference to processes of rationalization and evolutionary differentiation in modern society. We will examine Max Weber's conception in full in chapter 6. But we must first turn to the work of the most important contemporary sociological critic of Kantian aesthetics: to the work of Pierre Bourdieu.

Art and cultural capital: Pierre Bourdieu

Pierre Bourdieu's studies of arts consumption habits are part of Bourdieu's broader sociology of cultural structures of material inequality in society. Bourdieu follows Max Weber in defining social inequality not only by possession of economic capital but also by possession of status and prestige, or by what Bourdieu notably calls 'cultural capital'. Bourdieu adopts Weber's conception of an emergent 'sphere' of aesthetic value in modern western society and applies to his analysis of this sphere some of the techniques of Weber's own stratification analyses. Bourdieu shows how this sphere elicits expressions of taste that vary across classes and groups in society according to differential life chances marked not only by wealth and power but also by education and upbringing and by what Bourdieu calls cultural 'habitus' – a term earlier used by both Norbert Elias and Weber.

In *The Love of Art*, co-written with Alain Darbel in 1969, Bourdieu examines patterns of gallery attendance in France in the 1960s

(Bourdieu and Darbel 1991). Bourdieu finds that those respondents to his surveys who declare a liking for formally complex, experimental, abstract and expressionist art also declare a degree of background knowledge in art history and are most typically members of higher income groups. In contrast, those respondents who declare a liking for art of a more realist or functional or decorative character do not declare significant background knowledge of art history and are most typically members of lower income groups. Bourdieu observes that those respondents who possess less economic capital also tend to possess less cultural capital. They typically react to the more easily recognizable features of images. They make fewer distinctions between historical periods and movements of art. They tend to dislike ambivalence, play and (sexual) expressionism in art, although they may hold some passive moral respect for 'Culture' in the abstract. Their tastes are less individually distinctive and more standardized. In contrast, those respondents who possess greater economic capital also tend to possess greater cultural capital. They enjoy advantages of longer educational schooling and greater informal cultural socialization based on upbringing in 'cultivated families'. This enables them to develop a taste for 'pure', 'difficult', non-functional art that requires specific perceptual skills of appreciation. Their greater educational background knowledge enables them to decipher systems of signs in works of art. Bourdieu concludes that the Kantian attitude of 'disinterested contemplation' of works of art remains a privilege of those groups in society who possess greatest cultural capital. Aesthetic qualities in works of art are not immediately evident to everyone; and recognition of them is not an innate gift of nature. Recognition of aesthetic qualities in works of art is a learned ability, acquired under definite conditions of cultural socialization.

In a similar study, Bourdieu speaks of tastes in art as occupying a socially constructed 'hierarchy of legitimacies' (Bourdieu et al. 1990). At the top stand high-art forms that enjoy sanction by legitimate authorities. At the bottom stand low-cultural forms that lack generalized legitimacy. In the middle lies a zone of ambiguity marked by 'middle-brow' forms such as photography.

In *Distinction: A Social Critique of the Judgement of Taste* (1984), Bourdieu continues this line of analysis, alluding in his title to Kant's third *Critique*. The empirical centrepiece of Bourdieu's book is a survey of tastes in music among the French public in the 1960s and 1970s. Bourdieu examines some sets of preference responses in relation to three works of music: J. S. Bach's *The Well-Tempered Clavier*, George Gershwin's *Rhapsody in Blue* and Johann Strauss's

The Blue Danube waltz. Bourdieu sorts these responses into a three-tiered class division, consisting of the upper middle classes, the lower middle classes and the working class; but he subdivides this class membership into further occupational fractions, and supplies other indicators such as home and car ownership for economic capital and educational qualification and newspaper preference for cultural capital. Bourdieu finds that *The Well-Tempered Clavier* is most preferred by holders of upper middle-class occupations, although considerably more so by employees of educational institutions than by private sector executives. *Rhapsody in Blue* is most preferred by holders of lower middle class occupations, including technicians, engineers and administrative managers. *The Blue Danube* is most preferred by holders of working-class and lower middle-class occupations, including manual workers, shopkeepers and clerical workers.

Bourdieu again concludes that appreciation of formally complex and historically classical cultural forms depends on acquisition of perceptual skills of recognition, which in turn depends on possession of cultural capital and ultimately on possession of economic capital. The kinds of participants in Bourdieu's study who most like works of classical music such as *The Well-Tempered Clavier* are likely to have experienced some earlier exposure to classical music during an upbringing in relatively well-off middle-class families, able to afford supplementary educational activities for their children beyond formal instruction at school. Children of middle-class families are more likely to have the chance to learn to play musical instruments than children of working-class families; and they are more likely to be enabled and encouraged to pursue other supplementary activities such as learning foreign languages. In contrast, the kinds of participants in Bourdieu's study who become manual workers, shopkeepers or clerical workers are less likely to have been brought up in families possessing high economic and cultural capital, and they are less likely to increase their economic and cultural capital in the later course of their lives. Therefore they are more likely to respond to musical forms that demand no special skills of recognition and are more easily and standardly accessible, through commercial radio stations and the like. *The Blue Danube* is one such form, but most mainstream pop music forms would perhaps be more obvious examples.

Bourdieu proposes that class differentiation in skills of cultural recognition reflects a pattern of symbolic self-distinction between social groups. Different classes and groups in society distinguish themselves by their typical habits of consumption; and those groups in society who possess greatest cultural capital are typically those who most strive to make a display of these distinctions central to their way of life:

> Taste classifies, and it classifies the classifier. Social subjects, classified by classifications, distinguish themselves by the distinctions they make, between the beautiful and the ugly, the distinguished and the vulgar, in which their position in the objective classifications is expressed or betrayed.
>
> The science of taste and of cultural consumption . . . has to abolish the sacred frontier which makes legitimate culture a separate universe, in order to discover the intelligible relations which unite apparently incommensurable 'choices', such as preferences in music and food, painting and sport, literature and hairstyle. This barbarous reintegration of aesthetic consumption into the world of ordinary consumption abolishes the opposition, which has been the basis of high aesthetics since Kant, between the 'taste of sense' and the 'taste of reflection' . . .
> (Bourdieu 1984: 6)

In a later book, *The Rules of Art,* Bourdieu takes a different approach, characterized more by a focus on arts production than on arts consumption (Bourdieu 1996). Bourdieu investigates the tacit rules that make up the identity of artistic practices within fields of cultural production. He shows how modern artists have to believe that they are not following rules and are no longer mechanical providers of services, like medieval craftsmen. Modern artists have to see themselves as constantly breaking rules and constantly re-creating rules of their own, through acts of innovation. But Bourdieu shows how the rules that artists believe themselves to be spontaneously shaping and breaking are in reality socially reproduced rules that structurally regulate their field of production. Bourdieu illustrates this through extended analysis of a claim to aesthetic autonomy among French artists of the nineteenth century. Oppositional writers and painters such as the realist and impressionist painters and the symbolist poets felt themselves marginalized by an increasingly powerful class of mercantile industrialists in positions of public authority. Bourdieu shows how the French artists competed with one another in relation to this mercantile class, both economically and symbolically. Some artists perceived other artists as sacrificing their aesthetic integrity for privileges of friendship with the powerful. They found themselves caught in a skein of divided loyalties, personal dilemmas and irresolvable choices between public popularity and commercial success on the one hand and aesthetic authenticity, bohemian opposition and material poverty on the other hand.

Bourdieu analyses these dynamics at length in the writing of Gustave Flaubert, most notably in Flaubert's novel, *Éducation Sentimentale*. Flaubert's panoramic social novel tells the story of a young aspiring artist, Frédéric Moreau, who seeks his fortune in Paris with high political ideals and high ideals for art. Frédéric briefly takes part in the street demonstrations of the 1848 revolution but gradually becomes disillusioned with his world and his life after too many failed and half-hearted attempts at securing favour with patrons and employers. Bourdieu shows how Flaubert's novel of 'social ageing' is not an autobiographical novel but a sociologically reflexive novel in which Flaubert analyses his own condition as an artist caught between irreconcilable social fields of production. Bourdieu argues that it is the dynamic of these social fields of production that must be grasped if literary scholarship is to be truly reflexively aware of its institutional conditions of emergence and is not to relapse into the illusion of an unmediated attitude to history which lifts cultural objects out of their social relations of circulation and fetishizes them like magical charms in sacred exchange systems (see also Bourdieu 1993).

We will now move to some criticisms of Bourdieu's work. These are highlighted in part by recent American cultural sociologists, who propose some alternative approaches to the sociology of taste. After this, we discuss some further issues of a more normative rather than empirical kind, relevant to both Bourdieu and the American cultural sociologists. This second set of issues will return us to our initial discussion of the arguments for and against Kant's normative thesis of aesthetic autonomy.

Arts consumption in the US

Bourdieu's data for his studies on distinction and art gallery attendance are from France in the 1960s and 1970s. This raises the question of whether his findings can be generalized from their original context to the present day. The American sociologists draw different conclusions from their own data and also advance some methodological criticisms of Bourdieu's work. We may summarize these criticisms as follows.

First, Bourdieu is excessively deterministic in his assessment of the incapacity of working class and other underprivileged groups in society to make aesthetic distinctions. Drawing on his own study of arts consumption habits in New York, Halle (1993) argues that it is not the case that poor and working-class people's reduced educational opportunities predetermine them to a mostly functional and decorative attitude to art, without exercise of individual aesthetic discrimination. Family upbringing is not as formative for later cultural choices as Bourdieu contends, and lack of institutional legitimation for tastes by prestigious authorities is not as crucial for social esteem in contemporary society as he maintains. In general, Bourdieu exaggerates the extent to which a liking for fine art requires a specialized knowledge that is hard to acquire.

Further, Bourdieu asserts a direct correlation between taste prestige hierarchy and social class hierarchy which may well have existed in French society in the 1960s and 1970s but is harder to establish in the present day, particularly in the US but also in Europe. Lamont (1992) indicates in her study of the French and American upper-middle classes that while possession of cultural capital is more important for power and success in French society than in the US, it is not as important as Bourdieu maintains. In general, cultural stratification structures in western societies have changed since the time of Bourdieu's research. Humanistic non-vocational education at elite schools and universities plays less of a legitimating role in access to power and wealth than in the 1960s and 1970s. Widened access to higher education, together with rises in lower middle-class and upper working-class incomes, have led to broader public participation in fine arts institutions and a dismantling of some older status demarcations. On the one hand, Bourdieu's conclusions ignore significant increases in lower middle-class involvement in high-culture forms, through outlets such as blockbuster art exhibitions, commercial classical music radio stations, specialized TV channels. On the other hand, his conclusions exaggerate upper middle-class involvement in high-culture forms and underestimate upper middle-class involvement in 'middlebrow' forms, such as film, photography, dance, jazz and rock music.

According to Peterson (Peterson and Simkus 1992; Peterson and Kern 1996), most of the expanded middle-class public today have become 'omnivores'. Upper middle-class groups now not only patronize high culture but also dip into a broad spectrum of categories of cultural products that can include classical music as much as country music – and classical opera as much as soap opera. Conversely, lower middle-class groups now have considerably more leisure time, money and education at their disposal to shop around in their cultural choices, especially in the youth age groups. Daniel Bell (1976) once described these processes in terms of a 'disjuncture of culture and social structure', based on erosion of distinctions between 'high' and 'low' and the emergence of a broad middle-brow ground. Gans (1999) argues that it is more correct to speak of processes of both convergence in cultural taste and renewed divergence in cultural taste. Taste cultures have lost part of their character of vertical prestige ordering and have become more horizontally differentiated. While class remains the most significant factor in hierarchical social structure, cultural consumption habits, choices and status markers do not directly correlate with class structure. Gender, ethnicity and age have become as important as class in patterns of cultural consumption differentiation (Lamont and Fournier 1992).

Levine (1988) and DiMaggio and Useem (1978) examine structures of arts reception in the US in a more historical context. DiMaggio (1982) shows how American society knew no palpable distinction between high and low culture until late in the nineteenth century when Boston, the oldest city of the US, set up a museum of fine arts and a symphony orchestra to cater for the tastes of elites of established wealth, in distinction to groups of more recently acquired wealth. The founding patrons of the museum and the orchestra set up institutional and organizational structures that secured at once the educational authority and legitimacy of fine art and the social distinctness of its connoisseurs. These institutional and organizational structures generated systems of 'ritual classifications' in the exhibition and performance of different types of cultural products that soon dovetailed with social differences in the types of attending audiences. DiMaggio (1987) proposes that sociology should study the ways in which administrative organizational structures generate classification systems around cultural goods which in turn sustain symbolic markers between social groups through practices of cultural consumption. These classification systems are generated both by art worlds and by commercial agents such as dealers, promoters, sponsors, publishers and production company executives. Depending on circumstances, classification systems may be more or less differentiated in the numbers of categories and niches they articulate; more or less hierarchical in their distributions of prestige; more or less universalizing in the extent of their involvement of audiences; and more or less ritually bounded in their restrictions on mixing of categories.

Aesthetic validity versus the sociology of taste

We have now discussed several critical observations about the thesis of aesthetic autonomy. First we have considered some observations about how aesthetic autonomy relates to consumption habits among elite strata of eighteenth- and nineteenth-century European society, as well as some arguments about art's relationship to moral and political criticism. Second, we have considered some observations about relationships between arts consumption habits and differences of educational advantage and 'cultural capital', notably in the work of Bourdieu and recent American sociologists. All these observations indicate some important empirical facts about the relationship of aesthetic evaluation to dimensions of socioeconomic inequality and to differences of leisure, lifestyle and 'habitus' among social groups.

The question we must now address is what bearing these facts have on the idea of aesthetic autonomy as a *normative* thesis. Do they show that aesthetic autonomy is meaningless as a normative idea? Do they remove all sense from the injunction that works of art *ought* to be approached 'for their own sake', rather than for the sake of some ulterior social function or interest? Do they show that it is meaningless to say that aesthetic judgements *ought* to aspire to universal validity and not remain only expressions of particular consumption habits on the part of particular social groups?

In the following, we will propose some arguments for the view that aesthetic judgements can still be said to possess independent normative validity with respect to their functions of distinction for social groups. We will argue that works of art can still be said to possess aesthetic value in themselves and do not possess value *only* in virtue of different social *perspectives* of valuation. We will propose that while the normative thesis of aesthetic autonomy needs to be *contextualized* by sociohistorical and sociological considerations, it is not *refuted* by these considerations.

These considerations continue our remarks at the end of chapter 2 about the relative distinctness of questions of aesthetic value from questions of cultural domination in society. They continue our conclusions about the pitfalls of relativistic arguments which reduce questions of value to questions of power and perspective. In the following, we will not suggest that either Bourdieu's or any of the American cultural sociologists' contributions necessarily imply relativism. But we will concentrate on showing why relativism is a

problem, and we will argue that one of the reasons for the importance of Kantian philosophy is that it helps us to see why. We will
proceed first with some additional remarks on Kant's arguments;
second with some remarks on questions of democracy in culture;
and third with some concluding remarks on Bourdieu.

A first additional consideration about Kant's position concerns
his insistence on a presupposition of universality in aesthetic judgements. Kant sought to demonstrate that whenever I – a judging
person – make an aesthetic judgement, I implicitly declare not only
that I like X but also that I find X good, and furthermore that I
am prepared to propose reasons to *you* for X's being good. These
reasons may or may not be reasons for your liking X, but they ought
to be reasons with which you could have a critical debate with me if
you so wished. I cannot say that I find X good and then immediately back out of my claim by saying 'but this is only what I think',
or 'this is just how I am'. Even though it is conceivable for me that
you may not endorse my claim, I have to be prepared to stand
up for my claim in the event that I am challenged about it by you,
or by hundreds of people, or even – in principle – by everyone in the
world. People who make an aesthetic judgement must therefore
presuppose that their judgement is generalizable beyond their
immediate subjective situation. If this were not the case, people's
aesthetic judgements would have to be considered merely reflections
of their psychological and behavioural peculiarities. But aesthetic
judgements are not merely reflections of people's psychological and
behavioural peculiarities; they are claims to *validity*. Peculiarities of
age, sex, class or national background are all relevant to the judgements people make; but they are not the *ground* of those judgements. Therefore when I make a claim for a work of art, I cannot
relativize or withdraw my judgement by saying 'but this is only
because I am a man' (or a woman), or 'but this is only because I am
a member of the middle classes' (or the working classes) – any more
than I can rationally say '2 + 2 = 4, but this is only what I think', or
'murder is wrong, but this is only my opinion'.

Here let us once again consider how aesthetic judgements compare with statements in science and with moral judgements. Much
twentieth-century post-positivist philosophy of science has highlighted
ways in which scientific theories are embedded in sociohistorically
salient discursive 'paradigms'; for example, in the writings of Thomas
Kuhn. Similarly, much twentieth-century moral philosophy has
highlighted ways in which moral norms hold different meanings in
different, historically concrete situations; for example, in the writings

of Wittgenstein and Alasdair MacIntyre. However, very few except the most sceptical philosophers today argue that the physical mechanisms to which scientific theories seek to refer have no existence in objective reality and are nothing other than names in the discourses of scientific actors. Similarly, very few except the most sceptical philosophers today argue that moral norms are nothing other than social conventions, on the same level as, say, a social convention to drive on the right in some countries and on the left in others. Thus very few contemporary philosophers reduce validity in scientific statements and moral norms wholly to facts of social behaviour. Now aesthetic judgements certainly differ from scientific statements and moral norms in so far as they express subjective responses of pleasure and displeasure to sensory objects that cannot be deemed to be either true or false (as in science), and cannot be deemed to lay prescriptions for right or wrong actions (as in morality). Instead they assert other positive-negative predicates such as beautiful/ugly, elegant/crude, profound/superficial, and so on. In this respect they articulate a different *kind* of validity from scientific and moral statements. But they articulate validity nonetheless, and they are no more reducible to the behavioural peculiarities of the agents who assert them than scientific statements and moral norms are reducible to the behavioural peculiarities of the agents who assert them.

A second consideration about this dimension of validity concerns the relevance of differences of educational advantage to valuations of cultural objects. We may certainly accept the reasons for the view that university entrance authorities should recognize differences of advantage in socioeconomic background among the candidates they consider for admission to courses. However, it would not appear that there are reasons for arguing that university entrance candidates' differences of socioeconomic background advantage have any bearing on the validity of the academic contents students study in such courses, once they are admitted to university. It would not appear relevant to the validity of Newtonian calculus equations taught in mathematics courses that statistically fewer black working-class entrance candidates enjoy a prior acquaintance with Newtonian calculus than white middle-class candidates. It is therefore hard to see why the fact that statistically fewer black working-class school-leavers acquire an acquaintance with Shakespeare's plays than white middle-class teenagers should have any bearing on the aesthetic validity of Shakespeare's plays as poetic works.

If some agents in society were to advance arguments for persuading people to revise their acceptance of the mathematical coherence of Newtonian calculus – on the grounds, say, that it contains a false deduction – or to revise their acceptance of the aesthetic accomplishments of Shakespeare's plays – on the grounds, say, that his metaphors are contrived – these would be serious candidate arguments for impugning the validity of Newton's and Shakespeare's works. But this would be a very different type of discursive intervention from the claim that the validity of Shakespeare's and Newton's works can be impugned solely because some social strata possess greater opportunities to acquaint themselves with their works than other strata. It is true that it would be less meaningful to teach only Shakespeare and only the Bible to school cohorts composed entirely of pupils from Muslim backgrounds, just as it would be less meaningful to teach only the Koran to school cohorts composed entirely of pupils from Christian backgrounds. But the fact that it would be less meaningful to teach these texts to these sets of agents does not mean that the texts do not possess intrinsic validity as cultural objects.

This is a first general level on which Kantian philosophy retains importance for sociological thinking about aesthetics. But we will now consider a possible objection to our arguments so far.

It might be objected that our arguments so far have made aesthetic judgements look more obligatory on people than they really are. It might be argued that when I express a taste in something, I am not really making a *claim* on anyone else. I am merely giving voice to the things I like. I am not expecting other people to share my tastes. Different individuals have different tastes and they cannot be expected to be either able or obliged to arrive at agreement among themselves as to what tastes are the most valid and which tastes the least valid. This objection hints at something problematic in Kant's distinction between 'pleasures of sensation' and 'pleasures of reflection'. From the standpoint of contemporary sympathies towards lifestyle pluralism, the distinction appears contentious. It appears to command greater unanimity in value-orientation than is desirable from the standpoint of respect for lifestyle diversity. But let us examine the distinction more closely.

Let us consider the following random list of types of objects that might be said to invite cultural valuation: food, wine, coffee, clothes, perfume, apartment furnishings, soap opera, disco music, expressionist painting, symbolist poetry, Greek tragic drama. A case could be made for arguing that none of these types divide either exclusively on the side of 'pleasure of sensation' or exclusively on the side of 'pleasure of reflection'. A case could be made for arguing that all such types support aesthetic choices equally worthy of respect. We might say that people who build lifestyles for themselves around a tasteful choice of apartment furnishings, a stylish choice of designer suits and a discerning line in French wines make a set of aesthetic judgements equally deserving of respect as those of people who rank expressionist painting, symbolist poetry and Greek tragic drama above all else. But now let us consider some reasons for criticizing and qualifying this proposal.

Food, wine, coffee, clothes and perfumes certainly afford pleasure of sensation. Perhaps they also afford pleasure of reflection in the sense of a 'theme' or 'image' that I can express in the way I intelligently combine them. But do they do so to the degree that symbolist poetry does? Do they 'induce much thought', in Kant's phrase? Further, can I have a rational debate with someone about whether an Armani perfume is superior to a Christian Dior perfume in the way that I can have a rational debate with someone about whether Beethoven's last symphony is a more accomplished work than his first symphony, or the Beatles a more accomplished group of musicians than the Monkeys? I could exchange my Armani suit for an antique dinner table by selling the one and buying the other with the proceeds. But is it conceivable that the value of a Beethoven symphony could be exchanged for the value of a Picasso portrait? Could a Beethoven symphony be exchanged for a quantity of money in the way that a Ferrari sports car could be exchanged for a quantity of money? Are all cultural goods conceivable as equivalent to one another in the way that some objects are capable of equivalence to one another via the medium of money? Could one imagine a quantitative equation between, say, a Picasso portrait, a Beethoven symphony and an Emily Dickinson poem in the same way that one could imagine a quantitative equation of the form '6 Dior perfumes = 2 Armani suits = 4 Prada boots = $1000'? It appears not. It appears that there are differences. To be sure, these differences appear to be only ones of degree. If it is right to say that a Picasso cubist painting cannot conceivably be exchanged for a Braque cubist painting, it is not significantly less right to say that one soap opera series (say, *Dallas*) cannot conceivably be exchanged for another soap opera series (say, *Neighbours*). But there are differences nonetheless; and the differences seem to refer to the way in which those objects that are least capable of equivalence are precisely those about which it is most meaningful for people to have a discussion – because it is those objects that most make it possible for people to stake a claim for them as being not only objects of their own personal taste but as being objects of great intellectual and emotional worth and distinction that everyone could appreciate if they were only to acquaint themselves with them.

This is a second general level on which Kantian arguments retain importance for thinking about aesthetics. We now move to a third level.

We will now propose a normative distinction between questions of democratic parity of esteem in respect of *categories of cultural production*, on the one hand, and questions of differential aesthetic merit in respect of *individual objects* of cultural production, on the other hand. First some considerations on democratic parity of esteem in respect of categories of cultural production.

From a normative point of view, there would appear to be no superordinate basis of comparison on which any one *category* of cultural production can be deemed 'higher' or 'lower' in value than another. There would appear to be no basis of comparison for discriminating Greek tragedy, symbolist poetry and expressionist painting as either 'better' or 'worse' than rock music, soap opera, jazz or pantomime. Nor would there appear to be any basis for accounting the distinctive habitus practices of social groups in respect of these categories as being either more or less worthy of respect. Each habitus practice would appear to be equally worthy of esteem. There would appear to be no basis for saying say that the generally distinctive preferences of working-class and lower-middle class audiences for 'low-brow' culture are lower in value and less worthy of esteem than the generally distinctive preferences of upper middle-class audiences for 'highbrow' culture. In this respect, use of the spatial metaphors of 'high' and 'low' is a linguistic residue of pre-democratic thinking. From a normative point of view, assertions of value hierarchy across high and low culture are not democratically defensible; and they derive no normative foundation from their sociological correlation with social stratification. High culture is not higher in value because it is typically enjoyed by higher classes in society, and low culture is not lower in value because it is typically enjoyed by lower classes in society. And furthermore: high culture is not lower in value than low culture because it is typically enjoyed by classes who have historically dominated and exploited lower classes in society, and low culture is not higher in value than high culture because it is typically enjoyed by classes who have historically suffered domination and exploitation by higher classes in society. Value hierarchy in categories of culture is not justified by hierarchy in social structure, and neither is *inverted* value hierarchy justified by hierarchy in social structure. The former assumption is usually known as snobbery or elitism. The latter assumption is often known as inverted snobbery. The latter assumption can be compared with what Nietzsche called *ressentiment*, or petty resentment of other people's values. (We will discuss Nietzsche's contribution to aesthetics at length in chapter 5.) We can say that in each of these respects a democratic principle of parity of esteem obtains, and ought to obtain, across categories of cultural production and across the distinctive habitus practices of social groups in respect of these categories.

(One possible exception to this principle might be categories of dubious moral value, however. It might be argued that pornography is not worthy of parity of esteem, in so far as pornography constitutes a category of cultural objects at all. This case at least demonstrates that what is held to constitute a category of cultural objects has some relationship to debate about ethical value in such objects.)

However, the picture is different when we turn to questions of value in *individual objects* of cultural production. We have argued that some cultural objects are conceivable as being capable of equivalence to one another in a way that some other objects are not so conceivable. We must now try to establish more precisely what 'non-equivalence' might mean in this context.

There would seem to be two senses. Some objects would appear to be non-equivalent in the sense of the *distinctiveness* of their sensory qualities and in the sense of the *merit* of their sensory qualities. It is possible to think of one film or play or novel or photograph as being both aesthetically 'distinctive' and aesthetically 'better' in relation to others. It might be thought that these two senses stand in tension with one another. If two objects are each very distinctive in relation to one another, how could either object be viewed as 'better' or 'worse' than the other? However, this tension is more apparent than real. If an object A is very distinctive and an object B is very distinctive, then indeed A cannot be viewed as better than B and B cannot be viewed as worse than A. But if A is very distinctive and another object C is not very distinctive, we *can* speak of A as being better than C and of C as being worse than A. We could say that C is worse than A in the sense that we could say that it is 'not original', 'follows a formula', is 'derivative'. And conversely we could say that A is better than C in the sense that it *is* 'original', does *not* 'follow a formula', is *not* 'derivative'. Thus distinctiveness implies 'better-best' in relation to objects which are not distinctive; and non-distinctiveness implies 'worse-worst' in relation to objects which are distinctive. If any two objects C and D can be compared to, equated to, or replaced for one another, they are lower in aesthetic value than any two objects A and B that cannot be compared to, or equated with, or replaced for one another. We must, however, immediately add that comparability and non-comparability between objects in this context does not refer merely to factual membership or non-membership of definite genres, forms or styles of production. Clearly *Apocalypse Now* and *The Deer Hunter* are both comparable to one another in the *factual* respect of both being members of the category 'film', and of the subcategory 'Vietnam film'. But there are still grounds for arguing that each are incomparably good works of art in a non-factual, *aesthetically value-relevant* respect of being more distinctive and accomplished in their aesthetic qualities than some other Vietnam films in particular and many other films in general.

We may conclude that value equality in respect of *categories* of cultural production does not entail value equality in respect of individual *object members* of these categories. If it were not possible to discriminate differences of aesthetic value in individual cultural objects, there would be no rational basis for aesthetic judgement. If no individual cultural object could be judged as being higher or lower in aesthetic value than another, there would be no basis for uses of positive predicates in ordinary language such as 'elegant', 'brilliant' 'inspiring', in distinction to negative predicates such as 'mediocre', 'dull', 'average'. It would follow from this that any person could produce any object which no other person could criticize, or even praise. Any person could affirm anything about any object which no other person could contest, or even endorse. People could assert the same things about objects of which they have some acquaintance as of objects of which they have no acquaintance. And the things asserted of objects by people who have no acquaintance of them would have to be accepted as of equal insight to the things asserted by people who do have some acquaintance of them. Then there would be no rational basis for art criticism. There would be no rational basis for the selections, acquisitions, prizes and contracting decisions of art galleries, publishers, theatres and music companies; nor for student qualifications at colleges of art, music and design. The situation would be one of universal equivalence and universal relativism. The democratic sense that equality of value should be recognized across categories of cultural production does not therefore entail that equality of value should be recognized in individual objects of cultural production.

We may conclude from the aforegoing that it is necessary to reconcile sociological observation and political contestation of historical inequalities of cultural valuation with aesthetic value-appraisal in respect of individual objects of culture. There are two sides to the study of value in sociology of the arts. There is the side of empirical social facts about differences of habitus in respect of categories of cultural production and consumption, and there is the side of the normative aesthetic validity of individual objects of culture. Sociological understanding of the arts ought to be capable of recognizing the integrity of both these sides of its investigation.

We will now end with a few remarks on the way in which these two sides are handled in the work of Bourdieu. It is clear that Bourdieu *does* recognize the two sides and embraces the tension between them. In *The Rules of Art* Bourdieu shows how the claims of nineteenth-century French writers to aesthetic universality articulated an emerging system of social distinctions between autonomous and non-autonomous art; but Bourdieu does not crudely reduce these universality claims to 'bourgeois ideology' or to 'bourgeois cultural consumption habits'. Bourdieu shows how some of the most socially self-conscious of these writers, chiefly Flaubert and Baudelaire, strove for critical insight into their social worlds through their poetic engagements, using their pen as their sword – in full knowledge of the likely recuperation of their engagements by representatives of the French mercantile elites and officers of state. Bourdieu thus allows for ways in which artists themselves can achieve sociological reflexivity in relation to their own cultural production. However, Bourdieu's analytical techniques still tend to be biased towards the side of functional sociological analysis at the expense of understanding for normative validity in aesthetic contents. *The Rules of Art* is difficult to reconcile with Bourdieu's earlier, more polemical critiques of Kantian aesthetics in *Distinction* and *The Love of Art*, which are more reductive in their tendencies. In general, although Bourdieu often mediates understanding of normative validity in aesthetic contents with functional sociological analysis in sophisticated ways, he usually tends to subordinate the former dimension of engagement to the latter. He certainly recognizes art as being more than purely an object for social science. It is precisely for this reason that he speaks of sociology and art as making an 'odd couple' (*la sociologie et l'art ne font pas bon ménage*) (1980: 207). However, Bourdieu's accounts of how art's normative claims against social science can come up for fair experiential appreciation are not always perspicuous. His concern to demystify conceptions of hermeneutic understanding sometimes leads him to caricature the positions of his intellectual opponents and to rely too heavily on polemical anthropological analogies of object fetishism and cultic secrecy. This sometimes hinders rather than enhances Bourdieu's basic intention to open up thought about culture to an arena of democratic enlightenment.

Conclusion

We have considered various arguments about the thesis of aesthetic autonomy which speak both for the thesis and against the thesis – in different ways and on different levels. On one level, it is clear that ideas of aesthetic autonomy are a product of modern western culture since the eighteenth century and are not applicable in any immediate way to other societies in history and around the world. Ideas of aesthetic autonomy are also contradicted by observations about differential social functions of arts consumption for stratified groups within modern western society. These include entertainment functions, status-marking functions and group habitus distinctions. Disinterested contemplation of works of art informed by skills of perceptual recognition presupposes a history of cultural and educational habitus advantages that have not been open to all classes and groups in society. Different classes and groups develop different habits of consumption of cultural goods that cannot normatively be deemed to be more or less worthy of respect than each other. Sociological analysis therefore suggests grounds for a principle of democratic parity of esteem for habits of consumption in respect of different categories of cultural production, 'highbrow' as well as 'low-brow'.

However, sociological analysis is not in a position to derive a principle of value equality in individual objects of cultural production from a principle of value equality across categories of cultural production and types of consumer habitus. It is not in a position to reduce intrinsic differences of aesthetic value in individual objects to practices and perspectives of valuation by social groups. Therefore we must reject both transcendentalism – the view that aesthetic contents in works of art hold validity *in no relation* to social facts; and we must reject relativism – the view that aesthetic contents in works of art hold *no validity other than* as social facts. Kantian thinking is open to contextualization by sociohistorical arguments, but is not open to refutation by sociohistorical arguments.

The position we have reached in this conclusion rests on what can be called an *antinomy*. An antinomy in philosophy refers to two orders of argument that stand in contradiction to one another but are each incontrovertible in their own terms. An antinomy here obtains between empirical sociological observation of arts consumption practices and normative aesthetic evaluation of individual art objects.

In so far as we have defined the task of social-theoretic thinking about art as being to facilitate dialogue between value-distanciation in social science and critical value-affirmation in humanities disciplines, we may say that social theory needs to mediate between these two standpoints of investigation and seek ways of resolving the antinomy. Logical procedures that seek to resolve antinomies are known in philosophy by the name of *dialectic*. In the next chapter, we therefore discuss several social theorists who develop a *dialectical* way of thinking about art in society. These theorists draw both on the sociological insights of Karl Marx and on the philosophical insights of German idealist thinkers who follow in the footsteps of Kant.

5

Ideology and Utopia

So far in this book we have been mostly concerned with practices of arts production, arts consumption and arts evaluation as empirical subjects of sociological analysis. In this chapter and the following two chapters, we address a variety of more decisively normative issues to do with ideas of modernity, rationality and enlightenment in art. Our discussion in this chapter centres on debates about 'ideology and utopia'. We examine a certain constitutive ambivalence in works of art between their frequent historical appearance as bearers of images of happiness in a free society ('utopia') and their frequent historical appearance as bearers of compensating distractions from lived suffering in the real world ('ideology'). We begin by outlining the relevance of this ambivalence to the critique of 'mass culture' in twentieth-century Marxist social theory, which we discuss further in chapter 6 with reference to the work of Theodor Adorno. Then we set out the significance of ideas of nature, freedom and truth in art among German idealist philosophers of the early nineteenth century. We investigate the ways in which these ideas are transposed into the idiom of materialist critique in the early philosophical writings of Karl Marx, as well as in the twentieth-century Marxist thought of Ernst Bloch and György Lukács. Next we enumerate some respects in which contents of religious and mythical belief can be said to make an ideological return in certain aspects of late nineteenth-century European high culture. We draw partly on Durkheim's reflections on processes of social evolution as well as on Richard Wagner's and Friedrich Nietzsche's aesthetic philosophies. We conclude with a discussion of the concept of 'sublimation' in psychoanalytic social theory, notably in the writings of Sigmund Freud and Herbert Marcuse.

Origins of the critique of mass culture

We concluded our previous chapter by proposing a certain case for defending normative autonomy in art. We described this case as having a 'dialectical' character in the sense that it recognizes contents of aesthetic validity in works of art as both related to social facts and relatively independent of social facts. The theorists we examine in this chapter develop this case in significant ways. They draw from a tradition of twentieth-century humanistic Marxism which mostly avoids the reductive tendencies of classical Marxist thinking. This is partly because they have not sought to reconcile Marx's ideas with strict empirical science and partly because they have sought to combine Marxian ideas with other twentieth-century intellectual movements such as psychoanalysis, phenomenology and existentialism. They include Walter Benjamin, Ernst Bloch, György Lukács, Siegfried Kracauer, Jean-Paul Sartre and the Frankfurt School theorists Theodor Adorno, Max Horkheimer, Herbert Marcuse and Jürgen Habermas. We will refer to all these theorists in shorthand as the 'critical theorists', after Horkheimer's influential essay of 1937, 'Traditional and Critical Theory' (Horkheimer 1972).

The critical theorists take their point of departure from Marx's materialist understanding of dialectical logic in post-Kantian German idealist philosophy. Their thinking is 'critical' in the sense in which Kant defined 'critique' in his *Critique of Pure Reason* as inquiry into the '*conditions of possibility* of knowledge and experience of the world'. Both the critical theorists and the post-Kantian philosophers begin from Kant's principle that empirical knowledge of the world is possible only under the condition of certain concepts and categories of human intellection. Kant held that human intellection does not know the 'noumenal' world of 'things-in-themselves'; human intellection knows only the 'phenomenal' world of things as they appear to us under these concepts and categories. Kant held that when human intellection tries to gain empirical knowledge of the things in themselves, *antinomies* arise. Things in the world appear to be both free and unfree, both causes of themselves and caused by other things. However, Kant proposed that 'dialectic' is capable of resolving these antinomies. Dialectic is capable of explaining how things and persons in the world can be both physical phenomena, determined by laws of nature, and free ends in themselves, free causes of themselves. Critical thinking in this sense is concerned not only with empirical knowledge of the world under concepts and categories of the intellect (*Verstand*). It is also concerned with the conditions of *reason* (*Vernunft*) that make such knowledge possible. The conditions of reason are logic, and logic is dialectic.

Beginning from this Kantian principle, the critical theorists develop a specifically materialist understanding of this work of 'reason', 'dialectic' and 'critique'. In their discussions of science, they show how science is made possible by concepts and categories which develop historically under specific social conditions. They show how positivism – what Horkheimer called 'traditional theory' – fails to reflect on these sociohistorically specific conditions of the possibility of science. They show how positivism treats sociohistorical conditions only as given objects of empirical knowledge. Positivism does not reflect on the ways in which sociohistorical conditions are themselves conditions of the very possibility of science's knowledge of objects. Because it does not think dialectically, positivism is not able to resolve the contradiction between sociohistorical life as an *object* of empirical knowledge and sociohistorical life as a *condition of possibility* of empirical knowledge.

The critical theorists deploy similar arguments in their discussions of art. They show how works of art are not only materially caused by sociohistorical conditions of production; they show how works of art also possess a normative content which has validity in relative independence of these conditions. They show how works of art are social both in the sense of being produced and consumed in society and in the sense of thematizing society in their forms and contents of communication. Works of art are not only conditioned by society; they are *about* society. Works of art not only exist as objects for judging subjects. They exist as objects for themselves. They exist as subjects in their own right. Like works of science and philosophy, works of art are *self-reflective objects*, which, in varying degrees of clarity and coherence, give accounts of their social conditions of possibility. Therefore, works of art cannot be treated solely as objects for that particular science known as 'sociology'. They must be treated as self-thinking subjects – which say things about society that may be relevant also to sociology's social conditions of possibility as a science.

Georg Simmel, whose contributions we discuss at length in chapter 6, argued that works of art are autonomous in the sense that at the same time as being produced and consumed under definite social conditions, they are 'laws unto themselves' (Simmel 2000). Simmel proposes that works of art possess *Gesetzmäßigkeit*. They are both caused by society and they are their own causes. They are conditioned and they are conditioning. They have a purpose, and they are their own purpose. In this sense they are analogous to freely self-determining human individuals who are both subject to society's laws and are at the same time self-responsible moral agents. Like human individuals who set themselves ultimate ethical ideals, works of art set up ideal laws for themselves; and the degree to which works of art fulfil these ideal laws is the degree to which their parts serve the purpose of the work as a whole, as an integrated totality. It is the degree to which the work holds its own against its 'external', social laws: against its social uses and functions of consumption. It is the degree to which the work preserves its aesthetic autonomy and is, for this reason, aesthetically great.

Some commentators have objected that this way of thinking expresses a characteristically mandarin perspective of 'old European thinking' about culture. Some commentators have argued that the critical theorists took an invidious view of use-oriented, function-oriented artistic forms, especially entertainment forms. We will discuss this objection fully in our assessment of the work of Adorno in chapter 6. However, we will first introduce some preliminary reasons for persisting with the arguments of the critical theorists. These have to do with their conception of processes of societal rationalization in cultural life; with their conception of aesthetic autonomy; and with their conception of 'ideology and utopia'.

We must note that the critical theorists do not censure popular culture as such. They criticize processes of economic transformation in modern society under which both high-cultural forms and low-cultural forms become subject to pressures of industrial utility and commercial profit. They argue that these processes break down shared horizons of evaluative communication in society. They argue that contemporary commercial mass culture substantially differs from popular culture in historical social settings. They maintain that contemporary divisions between high and low culture have to do not only with symbolic status marking between leisured and unleisured social classes but also with deep-seated structural changes following from the breakdown of collectively recognized value-systems in society.

In the Middle Ages, western society knew no clear division between 'high' and 'low' because sociocultural life was mostly unified under the religious institution of the Catholic Church. The church sustained a largely cohesive social body in which written and oral culture partook of largely the same stock of symbolic meanings, familiar to literate and illiterate people alike. However, with the decline in the social role and power of the church after the Renaissance and the

Protestant Reformation, a recognizable differentiation between 'high' and 'low' emerged which became increasingly entrenched by processes of capitalistic industrialization in the eighteenth and nineteenth centuries. Peasants in the fields and artisans in the towns increasingly found themselves dispossessed of their local oral traditions of cultural knowledge as they sought work in the factories of the expanding urban centres. Industrialization destroyed generations of orally transmitted popular creativity. In the twentieth century, industrial capitalism replaces this popular creativity with commercial mass entertainment forms, based on a principle of aggregated mass production and consumption.

The critical theorists are not nostalgic about any particular world that might have been 'lost' to these processes. They know these processes of economic rationalization to be irreversible. They know that what Max Weber called 'the disenchantment of the world' (1930: 105) is an irrevocable condition. Thus they do not lament culture's differentiation into 'high' and 'low' as such. Their position is not comparable to Tolstoy's, who saw degeneration in culture from the very moment of the breakdown of religious medievalism. However, they criticize a specific transformation of this differentiation into a condition of alienation and reification in society under rationalized capitalism. They criticize a specific reduction of horizons of evaluative communication in society to pure acts of subjective consumption among atomized members. They criticize certain specific structures of industrial capitalism that threaten to reduce cultural life to a sum of quantitatively equivalent consumer commodities.

The critical theorists look to autonomy in art as a weapon of resistance to these processes of commodification. Some theorists certainly attach greater importance to autonomy than others. Some, such as Adorno, see art as remaining most critical of society when it preserves its autonomy in the form of self-contained *works*. In contrast, others, such as Marcuse, put more emphasis on art's life-transforming readmission into everyday labour. But none uphold any absolute notion of autonomy in the sense of the bourgeois privilege of 'art for art's sake'. All assert that art should strive to speak for everyone in society, not exclusively for elites. All assert that art should strive to articulate the whole of society – in so far as it is possible for society to be a whole when it is divided and alienated by capitalism.

The critical theorists argue that art subsists in a certain relationship between *ideology* and *utopia*. They argue that art contains utopian aspirations. Art aspires to be the image of a free and just society. Art aspires to present images of a world in which all individuals are free and equal and at the same time reconciled to one another as members of a whole – like the parts of the work of art which serve the purpose of the work as a whole and make the work an autonomous end in itself. But art becomes ideological when it betrays these utopian aspirations by making them appear absolutely impossible to achieve in the real world: when it becomes a compensating distraction from suffering and injustice in real social relations.

We may compare this conception to Karl Mannheim's examination in his treatise *Ideology and Utopia*, of 1936. In his treatise Mannheim (1991) shows how Christian religious doctrines of the Kingdom of Heaven have utopian social meaning: they communicate yearning for emancipation from slavery in the real world. But Mannheim shows how these utopian contents of religion become ideological when they imply acceptance of the world as incapable of change in the here and now: when they imply that utopia is literally nowhere to be achieved – except in life after death. In a similar fashion, the critical theorists argue that art can communicate both potentially true promises of utopia and potentially false, mendacious promises of utopia. When art is ideological, it makes illusory promises of sensuous redemption from suffering, on condition of ongoing acceptance of the status quo. However, when art is critical, it makes potentially true promises of utopia. When art negates the social system to which it belongs, not abstractly but concretely, when it criticizes its own social conditions of possibility and does not take them for granted, when it reveals real sources of injustice in the world and does not mystify them, art is potentially true.

We will now consider how the critical theorists arrive at this conception by way of their reception of German idealist philosophy.

Art in German idealist philosophy

German idealist philosophy refers to the period of intellectual ferment in Germany in the 1790s through to the late 1820s. It is exemplified in the writings of J. G. Fichte, F. W. J. Schelling, Arthur Schopenhauer and G. W. F. Hegel, as well as more loosely in the writings of early romantic thinkers and poets such as J. C. F. Schiller, Friedrich Hölderlin, Novalis, F. D. E. Schleiermacher and Friedrich and A. W. Schlegel.

The German idealist and early romantic thinkers share with eighteenth-century English and Scottish thinkers a concern with the distinctness of aesthetic sensibility and with the role of art in the cultivation of this sensibility. However, unlike the English and Scottish thinkers, who conceive of art and beauty mostly in a psychological manner, in terms of states of feeling and sensation impressed on a perceiving subject, the German thinkers conceive of art more emphatically in terms of sensuous manifestations of ideal contents of thought.

The German philosophers begin from Kant's principle that aesthetic judgement discerns something of universal validity in something that is uniquely particular. In the experience of beauty, a unique object is experienced as if it were an end-in-itself possessing the appearance of *freedom*. The German idealists propose that in this appearance of freedom in the unique object, all that is general is reconciled with all that is particular. All that is conceivable only by abstract concepts is made manifest in concrete sensuous form. What is conceivable only as an 'idea of reason' is sensuously shown and intuited in art. Art sensuously shows the 'idea of reason' that the very beings who think freely about the world are at the same time finite mortal creatures within the world. Art shows the idea of the identity of mind and matter, of freedom and nature. And in showing this identity, art resolves the 'diremption' or 'duality' of mind and matter, freedom and nature. Art shows that all that is known is the same as all that is experienced: that consciousness is the same as the world, and at one with the world. It is in this sense that Kant saw his last *Critique* on beauty, nature and ultimate purpose in the cosmos as the resolution of his two previous *Critiques* on the foundations of knowledge and the foundations of morality.

One of the most celebrated documents of this idea of the identity of freedom and nature in art is a short anonymous text from 1797, attributed jointly to Hegel, Schelling and Hölderlin, known as 'The Oldest Systematic Programme of German Idealism'. The authors proclaim that 'the highest act of reason is an aesthetic act since it comprises all ideas.' Therefore, 'truth and goodness are fraternally united only in beauty.' The authors write that 'people without an aesthetic sense are only philosophers of the letter'; and further that 'one cannot reason in an inspired way about history without aesthetic sense'; and therefore that poetry is the real 'teacher of humanity'. Most influentially, the authors propose that art and imagination are needed to promote a new 'mythology of reason' and a new 'religion of the senses' in which those who live by their minds – rulers and clerics – are reunited with the multitude who work by their hands and feel with their hearts. Reason will be educated by sense and daily life will be elevated to the level of inspiration:

the enlightened and unenlightened must shake hands: mythology must become philosophical to make people rational, and philosophy must become mythological to make philosophers sensuous. Then eternal unity will reign among us. No more will there be the contemptuous glance, never more the blind trembling of the people before its wise men and priests. Only then can we expect equal development of *all* powers, of each individual as well as all individuals. No longer will any power be repressed, and then will rule the universal freedom and equality of the spirits! (Hegel, Hölderlin and Schelling 1996: 4–5)

This idea of art as communicator and facilitator of a higher condition, capable of liberating society from the division between mental and manual labour under repressive political states, is developed at length by J. C. F. Schiller in his *Letters on the Aesthetic Education of Man* of 1793.

J. C. F. Schiller on 'aesthetic education'

In the *Letters on Aesthetic Education*, Schiller considers art's contribution to the sensuous well-being of the human personality. Schiller sees art as reconciling reason with the senses. Art civilizes society between wild nature and repressive control. Art resolves contradictions in human experience between freedom and necessity. Art stands between law and order on the one hand and desire and compulsion on the other. On the one hand, Schiller holds that no ethical meaning can be derived from man's purely instinctual bodily life. On the other hand, he argues that Kant's austere 'categorical imperative', based on refusal of bodily impulse and inclination, is too abstract to motivate ethical conduct. Morality must be reconciled with pleasure and sensibility. Reason must be tempered so that sensuous life can in turn learn from reason. Schiller thus holds out an ideal of the many-sided human self, intelligent in feeling and sense. He declares that this ideal is to be reached through *play*. Play stands between idleness and calculation. Play is free expression of the self in the medium of sensuous appearances. Art communicates this play of freedom because art incarnates beauty as play. Art discloses the identity of the phenomenal world of objects determined by nature with the noumenal world of things-in-themselves that are free causes of themselves. Works of art, in their autonomous self-integration, are the embodiment of *autonomous sociality*. They show a condition of ethical solidarity in which all living creatures are reconciled to one another in what Schiller calls the perfect 'aesthetic state'. Art intimates this perfect 'aesthetic state' to actually existing society. Art enjoins society to fulfil its highest ethical destiny and to abolish injustice and oppression.

We shall shortly see how Schiller's ideas are important for the early Marx, as well as for Ernst Bloch's idea of art as a fore-image of hope for a better society and for Herbert Marcuse's vision of 'desublimated' aesthetic liberation.

F. W. J. Schelling and Arthur Schopenhauer

F. W. J. Schelling is the first philosopher to develop systematically the idea of art's reconciliation of mind and matter in its sensuous presentation of 'the absolute'. Schelling declares that art embodies in the world of nature what Schelling calls 'intellectual intuition'. Intellectual intuition is the possibility of sensuously understanding what cannot be known empirically, nor empirically perceived. Intellectual intuition discloses that the 'I' who thinks is the same as the world that exists. In a phrase first coined by the poet Novalis, Schelling declares that art 'presents the unpresentable': art shows what cannot be said. Unlike discursive thought, which subsumes particular objects under universal concepts, art 'reflects' universality in the uniquely particular. Thus in his *System of Transcendental Idealism* (of 1800) Schelling speaks of art as 'the organon' of philosophy in the sense that philosophy depends on art for its deepest truths. In later works, Schelling views art as the equal to myth, religion and philosophy in its expression of the collective mind of historical peoples. Art relates *logos* to *mythos*. Art relates logical thought to poetic allegory. In so doing, art reveals the ground of existence that precedes all determinate thought about the world.

Arthur Schopenhauer, by contrast, is the progenitor of a deeply pessimistic philosophy which influenced numerous nineteenth-century artists and composers, most notably Richard Wagner. In *The World as Will and Representation* (of 1819), Schopenhauer begins from Kant's principle that things-in-themselves cannot be known by mortal human intellection. Mortal human minds can only know the world as a system of phenomenal objects, under concepts and categories of the intellect. Mortal human minds only know the world as 'Representation'. They do not know the world 'in itself'. But Schopenhauer redefines Kant's world 'in itself' as 'Will'. Schopenhauer defines 'Will' as the one total Will of all being. Human minds cannot know this one total Will. They only know the world under a 'principle of individuation' which divides Will into discrete beings and creatures, all with *separate* wills. Therefore, in the world as Representation, all beings and creatures remain divided from one another. They are opposed to one another, and remain incapable of satisfying their separate wills. Life is a wretched struggle with pain and suffering until death. However, Schopenhauer proposes one exception to this futility of life. The exception is art. When works of art are experienced under 'disinterested contemplation', they afford momentary relief from pain. Works of art relieve their contemplators from the pain of their separate willing and desiring by performing this willing and desiring *for* them. Art thus gives some consolation for suffering. However, Schopenhauer does not propose that art removes suffering, and nor does he propose that art gives hope for any abolition of suffering in the real world.

We will shortly investigate Schopenhauer's importance for the aesthetic philosophies of Richard Wagner and the early Friedrich Nietzsche. Both these philosophies represent examples of fundamentally conservative worldviews which see the social world as incapable of enlightened amelioration – in stark contrast to the revolutionary optimism of J. C. F. Schiller. But we will now turn to the philosopher who enjoys greatest importance for the early Marx and for all social theorists in the tradition of Marxian critical theory: to G. W. F. Hegel.

G. W. F. Hegel and the 'end of art'

Unlike Schelling and Schopenhauer and other early romantic thinkers, Hegel does not place art on a pedestal above discursive thought. Hegel does not consider mind and consciousness to be essentially preceded by an infinity of existence that only art can disclose. Rather, Hegel argues that existence is necessarily thought by mind, by 'spirit' (*Geist*), and is thereby 'taken up' (*aufgehoben*) into spirit through systematic rational reflection. Hegel argues that spirit gains knowledge of itself in the world of its own works through history, in the world of objective social institutions and in the products of reflection on these institutions which are works of art, religion and philosophy.

In *The Phenomenology of Spirit* (of 1807), and later in his *Lectures on Aesthetics* (of 1820–9), Hegel states that 'art has the vocation of revealing *the truth* in the form of sensuous artistic shape' (1993: 61). In its sensuous form, art communicates the idea of the rational development of history. Hegel states that art belongs to the medium of 'absolute spirit'. Hegel distinguishes 'absolute spirit' from what he calls 'subjective spirit', which refers to the personal psychology of individuals, and from what he calls 'objective spirit', which refers to political and moral institutions of society. Like works of religion and philosophy, works of art belong to absolute spirit because they not only reflect the society from which they arise; they reflect *upon* their own reflection; and in reflecting upon their own reflection, they strive to be true in an absolute sense: not one-sided, not limited or transitory.

Hegel goes on to argue that art in modern times is not only aesthetic experience. It is not only free play, in Schiller's sense. It is not like the aesthetic life of the ancient Greeks, who, with their wine and their Dionysus, enjoyed freedom without thinking about their freedom in any definite way. Art in modern times is the knowledge and thought of freedom. Modern art expresses reconciliation between outward sensuous life and inward mental consciousness. Hegel states that in what he calls the 'romantic' art of modern times, which differs from what he calls the 'symbolic' art of archaic times and the 'classical' art of Greek and Roman civilization, art searches for the absolute idea of reason. Thus Hegel comments that beauty in modern art is reflected not 'once' – like beauty in nature – but '*twice*'. In so far as modern art reflects on its own surrounding world self-consciously, it is a double work of reflection. Modern art is sensuously thinking mind, sensuously thinking about its own thought of the world.

However, Hegel also contends that art is coming to an end. Hegel declares that 'art is, and remains for us, on the side of its highest destiny, a thing of the past' (1993: 13). Art is taken up into the two higher forms of absolute spirit: into religion and into philosophy. Art communicates truth essentially only through sensuous media. Therefore art cannot fully mediate sensuous experience with conceptual thought; and therefore it cannot complete spirit's search for absolute self-knowledge. Religion mediates sensuality with conceptuality more completely than art because it unifies sensuous life in contemplation of the abstract idea of the infinite. However, religion also relies on sensuous representations, on metaphors, parables, icons. Therefore, religion too cannot complete spirit's search for absolute self-knowledge. Only philosophy can fully mediate sensing with thinking. Only philosophy can complete the journey of history and state the truth of history. Only philosophy can demonstrate completely that subject and object are one, and that 'what is rational is actual and what is actual is rational' (1991: 20).

To contemporary minds, Hegel's thesis of the end of art appears counterintuitive. Art has not come to an end since Hegel's death in 1830 in any obvious sense. However, Hegel's thesis is not as implausible as it first appears. Hegel is right to point out a general tendency towards increasing ideality in western art history. Admittedly this is not the same as saying that art has come to an end, in the sense of 'cease to exist'. But it is true that since the Renaissance, successive art movements incorporate reflection on previous ideas of art into the making of art, so that with the passing of each movement, art forms have become more and more self-referential. We have discussed one version of this thesis in the work of Robert Witkin and the early twentieth-century German art scholars. A further version occurs in the work of Arthur Danto (1987, 1991, 1997), who applies Hegel's thesis to the diminishing importance of material execution in nineteenth- and twentieth-century visual art and the rising importance of idea and intention. Danto shows this first in the idea of vision among the impressionists; then in the idea of the self-subsistent canvas surface among the early abstractionists; then in the idea of art as provocations about the meaning of 'art' among the dadaists; then most recently in minimalist and conceptual art of the 1960s and 1970s.

We can say that in these respects Hegel is generally right to propose that 'form' and 'content' in modern art do not add up to each other in an organic totality. In modern art, form and content, or medium and idea, do not determine each other organically in the way that the social content of Greek mythology organically determines the form of classical Greek tragedy. We can say that in modern art, no one 'content' corresponds to any particular 'form'. There can be a multitude of forms for expressions of the same content, and there can be a multitude of contents expressed in the same form. Modern art is a constant search for new forms for the same content, and a constant search for new contents in the same form.

Like all the ideas of the German idealist philosophers, Hegel's philosophy of art is fundamentally speculative and metaphysical. It is not compatible with empirical art history except with serious qualifications. It is dictated by a totalizing conception of metaphysics according to which all change in the real world occurs by logical contradictions within concepts. It is also a teleological, eurocentric philosophy of history in which all world culture is said to achieve its highest goal in the culture and society of Enlightenment Europe. However, it is not incapable of critical adaptation in more acceptable terms. Writers such as Danto, Witkin and the early twentieth-century Geman scholars and contemporary scholars of philosophy, such as Gadamer (1975) and Henrich (1966, 2001) (see also Bungay 1987) point to numerous ways in which it can be said to illuminate general tendencies in modern western art history. Not all of these reconstructions can be said to be fully successful in social-scientific terms. But not all of them need to be judged by strictly empiricist criteria of acceptable argument in social theory and philosophy.

We now discuss the ways in which Hegel's and other German idealist reflections enter into the early writings of Karl Marx and provide the foundation for dialectical materialist understandings of art among the critical theorists.

Marx, Bloch and Lukács

There is a way of reading Marx's fragmentary remarks on aesthetics that does not reproduce the reductive tendencies of his more dogmatic followers in the twentieth century. Marx's own reflections on questions of aesthetics do not correspond in every respect to the paradigm of 'classical Marxist thinking' discussed in chapter 3. 'Classical Marxist thinking' and 'vulgar Marxism' are products of doctrinaire readings of Marx disseminated partly by Friedrich Engels and later institutionalized in official Soviet propaganda.

In *The German Ideology* (of 1845), co-written with Engels, Marx criticizes German idealist philosophy for its metaphysical view of the world which distorts and mystifies real relations of subordination in society. Marx famously declares that 'the ruling ideas are in every epoch the ideas of the ruling class' (Marx and Engels 1965: 64). However, in the same text, Marx holds on to Schiller's idea of the many-sided human being, extolled also by the authors of the 'Oldest Systematic Programme of German Idealism'. Marx speaks of a 'free association of producers' in which all individuals would have the chance to 'hunt in the morning, fish in the afternoon, rear cattle in the evening and criticise after dinner . . . without ever becoming hunter, fisherman, herdsman or critic' (Marx and Engels 1965: 54). Marx here affirms the idea of the cultivated personality, rich in aesthetic sensibility, not reduced to a one-sided function in the division of labour, not degraded to the position of lifelong technician in the system of production. Marx holds out a vision of a free and equal society in which art would cease to exist as a separate realm of objects set apart from daily practices. Art would no longer be the privilege of an elite few. Art would express the creative capacities of everyone. It would be reunited with the working life of all. Intellectual labour would be reunited with manual labour, and every individual would be able to enjoy a spiritually fulfilling sensuous life.

Similar themes appear in Marx's *Economic and Philosophic Manuscripts of 1844* where Marx speaks of the power of art to 'awaken humanity from its animal slumbers'. Marx echoes Hegel in speaking of 'the education of the five senses' as being 'the work of all past generations' (1975b). Under communism, sensory cultivation would cease to be the privilege of an elite while the rest of society toils at the level of the sub-human, working, eating, sleeping and reproducing. Human beings' natural way of existing is to be social, to communicate and share experience through the objects of their labour, in the present and across history. Capitalism, however, alienates human beings from their social nature, their 'species-being'. Capitalism denatures the social character of human *aisthesis*. Capitalism destroys the true communal character of sensing, feeling and perceiving. Capitalism alienates society from universal communication.

In the short 'Contribution to the Critique of Hegel's Philosophy of Right' (of 1843–4), Marx famously refers to religion as the 'opium of the people' (1975a). Like a misused drug, religion administers to true needs in false ways. Religion promises something that the system it serves has no ability ever to deliver. Religion is at once 'the *expression* of real suffering and a *protest* against real suffering'. It is 'the sigh of the oppressed creature, the heart of a heartless world, and the soul of soulless conditions':

> The abolition of religion as the *illusory* happiness of the people is the demand for their *real* happiness. To call on them to give up their illusions about their condition is to *call on them to give up a condition that requires illusions*. The criticism of religion is therefore in *embryo* the *criticism of that vale of tears* of which religion is the *halo*. (1975a: 244; emphasis in the original)

Marx thinks of art before communism in similar terms. Like religion, art presents images of peace, love, harmony, community, freedom and equality. Like religion, art is 'at once the expression of, and the protest against, real suffering'. Like religion, art contains an injunction to its spectators to throw away the illusions about their condition that this condition requires, and thus ultimately to abolish the condition itself. Art is illusory when it presents this condition as natural and eternal, as incapable of abolition except in life after death, on the other side of the valley of tears. Art is false when it uncritically projects images of lost Arcadia, images of the pastoral idyll, images of reconciliation with nature, images of subordination under the bountiful care of paternal princes and fairy godmothers, where every creature has its allotted place, its 'rank and degree'. But art is potentially true when it projects images that intimate *how* the ideal order might possibly be reached, that show *how* the community was lost and *how* nature was destroyed by exploitative relations: images that reveal the causes of conflict and the real preconditions of their resolution.

We now discuss two twentieth-century critical theorists who develop this Marxian idea of a dialectic of truth and illusion in art. They are Ernst Bloch and György Lukács.

Ernst Bloch and György Lukács

In *The Principle of Hope* (of 1954–9), Bloch searches deep within the roots of western and eastern culture for potentially true moments of desiring, wishing and yearning in art for a free and just society. In many diverse contexts, Bloch (1986) interrogates Judaeo-Christian gnostic theologies of salvation for the poor and oppressed through the lens of Marx's critique of Hegelian dialectics. Bloch begins from Marx's famous last thesis on Feuerbach about 'changing the world' and not only 'interpreting the world'. He searches for possible moments of truth, glimmers of hope, in religious discourses that have become encrusted by ideology and betrayed by the forces of control. He proposes that the illusory character of religion might itself be redeemed through art. Art might be capable of redeeming religion from ideology and thus of keeping alive society's hope for a better world. Bloch theorizes the redemptive capacity of art in terms heavily indebted to Hegel. He proposes that art is the 'semblance' (*Schein*) that truth requires in order to appear to human practices in meaningful form. By 'truth' Bloch means the truth of history: in Marx's terms, the truth of class struggle. Art can release this truth within semblance because art is a sensuous medium of appearing, and furthermore because it is a *self-reflective* sensuous medium of appearing. Unlike capitalist consumer culture, art is not purely semblance and appearance. It is self-conscious semblance and appearance. However, Bloch adds that art too is capable of ideology, and therefore that art too will not fully release its redemptive powers unless it is in turn redeemed by revolutionary critical practice. Bloch explores these arguments through prolonged discussion of cases such as German expressionist painting, Grimms' fairy tales, J. S. Bach's Lutheran church music, Ibsen's and Chekhov's bourgeois dramas, Mozart's *The Magic Flute*, Brahms's *Deutsches Requiem* and Dante's *Divine Comedy*.

György Lukács also reads art's utopian truth-potential through the prism of Marxian dialectics. Lukács was the first to attribute a systematic aesthetic philosophy to Marx, especially in the *Economic and Philosophic Manuscripts*, which had not been published in Marx's lifetime and only came to light in the 1920s. In early works, including *Soul and Form* and a lengthy study of Hegel's aesthetics, Lukács synthesizes Georg Simmel's analyses of formalization and aestheticization in modern culture with a Hegelian interpretation of Marx's concepts of reification and alienation. Lukács begins from Simmel's thesis of a 'tragedy of culture' brought about by the socializing power of money which draws individuals into relations of exchange with one another and at the same time destroys their communal bonds to one another. Lukács's proposition is that individuals under capitalism cannot reappropriate their inner essences from the objective cultural forms in which they have externalized them. Individuals under capitalism lead superficial lives dominated by ephemeral forms of interaction divested of personal reflective meaning over time.

In *The Theory of the Novel*, from 1914, Lukács compares three ideal-types of artistic form: archaic epic, classical tragedy and the modern novel. This typology owes something to Schiller's essay of 1795 'On Naïve and Sentimental Poetry' which distinguishes between archaic oral narrative, represented by Homer's epics, which are 'naïve' in the sense of wholly accepting of nature as an inevitable cycle of life and death, and modern 'sentimental' art which is concerned with the passions of the individual self, estranged from both nature and society. Lukács describes epic as narrating mind and world as part of an organic totality in the collective mythic life of a people. Classical tragic drama – by which Lukács means ancient Greek drama as well as Shakespeare and seventeenth-century French drama – unfolds the total unity and coherence of a life project even as the hero is brought down by a fatal flaw of character. The modern novel, however, can only affirm unity of experience at a price. Lukács shows how in Cervantes' *Don Quixote*, totality is achieved only on condition of a subjective delusion. Though noble in comic defeat, the mad knight is radically estranged from his social world. Likewise, in Flaubert's *Éducation Sentimentale*, Frédéric Moreau ends up disillusioned with his friends, his society and himself. He is worn down not by any dramatic event but simply by time, boredom and everyday life. 'The hero's inner life', Lukács comments, 'is as fragmentary as the outside world; his interiority possesses no lyrical power of scorn or pathos that might set it against the pettiness of reality' (1971: 125). Thus the modern novel expresses the transitory, indeterminate character of modern life experience in the face of disenchanted social forms. Lukács speaks of the 'transcendental homelessness' of modern man.

In later books from the 1940s and 1950s such as *Studies in European Realism* and *The Meaning of Contemporary Realism*, Lukács's thinking becomes less sophisticated. It comes closer to the more dogmatic paradigm of classical Marxist thinking. He now seems to have forgotten his earlier subtle analyses of the difficulty and complexity of totality in modern art. He criticizes formal experimentation in art in favour of the nineteenth-century social realist novel – exemplified by authors such as Goethe, Balzac and Tolstoy. He now sees not Kafka but Thomas Mann as carrying the torch of authentic social consciousness. We may say that Lukács's later work illustrates three particular problems with mid-century socialist discourse about art.

First, Lukács's later work tends to equate truth-to-society exclusively with social realism. Lukács disregards the sense in which non-representational artistic languages can be just as true to suffering as realism. Lukács implicitly privileges message above medium. He interprets formal experimentation too readily in terms of symptoms of social decay. He overextends Hegel's conception of the tendency of modernist forms not to coincide with their contents in an organic structure.

Second, Lukács holds an excessively didactic idea of art's value for society. Although he criticizes writers such as Émile Zola for preaching to the reader, his own writings tend to expect artists not only to show injustice but also to *instruct* their audiences to abolish it. Here Lukács is not sensitive to the problem that works of art cannot dictate particular messages without undermining their existence as objects of polysemic possibility. We may say that in so far as works of art consist of open-ended sensory polyvalence, they defy translation in terms of unequivocal political lessons. We may say that they are more effective as critique when they exploit their aesthetic resources in order to examine society just as it is – without, however, suggesting that society can be left just as it is. Adorno and Benjamin both discern more astutely than Lukács that social justice can at best be intimated in art: it cannot be preached or prescribed. This didactic tendency is at least a latent problem in other socialist writers such as Orwell, Sartre and Brecht.

Third, Lukács tends to alternate between criticizing works of art for reflecting social contradictions of their time and praising them for the same reasons. There are some works which Lukács regards as little more than documents of their age, and there are others to which he awards independent aesthetic merit but in which he equates this merit with their reflection of the class struggle. Thus he applauds Balzac's novels for exposing egoism and hypocrisy in early nineteenth-century French society under the Restored monarchy; but he alternates between praising Balzac for this exposure and explaining the exposure as an unwitting outcome of Balzac's actual personal affiliation to royalism. Following Adorno (1997), we may say that Lukács mistakes the sense in which works of art are most effective as mediators of revolutionary practice when they are recognized as contents of relatively autonomous aesthetic possibility, standing in relatively autonomous relations to political advocacy. Lukács tends to collapse aesthetic value into political value without mediation.

In general we may say that while Lukács and Bloch both recognize the obsolescence of totalizing teleological philosophies of history in contemporary social consciousness, both thinkers are not sufficiently reflexive in their writing to notice a partial return of totalizing teleological thinking in their own texts. In *History and Class Consciousness* Lukács presents an at once tragic and triumphalistic understanding of history as driven relentlessly forward by dialectical contradictions between class consciousness and class interests. Similarly, in *The Principle of Hope*, Bloch is too programmatically concerned with the futurity and forward directedness of history. He is too attached to the meaning of the very last word in his long text: *Heimat* – 'homecoming'. Bloch and Lukács do not conceive of the difficulty of homecoming, finality and narrative closure in modernity with the same complexity as modernist writers such as James Joyce, Franz Kafka, Robert Musil or Samuel Beckett.

Bloch and Lukács do, however, indicate some interesting respects in which mythical and religious contents of belief can be said to make an ideological return in certain aspects of nineteenth- and twentieth-century modern art. It is to this phenomenon that we now turn.

Art, myth and religion in nineteenth-century European high culture

We have referred to some ways in which ideological constructions in art share features in common with myth and religion. The critical theorists argue that when utopian contents in works of art shade over into a false ideological form based on compensating distraction from lived suffering in real social relations, art repeats some functions of myth and religion for earlier stages of historical life and for non-rationalized societies. We will now try to sharpen the focus of this proposal. We will propose a distinction between a relatively organic relation of art to myth and religion in pre- and non-modern societies and an ideological (false, illusory) relation of art to myth and religion in high modern, high capitalist societies. We draw partly on some reflections of Émile Durkheim and partly on some reflections of Max Weber on rationalization and disenchantment.

We have seen that before the onset of processes of societal modernization in Europe around the fifteenth and sixteenth centuries, art remained integrally linked to the central religious institutions of society – in Europe, primarily to the Christian church, but also the synagogue of Judaism and the mosque of Islam. The same is true, *mutatis mutandis*, of artistic practices among the non-monotheistic civilizations of India and China and the pagan civilizations of ancient Greece and Rome. In Greece and Rome in particular, painting, sculpture, poetry, music and drama existed for shared public veneration alongside worship of mythical gods. They occupied a central place in communal life beside eating, drinking, dancing, leisure and sport as well as warfare and politics. In ancient Greece, dramatic performances were religious occasions. Actors, narrators and chorus would follow set traditional rituals but there would be no clear differentiation between spectators and audiences on the one hand and artists and performers on the other. Although certain processes of differentiation occur in late Roman civilization as polytheism becomes more codified around official deities and is gradually absorbed into Christian monotheism, official religious art remains intertwined with non-official folk custom, lore and myth. This basic structure continues throughout the Holy Roman Empire of the Middle Ages and in the Orthodox Church of the East.

It is helpful to think of these organic links between art, myth and religion in non-modern societies with the aid of Durkheim's concept of *conscience collective*. Although Durkheim never discusses art as such in his writings, in his last major work, *The Elementary Forms of Religious Life* (of 1915), Durkheim suggests that music, dance, song and visual imagery and decoration constitute part of the fabric of 'collective representations' through which societies symbolically picture to themselves their own inviolate identity (Durkheim 1995). In the image of God or gods and other entities such as angels, saints, spirits and demons, societies bear witness to their own moral solidarity. In rites of passage from baptism and other initiation rites through to marriage and burial, societies ritually reaffirm this moral solidarity in their daily lived codes and customs of behaviour. Thus Durkheim suggests that societies sensuously depict and dramatize this solidarity in their visual representations and other expressive activities – in ways immediately intelligible to all members of the social body, literate as well as illiterate.

We may say that Durkheim's conception throws much light on art under premodern social conditions. However, it is less applicable to the early modern period when social relations begin to change dramatically. From this time onwards, art no longer has the same comprehensive reach over life through the arm of the church and folk tradition. Although Durkheim's reflections still have great relevance to popular cultural symbolism, embodied in group gatherings such as festivals and sports and other assertions of ethnic and national group identity, art begins to differentiate from these wider symbolic practices of society. Art becomes institutionalized as 'fine art', distinct from myth and religion. From this time onwards, it is more instructive to turn to Max Weber's reflections on society and religion, rather than to Durkheim's. Max Weber indicates that once social relations begin to crystallize around institutionally differentiated spheres, cultural movements in society that attempt to reintegrate these spheres become conflictual and problematic. Once science, art, politics, morality, law and the economy begin to emerge as institutionally distinct spheres, their mutual differentiation cannot be reversed. Once myth and religion cease to play any legally sanctioned role in the political structures of the state and henceforth survive only in the role of diverse lifeworld practices of voluntary group association, their reassertion in collective public life becomes socially problematic. We can say that as lifeworld practices of personal belief and voluntary group association, myth and religion are compatible with modern self-understanding. But we cannot say that myth and religion are compatible with modern self-understanding when they are institutionally reinserted into the spheres of science, politics and law. When this occurs, they become cases of pseudo-scientific mysticism (theosophy), or cases of political atavism (fascism), or cases of theocracy (religious fundamentalism).

Up to a point, it is possible to suggest that art in modern culture rationally replaces some of the evolutionary functions fulfilled by myth and religion in pre- and non-modern societies. Up to a point, it is possible to say modern art preserves mythical and religious

contents of belief in the only form in which these contents can
still be rationally defended in modern society. In the twentieth century, painters, writers and composers such as Klee, Chagall, Joyce,
Broch, Pound and Messiaen transmit the ideational contents of
Christian, Jewish and pagan belief-systems in the only form in which
these contents can continue to be valid for a society that holds to
Darwin, Einstein and Crick and Watson for its explanations of the
physical origins and mechanisms of life, and to the self-evident rights
of life, liberty and the pursuit of happiness and the self-evident
wrongs of slavery and violent conquest in its fundamental political
principles. In this sense we can say that modern art redeems mythical and religious beliefs by transmuting them into states of aesthetic
experience and stripping them of their claims to cognitive validity
and moral validity. Art thus reconciles mythical and religious contents with the spheres from which they have become differentiated.
By transmuting them into aesthetic values of imagination and interpretation, art reconciles myth and religion with the autonomous
spheres of science, politics and law in the only institutionalized form
in which they can continue to coexist with the latter in a condition
of peace.

However, we must note some limits to this evolutionary thesis.
There are problematic formulations of the thesis that effectively
reproduce the same confusions of spheres that the thesis seeks to
distinguish. These are the chauvinistic formulations which we may
associate with the nineteenth-century positivistic philosophies of
Auguste Comte and Herbert Spencer. They are particularly evident
in Comte's 'law of three stages', according to which all societies are
said to progress from a stage of myth to a stage of theology, and
from a stage of theology finally to a stage of science. Here the
proposition that art 'redeems' mythical and religious contents by
transmuting them into aesthetic values takes on an ideological
form. Myth and religion are here said to achieve their highest
destiny in art. Art is itself said to redeem the world in a quasi- or
pseudo-religious sense.

We may associate this ideological form of the thesis with art
for art's sake in nineteenth-century France, with gothic revivalism
in Victorian England, with aesthetic neo-medievalism and neo-
Catholicism in many European countries, with nineteenth-century
national identity movements, and in general with what Hobsbawm
has called the nineteenth century's characteristic 'invention of tradition' (Hobsbawm and Ranger 1983). In all these contexts, art comes
to be seen as preserving and elevating myth and religion to their

highest, most sublime forms; or art itself comes to be venerated in pseudo-religious terms. In the latter case, works of art themselves come to be treated like religious objects. The work of art becomes a sort of altar to be worshipped at. It becomes the object of a sacred cult, with its ritual performances, its charismatic virtuosi, its avatars and its epiphanies.

We may say that all these ideological conceptions of myth and religion in art embody what Adorno (1997) calls 'religion of art' (*Kunstreligion*) (a term originally propounded by Hegel). *Kunstreligion* offered nineteenth-century European middle-class publics a means of coming to terms with rootlessness, anomie and the 'crises of faith' brought about by scientific rationalism and economic individualism following in the wake of secularization and industrialization. *Kunstreligion* effectively performs the opposite of the evolutionary conception it invokes. Far from distinguishing art from myth and religion, *Kunstreligion* de-differentiates art, myth and religion. According to the critical theorists, *Kunstreligion* is a precursor to similarly unreflective, unmediated reproductions of archaic mythical and religious contents in twentieth-century 'mass culture'. It is paralleled in other paradigmatic nineteenth-century cultural forms such as in Grimms' fairy tales and in the castle of the mad prince of Bavaria at Neuschwannstein. These in turn have their analogues in twentieth-century contexts as diverse as Hollywood film, in the cartoon images of Walt Disney, in the fantasy fiction of J. R. R. Tolkien, and – most sinister of all – in fascist mythology.

We will now examine one case of this ideological de-differentiation of art, myth and religion in one of the most representative nineteenth-century high-cultural forms: the opera. In particular, we will examine Richard Wagner's programmatic philosophy of the opera in nineteenth-century Germany. Then we turn to the more subtle vision of art, myth and religion articulated in the philosophy of Wagner's initial enthusiast in the 1870s, Friedrich Nietzsche.

Richard Wagner and Friedrich Nietzsche

Richard Wagner described his operas as totally self-contained aesthetic universes, uniting poetry and drama with music and visual imagination in an absolute unity of form and content. Wagner declared the opera of the future to be a 'total work of art' (*Gesamtkunstwerk*). This vision is immediately apparent in the character of Wagner's music. In its use of intense close harmony, rich orchestral texture and repeatedly drawn out and re-echoed phrases called leitmotifs, Wagner's music has a highly atmospheric character dominated by mood and effect which in some respects anticipates twentieth-century film music. It has an all-absorbing emotional power over the audience which Adorno (1981) notably compares to the techniques of total sensory gratification exploited in fascist propaganda film and Hollywood cinema. It is comparable to the kind of experientially overwhelming focus-blurring techniques famously evoked by Aldous Huxley in his account of the 'feelies' in *Brave New World*.

In the synopses of all his operas, Wagner draws from archaic sources of legend and myth in order to construct grand aesthetic statements about the spiritual needs of the present and the place of man in the cosmos. In *The Mastersingers of Nuremberg* Wagner hearkens back to the world of the medieval guilds of skilled crafts-men. Nuremberg's old master singers have become stuck in their ways; but when a younger outsider singer beats the masters at their own profession and then joins company with them, their world is apparently organically rejuvenated. In the tetralogy of *The Ring of the Nibelungs*, based on ninth-century Teutonic legend, Wagner opens his first opera in the cycle, *Rhinegold*, with an idea of the emancipa-tion of a race of oppressed miners, the Nibelungs. The Nibelungs try to come into possession of an all-powerful ring: an idea borne of the spirit of the 1848 revolutions. However, when Wagner finished his last opera in the cycle twenty years later, *Twilight of the Gods*, he had definitively shed all revolutionary sympathies. By this later date, Wagner embraced Schopenhauer's philosophy of art as metaphys-ical compensation for ineradicable suffering. In the later stages of the Ring cycle, Wagner portrays all attempts to change the world – by gods as well as by mortals – as fundamentally *against nature*, and therefore condemned to the corrupting power of evil. In *Tristan and Isolde*, based on a medieval romance from the songs of the Troubadours about a Cornish warrior-hero who falls in love with the daughter of his Irish enemy and betrays his king, Wagner links love with death, passion with fate, transcendence with destruction. In *Parsifal*, based on the crucifixion but retold through Teutonic legend, Wagner concludes his life project with the story of a young innocent forest boy who heals the older priests of their weariness with the world. Christianity is in this sense redeemed by 'nature', and 'nature' is redeemed through music.

In each of these synopses, Wagner evokes the idea of spiritual healing through art and music. Art is seen as saving modernity from

arid reason and re-enchanting a disenchanted world. But Wagner
traduces the truth-potential of his conception by raising art to the
level of something absolute, something unlimited in its claims over
life and superior to all critical historical self-understanding. Wagner
attempts to restore wholeness for modern times through sinister
ideas of authentic racial communities. He profoundly mystifies the
social conditions of human existence by projecting them onto an
order of unchanging natural eternity. His aesthetic worldview
attempts to roll back stages of rational cognitive and institutional
differentiation between art, myth, religion, politics and science. The
cultic character of his art is directly embodied in the tradition of
invitation-only performances of his epic works at the opera house he
arranged to be built at Bayreuth in Germany, which continues to
this day.

Friedrich Nietzsche is the first and most important critic of Wagner
because he begins his philosophical career by celebrating Wagner.
In his first book, *The Birth of Tragedy out of the Spirit of Music* (of
1871), Nietzsche extols Wagner's music for its reawakening of the
sense of the tragic in modern life. Nietzsche revives the spirit of
German romantic thought, castigating J. J. Winckelmann's eighteenth-
century classical norm of 'noble simplicity and quiet grandeur'.
Nietzsche contends that like the passionate violent love between
Tristan and Isolde, modern human beings need art's transcendent
aesthetic intensities to raise themselves above the pettiness of
everyday life. 'It is only as an aesthetic phenomenon', Nietzsche
declares – echoing Schopenhauer – 'that existence and the world
are eternally justified' (1993: 32). Art must strive to tear away the
protecting veil of frozen concepts, words and distinctions which
underpin pragmatic common sense and scientific objectivity. This
Schopenhauerian 'principle of individuation' is symbolized for
Nietzsche by the Greek god of rationalism, Apollo. Art must reveal
the truth of life and existence, where all is in flux, chaotic and
indistinct, ecstatic and intoxicating in its eternal cycle of death,
nothingness and violent creative destruction and rebirth. This is
symbolized for Nietzsche by Dionysus, Greek god of wine, passion
and flux, and embodied in the drama of the oldest Greek tragedian,
Aeschylus, author of the *Oresteia*.

However, less than three years after *The Birth of Tragedy*, Nietzsche
emphatically turned away from this youthful romantic philosophy.
In all subsequent works, from *Untimely Meditations* and *The Gay
Science* to *Thus Spake Zarathustra*, Nietzsche questions and criticizes
the attitude that confuses intensity of emotion with clarity and insight

of emotion, and that automatically privileges depth, wholeness and seriousness above surface, play, wit, irony, laughter, style and lightness. Nietzsche now stresses the ambiguity of art's relation to truth. On the one hand, image, metaphor, narrative and aesthetic experience open up the world for us: they forge connections and correspondences between disparate elements. On the other hand, art remains fiction, illusion and deception. Nietzsche declares that human beings need art and illusion in order to live – 'we have need of lies', he says, 'in order to live' (1968: 451) – but he warns that we should not flatter ourselves that our illusions are true. Art may have something to communicate about science, and perhaps art may even creatively subvert science, revealing the illusions on which science depends – 'there are no facts, only interpretations', Nietzsche declares (1968: 267) – but art is not science, and whatever knowledge art may have to impart, art's knowledge is never assured. 'Art is worth more than truth,' he says; but art is not truth (1968: 453). Art is as fickle and elusive as it is seductive and enchanting.

Nietzsche rails against the *Kulturphilister*, against 'culture vultures' who consume art for its perceived moral certainties. But Nietzsche does not unconditionally celebrate decorativism and surface in art. Nietzsche argues that art is intrinsically ethically challenging. In *Beyond Good and Evil* and *The Genealogy of Morals* Nietzsche uncovers complexes of ascetic self-abasement in conventional Judaeo-Christian morality. He sees these complexes as founded in guilt and in what he calls *ressentiment*, or petty resentment of individual excellence masquerading as 'brotherly love'. Nietzsche sees art as disclosing alternative visions of ethical character, oriented to sovereignty of the self and will and power of personality. He proposes that rather than passively accepting moral imperatives without question, individuals should be capable of finding meaning in morality for their own lives as 'free spirits'. They should be capable of treating morality in the same sense in which they argue for their tastes in art. Individuals should strive to raise their personal ethical styles of life to the level of something aesthetically exemplary and impressive.

Nietzsche's thinking about aesthetics and ethics is difficult to evaluate because it is in every respect equivocal. At the core of Nietzsche's thinking is an inspiring idea about the integrity of transience, uncertainty and contingency in life, over against metaphysical essence and Christian Platonism. It is an idea expressed in the poetry of Rainer Maria Rilke in terms of transfigurations of everyday life by song – through a rescuing of beauty not from the heavens but from *this world*, from the shadowy fleeting world of finite life. In this sense we can say that Nietzsche's concern is not to confine aesthetic experience within a lawfully policed domain of reason – in the manner of Kant or Hegel – but rather to allow aesthetic experience to spill over anarchically into the structures of everyday life, so as to liberate life from the banalities of routine habit, planning and security. However, the problem with this proposal is that it makes it difficult to see where carefree affirmation and unconditional generosity of spirit might appropriately end and practical responsibility and economy appropriately take over. Nietzsche does not create a religion out of art; but he makes it difficult to see where and how it might appropriately count against aesthetic understanding that science has a normative orientation to facts (not to fiction); that law and politics have a normative orientation to equality and democracy (not to 'supermen' and 'aristocracies of genius'); and that morality has a normative orientation to peaceful collective life (not to 'power' and 'strife'). Although Nietzsche's texts provide no foundation for the irrationalist misappropriations of his ideas in early twentieth-century European fascist and proto-fascist movements, they remain fundamentally equivocal about the claims of reason over modern life.

In chapter 7 we will discuss elements of Nietzsche's aesthetic critique of reason in the debates of more recent thinkers such as Bataille, Foucault, Habermas and Lyotard about modernity and 'postmodernity'. In the following, we turn now to a final constellation of ideas about myth and religion in art which revolve around themes of 'sublimation' in psychoanalytic social thought.

Sublimation and civilization: Sigmund Freud and Herbert Marcuse

Since the pioneering writings of Sigmund Freud, psychoanalytic thinking about art has been central to numerous social theorists, to literary theorists and cultural critics as well as to numerous artists and poets. Here we confine ourselves to an overview of some of Freud's most recognizably sociological reflections on art and their relationship to the philosophies of Marx and Nietzsche. We conclude with the psychoanalytic aesthetic thought of Herbert Marcuse.

Freud, Nietzsche and Marx are often conjoined in the history of ideas because all three espouse forms of what Ricoeur (1970) has called 'hermeneutics of suspicion'. Marx interprets social behaviour and belief in terms of concealed class interests. Nietzsche interprets social behaviour and belief in terms of hidden complexes of moral self-deception. Freud interprets social behaviour and belief in terms of unconscious wishes and desires. Marx speaks of mystifications of material social needs. Nietzsche and Freud speak of complexes of displacement, repression and 'sublimation'. In *Civilisation and its Discontents* (of 1930) and *The Future of an Illusion* (of 1927), Freud speaks of culture as encoding sources of unconscious desire and yearning for pleasure which would threaten social order if they were allowed free reign. Freud argues that these motives must therefore be repressed and displaced into more pacific forms – such as in dreams, and in works of art, in mythical stories and moral fables. As Nietzsche speaks of beauty and truth as 'necessary illusions' for life, so Freud speaks of art, myth and religion as necessary forms of sublimation that compensate for repressed wishes and channel these wishes into socially more acceptable forms. In this sense we can say that Freud and Nietzsche throw further light on Marxian ideas of an internal relationship between utopia and ideology. Although Freud and Nietzsche do not share Marx's specifically political philosophy of collective emancipation, both Freud and Nietzsche espouse a certain idea of a social pathology of repression and a certain idea of a cure from this pathology.

Freud developed some of his founding pyschoanalytic principles from his reflections on classical artists and writers such as Sophocles, Michelangelo, Leonardo, Shakespeare and Dostoevsky (Freud 1985). In *The Interpretation of Dreams* (of 1899) Freud famously derives his theory of the unconscious desire of sons to murder their fathers and sleep with their mothers from Sophocles' tragedy *Oedipus Rex*. Freud reads Shakespeare's *Hamlet* in this sense as the dream of a man who displaces his real desire to murder his father onto an imaginary action of his uncle. In essays such as 'Mourning and Melancholy' and 'Creative Writers and Day-Dreaming', Freud speculates on experiences of grief, depression, delusion and hysteria in 'artistic personalities'. In *Jokes and their Relation to the Unconscious* he interprets humour in terms of sudden irruptions of unconscious desire into the workings of everyday language. In his essay on 'The Uncanny' he examines artistic representations of things experienced as alien (*unheimlich*) within contexts felt to be most intimate and secret (*heimlich*), notably in ghost stories. In his last published text, *Moses and Monotheism* (of 1939), Freud examines religious discourses of idolatry and sacrilege in art. He examines the Jewish Mosaic ban on graven images of God that attempt to represent that which is beyond representation: the one and only God, hidden from this world.

Although Freud's ideas pose many problems for social theory, they have had a lasting impact on sociological canons of thought. Although they are compromised by Freud's tendency to generalize from situations of individual clinical analysis to sociohistorical conditions of collective human behaviour in speculative and usually reductive ways, they occupy an important place in the work of the Frankfurt School, in American functionalism, in French poststructuralism and notably in Nobert Elias's conception of 'civilizing processes'. In particular, although Freud's own pronouncements on sublimation in art tend to presuppose a positivistic methodology that interprets creative intentionality in excessively physiological terms, they have inspired several social theorists of art to deploy parts of his ideas in ways that try to avoid both his more problematic methodological precepts and his rather obscurantist, sociologically problematic conception of intrinsically violent human 'instincts'. Many theorists have seen emancipatory political potential in Freud's lapidary statements at the end of *Civilisation and its Discontents* about the limits of sublimation and the tendencies to neurosis in repressive moral culture.

Among the first to develop Freud's ideas on art and creativity in this more sociocritical direction is Erich Fromm, an early associate of the Frankfurt School. Eschewing Freud's Manichean dichotomies between instinct and order, nature and culture, individual and society, Fromm sought to distinguish between destructive-repressive forms of sublimation in society and creative-expressive forms of sublimation. This same basic move continues in the writings of Adorno and Horkheimer, among anarchist and French Situationist intellectuals of the 1960s such as Guy DeBord, Raoul Vaneigem and Cornelius Castoriadis, in the ideas of radical musicians of the 1960s such as Frank Zappa, and perhaps above all in the writings of the intellectual spokesman of the American 1968 movement, Herbert Marcuse.

In *Eros and Civilisation* (1956) and *One-Dimensional Man* (1964) Marcuse fuses Freudian ideas of repression of libidinal energy with Marx's critique of capitalist exploitation and competitive accumulation. Marcuse argues that capitalism reduces expressive creativity to mechanistic mass production. Capitalism reifies desire and turns it into commodity fetishism. Capitalist rationalization degrades eros to functions of sexual reproduction of the labour force. It also incites destructive forms of libidinal repression manifested in xenophobia,

racial prejudice and mass hysteria. Marcuse contrasts this with
Schiller's vision of aesthetic education, rooted in play and freedom
and the many-sided personality. Marcuse fuses Schiller with Marx
and Freud in calling for a 'self-sublimation of sensuousness' and a
'de-sublimation of reason'. Reason and desire need to be reconciled
with work and play in an 'order of abundance' and in a 'free play of
human faculties', based on conquest of scarcity without repression
and inequality. Marcuse associates this order with Orpheus, the
singing god who liberates nature, in contrast to Prometheus who
dominates over nature.

Marcuse argues that capitalist consumption practices represent an
illusory form of aesthetic utopia. They trade on a 'happy consciousness' of passive audiences willing to surrender critical agency for the
sake of distraction from ongoing regimentation in Fordist workplaces.
Capitalist consumption attempts to replace what Hegel called the
'unhappy consciousness' of the early Christian slaves, who knew
freedom but did not possess freedom, with Hegel's vision of the
Greeks who possessed freedom but did not need to know freedom.
Capitalist consumption is the simulation of freedom, not the reality
of freedom. It is a condition of false 'positivity', a false state of
grace, a false promise of utopia, false deliverance from hell. In later
texts (1972, 1978), Marcuse argues that art's task is to communicate a critical vision of freedom, rooted both in sensuous catharsis
and in concrete negation of the prevailing social order. Art's task is
to evoke alternative horizons of perception, experience and action
that give courage to change the world.

Marcuse's aesthetic thought shares features in common with
Adorno's and Horkheimer's derisory attitude to 'mass culture' and
the 'culture industry'. It is consequently open to the some of
the same generic objections to the Frankfurt School which we will
consider in chapter 6. However, we must note that Marcuse's thought
is by no means dismissive of popular culture. It is conceived very
much in the spirit of the popular cultural revolutions of the 1960s.
It is certainly idealistic in this respect, and it is often associated
with a post-1968 culture of hedonistic disengagement. But its basic
political impulses are not naïve. Marcuse's vision is that art and
aesthetic experience bear witness to a struggle to realize utopianism's
no-place in *this* place; to realize heaven on this earth, in definite
social situations; not to defer justice, peace and happiness to an
ever-beyond; to negate the status quo concretely and determin-
ately, not abstractly and indeterminately; to refuse defeatism and
despair.

Conclusion

We have seen how critiques of 'mass culture' in European Marxian critical theory have their origins in the ideas of the early nineteenth-century German idealist philosophers about truth, beauty, freedom, reason and the absolute. The critical theorists filter these ideas through the prism of Marxian materialist dialectics. They fuse a Kantian conception of critique as inquiry into the conditions of possibility of knowledge and experience of the world with a Marxian sociohistorical understanding of the material conditions of human freedom. The critical theorists interpret aesthetic contents in works of art in terms of an ambivalent relationship between ideology and utopia. They follow Marx's understanding of religion as at once 'an expression of suffering and a protest against suffering' and they combine this understanding with ideas of illusion, deception, repression and sublimation in the writings of Nietzsche and Freud. They show how utopian contents in modern art sheer over into delusory constructions when modern art attempts to resurrect myth-ical and religious contents of belief in an unreflective, unmediated manner. They show how modern art thereby attempts to reverse irreversible processes of cognitive and institutional differentiation in social evolution – such as in the music of Richard Wagner and many other examples of nineteenth-century European high culture. The critical theorists argue that art in these cases assumes functions of distraction and mystification analogous to twentieth-century 'mass culture'. Such art celebrates its aesthetic autonomy but it in fact forfeits its autonomy. The critical theorists therefore argue that autonomy in art can only be defended dialectically and strategically, as a medium of critique against false celebrations of autonomy in bourgeois thought. They attempt to develop a dialectical conception of art as at once its own law and subject to laws: at once its own purpose and subject to purposes, at once conditioning and conditioned.

In the next chapter we examine some ways in which these same basic ideas are addressed specifically to concepts of modernity, modernism and modernization in art in the writings of Weber, Simmel, Benjamin, Kracauer and Adorno.

6

Modernity and Modernism

'Modernity' in social theory is generally understood to refer to experiences of radically changing times brought about by projects of collective transformation of the structures of society. 'Modernism' usually refers to a specific movement in the art, culture and thought of modernity that dramatizes, thematizes and often champions these experiences in various ways. 'Modernization' refers to the process of the emergence of modern society.

In this chapter we discuss the work of five influential social theorists who elaborate these interrelated themes of modernity, modernism and modernization in art. They are Max Weber, Georg Simmel, Walter Benjamin, Siegfried Kracauer and Theodor Adorno. These thinkers further develop the concepts of autonomy, ideology, utopia and 'mass culture' introduced in chapters 4 and 5. We discuss Adorno's thinking in conjunction with a broader assessment of the work of the Frankfurt School.

We first assemble a few preliminary considerations on some of the most general aspects of modernity and modernism in art before turning to these thinkers' more specific accounts. We begin with the themes of time and the metropolis as they appear in the writings of the influential French nineteenth-century poet Charles Baudelaire.

Aesthetic modernity after Charles Baudelaire

Modernism in art can be dated from around the 1850s. It is marked by the French realist and impressionist painters, by the first skyscrapers of Chicago, by the psychological novels of Dostoevsky, by the complex dissonant symphonies of Gustav Mahler and Charles

Ives, and many other cynosures. Modernism reaches its highpoint in the interwar period in the work of the Russian constructivists and the Bauhaus, in the dadaists and the surrealists, in the work of austere abstractionists such as Mondrian and Kandinsky, in the revolutionary projects of utopian architects such as Le Corbusier and Mies van der Rohe, in the atonal music of composers such as Stravinsky and Schönberg, and in the experimental writing of novelists such as Joyce, Kafka, Döblin and Dos Passos; and it continues after the Second World War in movements such as American abstract expressionist painting and French absurdist and existentialist theatre.

As we discuss in chapter 7, it is possible to say that modernism comes to an end around the 1970s as values of linear development and formal purity in art come to be discredited by a new idiom of creativity that has come to be known as postmodernism. However, to say that modernism is superseded by postmodernism around the 1970s is not to say that *modernity* comes to an 'end'. To say that modernist forms no longer have currency after about 1970 is to acknowledge postmodernism's real existence as a distinct style of imagining. But it is not to affirm the idea of a condition of postmodernity that comes 'after' modernity. The chief reason for this is that it is a mistake to think of modernity in an exclusively chronological sense. 'Modernity is a qualitative, not a chronological category,' Adorno writes (1974: 218). Modernity is not so much a period of time as an attitude to time. It is an attitude of critical distanciation from experience with an orientation to rationality and reflexivity. Thus there is a sense in which we can say that modernity continues in spite of, beyond, and even within, postmodernism.

The first most significant occurrence of the term 'modernity' is to be found in the writing of Charles Baudelaire. In an article for *Le Figaro* from 1863, titled 'The Painter of Modern Life', Baudelaire declares that modern artists will not find beauty in past convention and tradition. Ancient canons of beauty are not perennial. They are no longer for *our time*. They are not 'our mode'. The artist of our times must capture the spirit of modern life:

> And so away he goes, hurrying, searching. But searching for what? Be very sure that this man, such as I have depicted him – this solitary, gifted with an active imagination, ceaselessly journeying across the great human desert – has an aim loftier than that of a mere *flâneur*, an aim more general, something other than the fugitive pleasure of circumstance. He is looking for that quality which you must allow me

to call 'modernity'; for I know of no better word to express the idea
I have in mind. He makes it his business to extract from fashion
whatever element it may contain of poetry within history, to distil the
eternal from the transitory.
[. . .]
By 'modernity' I mean the ephemeral, the fugitive, the contingent
[*le transitoire, le fugitif, le contingent*], the half of art whose other half is
the eternal and the immutable. (1995: 12)

Baudelaire's painter of modern life experiences time as a line inexor-
ably rushing forward into the future. As each present moment is
cast into the past, the artist releases that which is classic and eternal
from that which is 'transitory, fugitive and contingent'. But time
breeds so many passing novelties and fashions that the artist is faced
with a constant problem of *ennui*. The artist tries to stop time so as
to rescue singularity from replication. The artist is more than a
dandy, a *flâneur*. The artist wanders the streets of the city in search
of grace; but the artist remains a spectator to the ways of the world,
entranced by sight, sound and sense and at the same time restless,
melancholy and solitary, unable to find union with the crowd. The
artist tries to rescue the accursed and dejected, to turn dirt into
gold, to pluck the 'flowers of evil', as Baudelaire evokes in the title
of his cycle of poems, *Les fleurs du mal*.

Baudelaire's reflections have been enormously influential in
twentieth-century cultural thought. Jürgen Habermas (1987) links
Baudelaire's reflections to Reinhardt Koselleck's (1985) thesis of
modernity as the time in which society comes to objectify its own
past as 'history'. Kosselleck argues that modernity is the time in
which society conceives its past as a definite sequence of events
culminating in the present, not a repetitious cycle. 'Our time'
becomes 'new time'; and 'new time' becomes that which places
the 'Middle Ages' in between modernity and antiquity. Time thus
becomes something of which society takes possession and makes its
own 'project'. Modernity sees itself as determining its own future,
continually expanding its 'space of experience' under more and more
ambitious 'horizons of expectation'.

We may add that time becomes a leading preoccupation of
modern artists because time appears to move faster than society's
ability to adapt to change. As individuals find themselves moving
faster through stages of life, not statically remaining in traditional
stations of life but *becoming* who they are – by choice and by force,
as migrants to the city, as waged labourers in the factories and

offices – the structure and unity of life becomes a problem. The life course becomes overdetermined by accident, contingency, possibility and complexity at every juncture. This raises the question of whether life has any overarching meaning, whether life can be narrated as a coherent whole. Modernist writers and painters tend to search inward for this narrative unity. They look towards sensation and affect, impression and expression. They frequently relinquish third-person omniscient narrators in favour of fragile first-person narrators. Yet they are frequently sceptical of unity, finality and closure in experience.

Time becomes central to modernism in the further sense that it is the complement to space, speed, movement, travel, transport and the machine. In an age of the railway, the motor-car, the steam ship, radio, cinema and the telephone, individuals move faster across space and come into communication more rapidly with other worlds. Space and time are no longer experienced as coordinating dimensions of a single unified manifold. They are experienced as kaleidoscopic moments of multiple worlds, anarchically juxtaposed to one another. As Einsteinian relativity supersedes Newtonian absolute space, so the cubists, the surrealists, the futurists and the first pioneers of film montage explore splintering, fragmentation, simultaneity and relationality of experience.

This sense of flux is above all experienced in the metropolis. Modern cities are experienced as spaces of relentless ferment, at once exhilarating to the senses and bewildering for the mind. Writing of Vienna in the early 1900s, the Austrian novelist Robert Musil speaks of

> irregularity, change, sliding forward, not keeping in step, collisions of things and affairs, and fathomless points of silence in between, of paved ways and wilderness, of one great rhythmic throb and the perpetual discord and dislocation of all opposing rhythms . . . a seething, bubbling fluid in a vessel consisting of the solid material of buildings, laws, regulations, and historical traditions. (1953–60: vol. 1, 4)

In the sprawling metropoles of London, Paris, Berlin, New York and Chicago, urban spaces divide between historic centres and monuments to state power and imperial tradition, on the one hand, and limitless unplanned zones of proletarian dwelling and industrial production, on the other. They are the melting pots of cultures, cosmopolitan nodes of socialization between migrant peoples, crucibles of change and synthesis. They are the engines of fashion that spark innovation, but they are at the same time spaces of crime and fear, of voyeurism and anomie, and also of violent insurrection and violent repression. In the cities, social change is shockingly accelerated as old regimes are discredited and traditional elites removed from power by mass political parties. Symbols and institutions of authority are defamed and exposed for corruption as new means of consumption, spectacle and political mobilization affront conventional social norms, civil as well as sexual, public as well as private. In Marx's oft-quoted words, 'all that is solid melts into air' (Berman 1982).

We will now consider how each of these themes acquires particular prominence in the work of the five German theorists. We begin with Weber.

Max Weber: rationalization and the aesthetic sphere

We have referred to Weber's reflections on art at earlier stages of this book, notably in chapters 4 and 5 in relation to aesthetic autonomy and to processes of rational differentiation between 'value spheres'. We now explore Weber's formulation of these concepts more closely. We begin with his late monograph, *The Rational and Social Foundations of Music*, first published as an appendix to *Economy and Society* in 1922.

Weber's monograph on music is a highly technical case-study of processes of rationalization in the theory of harmony in western music, and in the technology of western musical instruments. Weber (1958) examines how western music evolved a system of written notation which allowed melodies to be preserved and reperformed in more and more complex harmonic variations. In the early modern period, western court and church music began to evolve a stringent harmonic system organized around the diatonic scale of twelve tones and eight notes known as the octave. Weber notes that this octave system rests on a problem of a dissonant seventh note, preceding the resolution of the octave. Western classical music experiences this seventh note as irrational. Consequently, western classical music gives rise to a constant search for new rules of harmonic consonance.

Weber argues that such drives towards harmonic rationalization do not significantly occur in the musical traditions of other civilizations. Some musical traditions in other civilizations are based on a simpler five-note pentatonic system (for example in China and Japan). In other civilizations, variation in tone and pitch is concentrated into melody but not developed in the supporting harmonic accompaniment (for example in Indian quarter-tone music). In the European Middle Ages, harmonic intervals are much wider apart, and therefore create less of an experience of dissonance which has to be resolved. Weber argues that these technical rationalization processes in western harmonic theory explain the rise of the phenomenon of the individual composer, the technically accomplished virtuoso performer and the large symphony orchestra. Western classical music departs in these respects from musical activities in oral folk cultures where melodies, accompaniments and dance steps tend to be learned by informal example and imitation. Weber also notes similar corresponding rationalization processes in the technology of western musical instruments. Stringed instruments crystallize around the four-stringed violin and violin-cello with a bridge, frets and an exactly shaped resonant body. Likewise, the organ and the pianoforte are continually engineered and modified to produce the richest, most powerful sound.

Weber's monograph on music demonstrates empirically Weber's more general thesis of rationalization processes in modern western societies. This more general thesis is developed in the 'Preface' and 'Intermediate Reflections' to Weber's *Collected Essays on the Sociology of Religion* (of 1920). These essays examine changing historical relationships of the economy to religious belief across different civilizations, in India and China as well as Europe. Weber (1948a) argues that with the rise of ethical compromises between economic activity and religious rejection of worldly goods, especially in northern Europe after the Protestant Reformation, western society differentiates into increasingly distinct and autonomous spheres of cultural value, each following their own independent rational logics of development. Weber notes five spheres in particular: the political, the economic, the aesthetic, the erotic and the intellectual (science and philosophy). As the church concedes more power to the state, so politics becomes uncoupled from morality in the idea of 'reason of state'. Religion and conventional moral norms also lose more of their hold over art and erotic life. According to Weber, the two starkest outcomes of these rationalization processes are the autonomy of capitalism and the autonomy of science.

Weber observes that art once stood in close affinity to 'magical religiosity', for example in religious icons and other artefacts used as instruments of exorcism and holy ecstasy: in the chalice, the altar and the rood. In Catholic countries, this close relationship continues throughout the early modern period, especially during the Catholic Counter-Reformation. Elsewhere, however, religious teaching cannot tolerate art because art is seen as distracting attention from the holy towards the creaturely. Protestant cultures tend to suspect art of idolatry, of promoting worship of images of the divine rather the divine itself. Weber notes that art in Protestant cultures begins to sever its connections with the church much earlier than elsewhere. Art begins to form a separate value sphere. It begins to afford a this-worldly sense of salvation analogous to the Protestant sense of divine 'calling' but increasingly distinct from religious belief. In *The Protestant Ethic and the Spirit of Capitalism*, Weber describes this battle for aesthetic legitimation in the works of writers and painters from Puritan and Calvinist milieux, such as Shakespeare, Milton and Rembrandt. Weber remarks that in the nineteenth century, aesthetic values strive to break free not only from religion but also from secular moral teaching. In the writings of figures such as Baudelaire and Nietzsche, conventional moral values come to be replaced by aesthetic values. Moral and religious ideas of evil, sin and transgression become open to aesthetic redemption. Horror, violence, desire, eros and sexuality become legitimate aesthetic vehicles of redemption. Art is now a protest against moral hypocrisy, and against science and everyday rationality. Yet art itself remains deeply implicated in processes of rationalization.

Weber argues that these processes of autonomization of spheres create problems of radical value conflict in the modern world. Weber's ideas here follow a line of thinking traceable to the thought of the nineteenth-century Danish philosopher, Søren Kierkegaard. In his treatise of 1843, *Either-Or*, Kierkegaard argued that there can be no arbitration between an aesthetic understanding of the world and a moral understanding of the world (Kierkegaard 1944). Kierkegaard associates aesthetic understanding with music, seduction, sensuality and the myth of Don Juan. He associates ethical understanding with marital fidelity, the family and social propriety. Kierkegaard argues that from the point of view of morality, art is decadent, destructive and evil. On the other hand, from the point of view of art, morality is pedestrian and life denying. For every criticism of art by morality, art has an answer which morality cannot accept; and for every criticism of morality by art, morality has an answer which art cannot accept. Therefore the individual must choose: between *either* art *or* morality.

Weber interprets Kierkegaard's conception in a sociological sense. Weber speaks of new order of polytheism in which each one sphere of values becomes a kind of god and every other sphere becomes a kind of devil – between which individuals must decide their allegiances. Weber incorporates Kant's distinction between science, morality and aesthetics as three autonomous domains of reason, but he does not follow Kant and post-Kantian idealist philosophy in viewing these domains as composing a unity or a system. Weber argues that the ancient substantial unity of truth, goodness and beauty has today definitively broken apart. In *Science as a Vocation*, Weber declares:

> If anything, we realise again today that something can be sacred not only in spite of its not being beautiful, but rather because and in so far as it is not beautiful. . . . And, since Nietzsche, we realise that something can be beautiful, not only in spite of the aspect in which it is not good, but rather in that very aspect. . . . It is commonplace to observe that something may be true although it is not beautiful and not holy and not good. Indeed it may be true in precisely those aspects. But all these are only the most elementary cases of the struggle that the gods of the various orders and values are engaged in. (Weber 1948b: 148)

Weber illuminates his account of radical conflict between science, religion and art with various reflections on German romantic poetry, most notably on Goethe's *Faust*. In Goethe's version of the story of the presumptuous man of science seduced into compacting with the Devil for earthly power, Weber sees an allegory of the paradoxes of modern reason. Modern reason endows man with power and mastery over the world and nature, but only at the cost – the demonic, diabolical cost – of destruction of cosmic understandings and ultimate meanings. Weber's 'disenchantment of the world' (*Entzauberung der Welt*) (1930: 105) has similar romantic roots, most notably in the poetry of Hölderlin and especially in Schiller's poem 'Die Götter Griechenlands' about the exile of the gods from the world. It is also rooted in ideas in Tolstoy and Dostoevsky about science, atheism, nihilism and irreconcilable conflicts between politics and love, money and goodness, secular power and holy authority.

We will encounter similar themes of cultural crisis and 'tragedy' in the thought of Georg Simmel.

Georg Simmel: money, style and sociability

Georg Simmel's concerns in his sociological writings are with the role of cultural codes of conduct in socializing and 'civilizing' individuals into membership of particular social groups with particular social statuses and styles of comportment. Simmel is concerned with 'forms of association' and 'forms of interaction' in the structuring of social personalities. He shows how these 'forms of association' can serve both definite instrumental functions – such as for producing goods and exchanging them in the market-place – and indefinite expressive functions, such as in leisure, sport, courtship and entertainment. In the latter case, interaction involves open-ended conversation, etiquette and taste guided by tacit senses of group identity and group difference from others – such as from the 'crowd', the 'vulgar', the 'uninitiated' or the 'stranger'. Simmel is particularly concerned with the ways in which this mediation of behaviour by outward signs and codes of conduct begins to dominate over social life in the urban centres of high modernity. Simmel is fascinated with the atmosphere of the *fin de siècle* in affluent old European cities such as Vienna, Paris, Berlin and London. In impressionist painting and symbolist poetry, the Jugendstil and art nouveau, Simmel sees a culture of highly formalized, aestheticized social relations.

Simmel (1997) understands 'culture' in a wide and eclectic sense. His numerous essays on culture range across such diverse topics as style, fashion and design; photography, self-presentation and the face; cartoons and caricature; eating, courtship and coquetterie; gifts and letter-writing, secrecy and discretion; buildings, bridges and doors; the idea of youth, and the myth of the adventurer. In his essays on fashion, Simmel links forms of dress and adornment to practices of social emulation oriented to refinement and nobility in appearances. Fashion confers on its followers a sense of individual distinction and at the same time binds them into social groups. Fashion is a continual process of differential alternation between forms perceived as distinguished and forms perceived as standard. Similarly, Simmel shows how jewellery socially confirms the wearer's feeling of individual centredness within a circle of social attention. The piece of jewellery is rare but not unique; it belongs to the owner but is not personally expressive of the owner. It is a socially prized commodity and it is socially brilliant for the owner precisely because it cannot possibly be fabricated by the owner.

Simmel concludes that style and stylization represent a generalizing principle in aesthetic form. The stylized utility object such as the chair or wine glass is designed in its essence for general social consumption. It is not unique in its meaning and not made by individually significant creators like paintings or sculptures.

Simmel notes how similar social group dynamics take effect in the vogue for historical pastiche, imitation and nostalgia in architecture; in the nineteenth- and eighteenth-century passion for ruins; and in the touristic appeal of Italian cities such as Rome, Florence and Venice and the landscape of the Alps. These images imbue culture with the aspect of nature and nature with the aspect of culture. They turn history into myth and aesthetic artifice.

In his 1903 essay on 'The Metropolis and Mental Life' Simmel observes how communal relations give way to impersonal anonymous relations where experience becomes both more aestheticized – in so far as it is characterized by sensory plenitude and intensity, by spectatorship before surfaces, facades, windows and display, and by accelerated movement through space – and, at the same time, more *an*aestheticized, in so far as it is characterized by a 'blasé attitude' in which individuals form a need to protect themselves from nervous exhaustion, overstimulation and wasted emotion, by hiding their inner selves behind an indifferent exterior.

In *The Philosophy of Money* of 1900, Simmel expounds his theory of the socializing power of money in modern culture. Simmel (1978) proposes that money not only bears value; it socially constitutes value. Simmel does not subscribe to Marx's labour theory of value according to which value is essentially and originally invested in material substances by human labour. He does not argue that what Marx called 'use value' – use from labour, and use for labour – is more primordial than what Marx called 'exchange value'. Rather, Simmel argues that value only first comes to exist in social exchange. Value is first constituted in social interaction, and has no meaning in the absence of interaction. Things have value only to the extent that they are socially exchanged, and money is the most efficient medium for exchanging things because money systematically abstracts from qualitative differences between things. Unlike barter economies, which constantly have to renegotiate equivalences between things, money economies erect an invariant standard of equivalence. This universal standard of equivalence accelerates processes of socialization between individuals and groups as agents determine their lives more and more around travel towards centres of the market. These centres of the market are cities. Cities are the densest centres of monetary exchange, and therefore they are the fastest moving centres of all social and cultural change.

At the end of *The Philosophy of Money* Simmel considers whether money's increasing preponderance in urban culture might not ultimately destroy the preconditions of meaningful social interaction. Cities witness ever more complex patterns of stylization of life based on commerce and consumption. Yet these processes threaten to corrode individuals' sense of subjective continuity of experience over time. Money evacuates 'soul' from 'life'. Money disperses and freezes the fibres of individual personalities in temporally disconnected nodes of social intersection. Simmel therefore suggests that money, the very medium that creates a social possibility of value, might also be the very thing that destroys value. It is in this respect that Simmel's analyses finally complement, rather than contradict, Marxist accounts of reification and commodity fetishism in capitalist society, such as in the work of Lukács.

Simmel investigates some cultural consequences of urban money economies in *fin de siècle* aesthetic consciousness. In Stefan George's expressionist poetry, in Rodin's sculpture and Böcklin's painting, Simmel descries an attempt to reclaim organic 'soul' from static 'form'. Simmel interprets expressionism as an attempt to reunite form and soul, to rediscover primordial Gestalt in the inner life of the psyche, and thereby to draw together the dispersed fragments of the modern ego into a new unity, saved from alienation in the social machine. Expressionist works strive to incorporate the whole of life into their own self-subsistent being. However, in so far as their contents depend on flux of life, on contingency and openness to incalculable possibility, they cannot assure their autonomy.

Simmel argues that social reality today is too complex, labile and unstable, too much characterized by distance, transience and obscurity, to support any but the most fleeting efforts at universal summation of life. Art today cannot be what it was for such figureheads of humanistic culture as Michelangelo, Leonardo, Rembrandt and Goethe. A painter of the seventeenth century such as Rembrandt could reconcile form with soul, stasis with movement, pictorial space with narrative time, in a perfect symbiosis. Simmel argues that Rembrandt, in his portraits and self-portraits of the ageing human self, imprinted being into becoming and becoming into being. This is no longer possible for our time. Simmel argues that contemporary social actors are too much children of Schopenhauer's teaching on life's inexorable stream of unfulfillable desires, and of Nietzsche's ideas about repetition, difference and eternal return without wholeness and identity, to be capable of reviving Renaissance visions of centred personal harmony. For the great mass of people today, which includes artists and intellectuals as much as factory workers and functionaries, life is an obscure congeries of fractured identities and compulsions, devoid of any overarching order. Simmel famously calls this predicament the 'tragedy of culture':

> The concept of all culture is that the spirit creates something independent and objective, through which the development of the subject from itself to itself makes its way. But, in so doing, this integrating and culturally determining element is predestined to an autonomous development, which still consumes the forces of human subjects, and still draws such subjects into its orbit, without elevating them to its own height: the development of the subjects now can no longer take the path followed by the objects; where the former follow it nonetheless, the development runs into a cul-de-sac or a vacuity of our innermost and most genuine life.
> [...]
> There thus emerges the typical problematic condition of modern humanity: the feeling of being surrounded by an immense number of cultural elements, which are not meaningless, but not profoundly meaningful to the individual either; elements which have a certain crushing quality as a mass, because an individual cannot inwardly assimilate every individual thing, but cannot simply reject it either, since it belongs potentially, as it were, to the sphere of his or her cultural development. (1997: 72, 73)

Simmel proposes that such is the extent of aesthetic stylization in modernity that sociology must itself become aesthetic in its methods if it is to be adequate to social reality. He thus himself writes in an aesthetic, 'essayistic' style. Simmel here inaugurates a conception of sociological writing that continues in the work of Benjamin and Adorno, and in many contemporary postmodernist commentaries. The thesis is that theory will not capture its object for as long as theory attempts to remain a fully self-contained conceptual system. Rather, theory will have to become fragmentary, partial and ambivalent in relation to its object, because modern life itself has become fragmentary, partial and ambivalent. Theory will find truth not in totality but only in the tiny part, the fleeting episode, the forgotten, derided instant: in the disparity between thought and action, concept and impression (Adorno 1992).

At the same time, however, Simmel remains deeply committed to the possibility of systematic sociological explanation. He is a 'sociological impressionist' in his form of writing but not in his ambition of explanation. Underlying Simmel's penchant for illustration and vignette can be discerned an aspiration to explanatory objectivity and to the postulate of universal truth, goodness and beauty. Despite tendencies towards blurring and fragmentation of aesthetic validity in late nineteenth-century culture, Simmel holds out for the idea of beauty as an intrinsic universal value. Simmel argues that it is possible to account for social relativity in aesthetic taste and still to hold on to the idea of the universality and autonomy of aesthetic value. Simmel proposes that great works of art sublimate subjective appetitive necessity into objective spiritual necessity. Great works of art are unique and incommutable with any other object in so far as they embody social generality in their singular existence. They are embodiments of the general in the particular, not subsumptions of the particular under the general – like stylized utility objects produced according to repeatable formulae.

We will now see how these dialectical tensions between universality and relativity, autonomy and heteronomy, take on a more melancholy, almost mystical quality in the writing of Walter Benjamin.

Walter Benjamin: mourning and the messianic

Walter Benjamin's protean writings on art, literature and society have been rich sources of inspiration for many cultural critics. Benjamin read and admired Simmel's work, but did not generally engage with more academic sociological writers such as Durkheim; and he did not see his writings as contributions to 'social science' in any strict sense. He drew most of his inspiration from poetic, philosophical and theological sources. His writings are fragmentary and aphoristic, and they essentially seek concretion in disparate sensuous manifestations. They have their roots in a certain interpretation of Neo-Platonic metaphysics and Jewish messianic theology, blended with Marxian historical materialism.

Benjamin sees art and aesthetic life as ciphers of social relations. Artworks and artefacts are keys to the unlocking of social contradictions, but they are not crude reflections of socioeconomic structures. Social relations are encoded in cultural forms, as meanings are inscribed in texts, in allegory, symbol and collective dreamwork. This inscription is not arbitrary, accidental or superficial; it is the real constructing of social relations in contexts of material domination.

Cultural forms are part of the medium of affect, action and perception in which real social struggles are fought out.

The guiding intellectual figure in all Benjamin's writings is 'redemption'. However, Benjamin does not speak of redemption in any conventional religious sense, and nor does he defend a purely aesthetic concept of redemption. Unlike Wagner, Schopenhauer, Stefan George and the disciples of *l'art pour l'art*, Benjamin does not hold that art redeems the world in the sense of compensating for suffering, or making life happier, or playing proxy for God, or taking away sin, or reconciling creatures to each other. If artists are too convinced of their redemptive powers, believing in art as a kind of ersatz salvation, their work becomes ideological. Art does not sublimate pain into pleasure. Art is a protest against the world and a spur to change it. It can give hope, and it pays tribute to the memory of the forgotten and the oppressed; but it does not console. Art is redemptive in the sense in which Baudelaire and Marcel Proust think of literature. As Baudelaire's painter finds beauty in the fugitive and the vilified, rendering 'evil' into 'flowers', so art for Benjamin saves truth from the falsehoods of hypocrites, moralists, myth-mongers and power-seekers. As Proust finds narrative beauty in the search for lost time – not in the *recuperating* of lost time, as when a businessman thinks that lost time has to be made up because 'time is money', but in the *remembering* and *writing* of lost time *as lost*, as irretrievable – so Benjamin sees the artist as rescuing value from the machinations of capitalists, industrialists and ideologues who turn value into profit, cheap thrills and hollow cant.

In writings from the early 1920s, Benjamin's thinking revolves around themes of language, nature, history and representation. The essays 'On Language in General and the Language of Man', 'The Task of the Translator' and 'On the Mimetic Capacity' are allegorical reflections on alienation, modernity and domination over nature. Benjamin (1973a) recasts the story of the Fall from Eden, imagining that 'language in general' is the language of nature, the language of all animate and inanimate beings, which call out to Adam and invite Adam to respond by giving them names. Benjamin proposes that eating from the Tree of Knowledge implies loss of this original co-responsive relationship to nature in a thirst for possession and acquisition. The 'language of man' is a degraded instrument of invention by which man attempts to know nature by controlling nature. By 'the language of man' Benjamin means the primeval form of instrumental reason: natural science, technology and capitalism. God therefore punishes man by shattering the Tower of

Babel and scattering the language of man into a cacophony of languages across the earth. Benjamin concludes that the task of translators of languages and imitators of nature is to return voice to silenced nature, to return nature to its own speech. To return voice to nature is not to erect some universal language of objective semantic reference, in the spirit of positivism. To translate languages is not to map meanings onto objectively fixed references. To translate, and to imitate, is to create anew. Translation and imitation imply co-respondence to nature, but not possessive representation of nature. They imply 'presentation' (*Darstellung*), not 'representation' (*Vorstellung*).

In *The Concept of Art Criticism in German Romanticism* Benjamin develops these ideas into a conception of the truth-potential of works of art. Benjamin examines Schelling's and Friedrich Schlegel's conception of the relation of aesthetic judgement to aesthetic experience, and of art criticism to art object. Benjamin shows how art criticism does not translate poetic objects into definite fixed meanings; it brings poetic objects to completion of themselves by participating in their own poetic qualities. Discursive thought is particularized and concretized in aesthetic experience. In a later essay on Goethe's novel *Elective Affinities*, Benjamin deploys a metaphor of alchemy, alluding to the poetry of Rimbaud. Like the alchemist who discovers secret elective affinities between disparate elements, criticism releases truth from art by finding the conceptual in the sensuous, in the fleeting and the rare. Art's truth remains hidden without criticism; but criticism will not awaken this truth unless criticism itself takes the risk of becoming aesthetic and poetic.

In *The Origin of German Tragic Drama* Benjamin (1977) speaks of a rescuing of phenomenal appearances through art's lyrical presentation of Ideas. When art presents Ideas – Platonic Ideas, essences in themselves – art rescues the phenomena of this earth from their falling away into non-being under the scythe of time. But Benjamin says – like Nietzsche and Rilke – that Ideas can only appear in a medium of transient semblance (*Schein*): in phenomenal, illusory form, in difference and non-identity with themselves. This leads Benjamin to speak of the 'origin' as that which originates in time in sensuous appearance. Benjamin's 'origin' (*Ursprung*) is close to Goethe's 'original phenomenon' (*Urphänomen*). Origin means form that arises out of the flux of becoming; origination means a summoning up into seminal life out of the ebb and flow of time.

Benjamin reflects on the origination of the seventeenth-century German dramatic form called *Trauerspiel*, or 'mourning play'.

Trauerspiel dramatizes the predicament of political sovereigns swept up by events into situations of irresolvable aporia. The sovereign's attempt to preserve empire in the dignity of a heroic moment of decision is defeated by a greater empire: the empire of time. In this sense, dramatic works for Benjamin are allegories of history. Drama, writing and all art forms in general for Benjamin are allegories of social and political forces raging through time, wreaking death, destruction and betrayed hope in their wake. Like *Trauerspiel* in particular, art in general is a work of mourning for the victims of rationalization and regimentation. Art calls for remembering and atonement for violence to nature. But since mourning can never be completed until violence is abolished, mourning subsides into chronic persistent melancholy (Buci-Glucksman 1994).

In the later 1920s and 1930s Benjamin begins to write in a less allegorical vein, turning his attention to the more immediate world of material mass culture, especially in Berlin under the short-lived Weimar Republic. In *One-Way Street* Benjamin writes aphoristically about the shop window, the advertisement, the street junction, the petrol station, the photographer, the watchmaker, the antiques dealer. He also begins a monumental study which remained unfinished at his death known as the *Arcades Project*. The *Arcades Project* investigates the cosmos of art, politics, culture, consumption and capitalism in nineteenth-century Paris. Inspired by Louis Aragon's surrealist novel of 1926, *The Paris Peasant*, about the little passageways joining parallel streets in the area around the Opéra in Paris, Benjamin (1999) treats the arcade as a cipher of high capitalist modernity. Built after the 1820s, the arcades are iron structures that close off space between adjacent buildings. They create a covered walkway lined with miniature shops, each with facades made entirely of glass and iron. They are the ancestors of the present-day shopping mall. They create intimate commercial interiors, hived off from the municipal space of the city. They allow commodities to be put on display more densely and seductively than anywhere else in the city. Benjamin speaks of the arcades as 'phantasmagorias': little fairy-tale fantasies of personal happiness and gratification that draw in customers like voyeurs through a looking glass or a peeping hole. They are the embodiment of Stendhal's characterization of the beauty of the fashionable lady in the gaze of the possessive male lover: little 'promises of happiness' – *promesses de bonheur* (Stendhal 1975: 66). The arcades are the smaller cousins of the enormous glass structures of the great exhibitions of the 1850s, symbolized by London's Crystal Palace.

This leads Benjamin to write more broadly of the alliance between industrial finance capital and the imperialist European nation-state, taking his cue from Marx's *Eighteenth Brumaire of Louis Bonaparte*. Benjamin comments on the mythic imperial architecture of Napoleon III's populist dictatorship. Large quarters of obstreperous working-class Paris were bulldozed after the revolutions of 1848 and replaced by gentrified boulevards under the command of Baron Haussmann. Haussmann's gentrified boulevards are too wide to be crossed by makeshift barricades; but they create little interstitial pockets of resistance, little bohemias of the angry, the dispossessed and the creative. For the artist, Paris's boulevards and radial street junctions create carousels of possibility. Paris's streets, shops, fashions and facades become the dream work of a high capitalist society that displaces its utopian collective wishes and desires into little nuggets of consumption. Benjamin says that the task of the artist is to shock society out of this dream and awaken society to its own historical agency: to show the truth in the illusion, the reality in the surreality.

In his famous essay on 'The Work of Art in the Age of Mechanical Reproduction', from 1936, Benjamin (1973c) argues that art today no longer consists of inimitable works of singular 'aura'. Visual art today stands in a conscious reflective relationship to mass production because all artists now know that any image can be mechanically reproduced thousands of times over without difference from the original. The traditional 'auratic' work of art radiated a 'unique appearance of distance within nearness'. It had cultic status. Today, however, photographic reproduction is capable of lifting any image out of any historical tradition of reception and thereby nullifying its time-honoured charm. Capitalist mass culture attempts to re-enchant this disenchantment: in the cult of the popular performer, the star and the commodity fetish; but capitalism's strategies of re-enchantment produce only a perpetual same. Artists therefore need to reckon up to this massified reality and seek ways of illuminating by disrupting routine habit and mass toil in the factories and offices. In the mass media of film and photography, artists find possibilities of illuminating through shock montage. But Benjamin notes that film is ambiguous because it can stupefy and distract as much as shock. Fascism recognizes and exploits this in its propaganda. Through the mass media, both fascism and capitalism aestheticize politics. They leave artists with only one option: to fight the aestheticization of politics with the politicization of art.

In his 'Theses on the Philosophy of History', from 1939, Benjamin reaffirms this vision of a revolutionary art of political struggle. The future society is communism. But communism's arrival defies all prediction, all anticipation and all representation. Like the ban on images of God in Jewish theology, art can only hint at utopia. Just as the coming of the Messiah marks an absolute break with time, beyond all horizons of earthly expectation, so to narrate and represent history's steady advance towards utopia would be to legislate over time and contingency in a false way. It would be to blot out all possibility of radical newness in a lightning moment of the 'now'. In the famous ninth thesis, Benjamin interprets a picture of an angel by Paul Klee, entitled *Angelus Novus* (see illustration 6). Klee's angel, Benjamin writes, looks like the angel of history:

> His face is turned toward the past. Where we perceive a chain of events, he sees one single catastrophe which keeps piling wreckage upon wreckage and hurls it in front of his feet. The angel would like to stay, awaken the dead, and make whole what has been smashed. But a storm is blowing from Paradise; it has got caught in his wings with such violence that the angel can no longer close them. This storm irresistibly propels him into the future to which his back is turned, while the pile of debris before him grows skyward. This storm is what we call progress. (1973b: 249)

Siegfried Kracauer: the redemption of physical reality

Siegfried Kracauer's writings on popular literature and music, urbanism and especially film and photography are as penetrating as Benjamin's but have suffered neglect in contemporary commentary. Deploying his skills as a journalist for the *Frankfurter Zeitung* in Berlin in the 1920s, Kracauer developed a mode of cultural criticism that prizes moments of the fleeting and fragmentary within contexts of structural sociological import – 'exemplary instances of modernity', as he called them. Kracauer saw himself as paring off the crusts of idealizing obscurity that conceal real material conditions for the possibility of culture in an age of mass mechanization. This project culminated in two masterworks of the postwar period, written in English after emigration to the US: *From Caligari to Hitler: A Psychological History of German Film* (1947) and *Theory of Film: The Redemption of Physical Reality* (1960).

In an early study of the late nineteenth- and early twentieth-century detective novel, Kracauer (1971) begins from Lukács's conception of the 'transcendental homelessness' of modern man. Kracauer argues that characters in detective novels of this period are

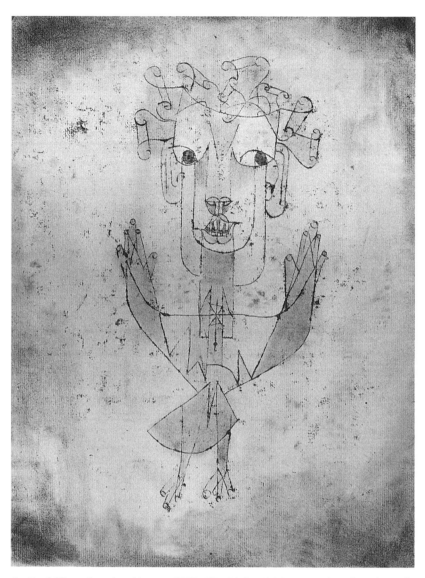

6 **Paul Klee,** *Angelus Novus*, **1920, 32.** 31.8 × 24.2 cm, India ink, coloured chalks and brown wash on paper. The Israel Museum, Jerusalem, Gift of Fania and Gershom Scholem, John and Paul Herring, Jo Carole and Ronald Lauder. Photo © Israel Museum/David Harris. © DACS 2003

typically atomized monads, lost in anonymous crowds of the metropolis. Their relations to one another are stripped of emotion and trust. They are caught up in anomic relations of secrecy, paranoia and voyeurism, behind an ongoing routine of business as usual. Kracauer comments on the significance of the hotel lobby in many detective novel scenarios. The hotel lobby is a place of congregation. It is like the nave of a church where members of the laity commune in worship of a higher truth and a higher reality. In the hotel lobby, however, there is co-residence but no community. There is a truth, a secret and a mystery – of the doer and the deed – but no transcendent reality. There is only fascination with the horror of a temporarily dismembered social body. Kracauer here applies Weber's concepts of rationalization and disenchantment. The detective is the personification of intellectualized *ratio*, playing God between the police and the suspects. The detective is solitary and shady with an aura of the genial. The detective calculates, extrapolates, deduces the laws of motivation that lead to the identity of the criminal; but his reasoning is of a purely abstract kind, bereft of emotive sensibility. The detective's psychological ratiocination delivers the correct result after a series of exhilarating suspenses; but his analyses – and the genre's analyses in general – bring society no closer to an understanding of the social causes of its spiritual desolation.

In an essay on 'The Mass Ornament', Kracauer (1995) writes of a reduction of articulated personal trajectories of experience to rehearsed formulae of behaviour, learned by imitation from the mass media and worn by their bearers like pieces of external adornment. The mass ornament is the flipside of de-substantialized social relations, in Simmel's sense of a preponderance of 'form' over 'life'. Shop window dressings, cabaret girls and dance fashions function as decorative role models for armies of regimented factory and office workers who themselves are potential clay in the hands of the capitalist, the bureaucrat and the Führer. The mass ornament connotes a mythical simulation of grace in the face of processes of mechanization. These processes are at once rational and profoundly irrational. They rest on a radical disjunction – not mediation – of *ratio* on the one hand and 'instinct' on the other hand.

In a study of the French popular composer of the *belle époque*, Jacques Offenbach, Kracauer (1937) traces some origins of these processes in French society of the Second Empire. He argues that Offenbach's operettas articulate collective hedonism in a society that has put aside revolutionary agitation at the barricades for spectacle and light entertainment, for coffee-house gossip and salacious scandal. But Kracauer argues that Offenbach's comic melodramas are not only to be seen as music of distraction. In their mischievous satirizing of parvenus, hypocrites and sycophants in French high society, they reveal a theatre of absurdities in a society capable at once of state-consecrated political individualism, Catholic neo-conservatism and virulent anti-Semitism. Kracauer shows how the passage across the Rhine from the frenetic *joie de vivre* of the Parisian cancan to the sinister psychosis of the Prussian goose-step is but a few years in historical time.

When Kracauer fled Germany for New York in 1933, he had already written dozens of reviews of European and American films and other essays on photography. Film was to become his dominant preoccupation until his death in 1966.

From Caligari to Hitler unfolds Kracauer's account of the development of German cinema after 1918 under the Weimar Republic and the rise of National Socialism. The expressionist silent film *Dr Caligari's Cabinet*, written and directed by Carl Mayer and Hans Janowitz in 1920, tells the story of a psychiatrist, Caligari, who appears as a showman hypnotist at a street fair, wearing a distinctive pair of horn-rimmed spectacles. Three murders occur, two of which include the friend and the lover of Francis, a student who visits Caligari's show and listens to Caligari's hypnotized medium, a man named Cesare. Cesare answers Francis's friend's question 'how long will I have to live?' with the words 'until dawn'. When the friend and then Francis's lover are both found murdered in mysterious circumstances overnight, Francis suspects first Cesare, then Caligari. Francis believes Caligari to be hiding in disguise in a lunatic asylum. But when Francis arrives at the asylum and meets the Director, he is shocked to recognize the benignly smiling face of Caligari. In a final twist to the story, added to the original Mayer–Janowitz script at the last minute, Francis appears at the beginning of the film as himself a lunatic in the asylum. Francis insists on the verity of the events he is about to relate, and then the main action follows. At the end, convinced of the identity of the Director and Caligari, the delirious Francis is brought to meet the Director for therapy. The Director bears no resemblance to Caligari, except at the moment when he dons a pair of horn-rimmed spectacles – and then removes them, at which point everything appears to return to normality and the film ends.

Kracauer interprets this as an allegory of the German people's uncertain relation to authority in the aftermath of the shock of the Great War. Unable to find authority within themselves as morally autonomous individuals, the German people abdicate responsibility for themselves. They turn to external instances of authority, to the Kaiser and the military generals, who manipulate them into murderous deeds, like Caligari and Cesare. At the same time, hyper-inflation, unemployment and chronic social dislocation induce a general retreat into inwardness, a quietism and timidity. Kracauer sees this in Caligari's ambivalence between demonic reality and neurotic hallucination in the mind of Francis. Kracauer sees similar motifs in other films of the 1920s, by Fritz Lang and others up to the rise of Nazi propaganda film, where storylines revolve around themes of tyranny and chaos, realism and escapism, normality and pathology. Kracauer's thinking here shares much in common with the accounts of Weimar Germany of Norbert Elias (1996), Hannah Arendt (1973), Elias Canetti (1984), and Adorno et al. (1950), as well as with Thomas Mann's late novel *Dr Faustus* and Klaus Mann's *Mephisto*.

In *Theory of Film*, Kracauer expounds a general theory of the aesthetic capacities of the cinematic medium. Like Benjamin and Hauser and more recent film theorists such as Deleuze (1986–9) and Rancières (2001), Kracauer sees cinema as the defining medium of high modernity in so far as film uniquely captures contingency of form, movement, fragility of vision, transience and discontinuity of lived time, everyday noise and materiality, and especially the cool, externalized, corporealized character of feeling and mentality in a world of anonymous crowds, machines, factories and urban spaces. By the 'redemption of physical reality', Kracauer means film's capacity for documenting, capturing and bearing witness to fleeting phenomena of the material world and thereby saving them from their aspect of oblivion, evanescence and stolid silence in everyday business. Kracauer contends that when film is true to its medium, it does not purport to compose and arrange its subject-matter, like painting or drawing. Film's telos is to capture fragments of experience in the raw flow of their occurrence, not to contrive experience by any preparatory touch of artifice or confection:

> The intrusion of Art into film thwarts the cinema's intrinsic possibilities. If for reasons of aesthetic purity films influenced by the traditional arts prefer to disregard actual physical reality, they miss an opportunity reserved for the cinematic medium.
> [. . .]
> [A]long with photography, film is the only art which exhibits its raw material. Such art as goes into cinematic films must be traced to their creators' capacity for reading the book of nature. The film artist has

traits of an imaginative reader or an explorer prodded by insatiable curiosity. He is a man who sets out to tell a story but, in shooting it, is so overwhelmed by his innate desire to cover all of physical reality – and also by a feeling that he must cover it in order to tell the story, any story, in cinematic terms – that he ventures ever deeper into the jungle of material phenomena in which he risks becoming irretrievably lost if he does not, by virtue of great efforts, get back to the highways he left. (1960: 301, 302–3)

One might argue that Kracauer is excessively prescriptive in his claim that all film genres that do not directly address physical preconditions of the possibility of experience remain 'inauthentic' uses of their medium. One might argue that he is excessively purist in his account of film's difference from other art forms such as painting, drawing, writing and theatre. Kracauer is indeed characteristically modernist in his antipathy towards blurring of boundaries between genres and media. But Kracauer is nevertheless right to point out that in an age in which sacred systems of metaphysical belief have been conquered for a radically mechanized order of science, industry, technology, economy and utility, it is appropriate that film should interrogate this machine reality through its intrinsic resources. Of all visual art media, film and photography are the most implicated in technology – that is, before the invention of television, computers and the internet. Therefore it is appropriate that film should seek inner meanings in experience only from the starting-point of life's outward structures of technological mediation.

We will now see how these themes of truth to material mediation of life continue in the writings of Theodor Adorno.

Theodor Adorno and the Frankfurt School

The central founding members of the Frankfurt School were Max Horkheimer, Herbert Marcuse, Leo Löwenthal, Franz Neumann, Otto Kirschheimer and, above all, Theodor Adorno. Adorno is the figure most responsible for the dissemination of Benjamin's ideas among the research programmes of the Frankfurt School. Adorno's thinking owes a profound debt to Benjamin, but Adorno is generally more severe than both Benjamin and Kracauer about possibilities for emancipatory redemption from and through industrial mass production and consumption. Partly for this reason, Adorno remains a controversial figure in social theory. Adorno is repeatedly accused of mandarin prejudice against what is today called 'popular culture'. This charge is not without substance, but it requires important qualification. We will first discuss Adorno's late philosophical treatise on art, his *Aesthetic Theory* of 1969, and then his earlier classic work, *Dialectic of Enlightenment* of 1947, written with Horkheimer, which unfolds his critique of the 'culture industry'. We conclude with a critical assessment of the work of the Frankfurt School.

Adorno's aesthetic theory

Adorno's *Aesthetic Theory* can be understood as a critical restatement of Hegel's philosophy of art. Adorno makes at least three critical emendations to Hegel's aesthetics. We will first enumerate these and then examine them more closely.

First, following Marx, Adorno holds that art's way of revealing truth in the world is real and material, not ideal. Second, against Hegel's thesis of the end of art, Adorno holds that art is both always 'at an end' and never 'at an end'. Adorno holds that even as art is subsumed into philosophy, philosophy depends on art. Therefore, philosophy cannot complete its subsumption of art: art always remains a moment of excess. Third, Adorno follows Hegel in asserting that art strives to be the rule of freedom in nature; but Adorno opposes Hegel in insisting that this striving cannot be true unless art shows the reality of non-reconciliation between freedom and nature under real conditions of instrumental reason.

Like Bloch and Benjamin, Adorno holds that art opens to truth in so far as it moves in the medium of 'semblance' (*Schein*). Art can reveal the truth of the 'system of illusions' (*Verblendungszusammenhang*) that is capitalist production and consumption because art itself partakes of semblance and illusion. Therefore, art is able to make illusion self-reflective. Like mass culture, art reflects society; but unlike mass culture, art reflects *on* its reflection. Art is like an intelligent second mirror reflecting images reflected in an initial mirror, and not mistaking these images for real things. Thus Adorno's aesthetics is a theory of sociological mimesis. Adorno argues that instead of holding a mirror to nature, art holds a mirror to society, and does not mistake society for nature – as mass culture does. Mass culture reflects the status quo as if it were nature, whereas art is capable of showing the status quo for what it is: contingent, changeable and fraudulent.

Art moves in the medium of semblance because art evokes aesthetic experience. This is Nietzsche's importance for Adorno.

Art cannot enlighten without playing with sense and sensuality. But at the same time, art is not solely sensuous life. Art stands at one remove from aesthetic experience because art consists in autonomous *works*. Adorno does not share Brecht's, Marcuse's and the surrealists' view that art should dissolve into life and reunite with everyday labour – while capitalism still exists. Art should preserve its autonomy, not in the sense of bourgeois 'art for art's sake' but in the sense of a fore-intimation of the possibility of real autonomy in social relations. To gain critical purchase on social reality, art must stand apart from this reality. Art comes closer to life by keeping a distance from life – just as critical theory remains most effective when it is not collapsed into praxis but mediated with detached analysis.

Art also holds a distance from aesthetic experience for the further reason that art seeks to relate sense perceptions to concepts. Although aesthetic contents in art cannot be translated into determinate concepts because they are always excessive, they are not ineffable. If they are contents at all, they are capable of critical articulation by philosophy, and they are in need of such articulation. Adorno writes:

> Philosophy and art converge in their truth content: The progressive self-unfolding truth of the artwork is none other than the truth of the philosophical concept.... For contemporary consciousness, fixated in the tangible and unmediated, the establishment of this relation to art obviously poses the greatest difficulties, yet without this relation art's truth content remains inaccessible: Aesthetic experience is not genuine experience unless it becomes philosophy. (1997: 130–1)

Adorno does not, however, accept Hegel's absolute sublation of art into philosophy and conceptuality. For as long as social reality remains traduced by ideology, there can be no ultimate identity of sense perceptions with their concepts. Just as the reality of freedom today is not identical with the *concept* of freedom, so art is true to reality only when it reflects back this non-identity of the world with its concepts, with the world as it could be. Art is true to itself only when it reflects back its own non-identity with its concept, when it negates itself and becomes anti-art – such as in the work of experimentalists such as Marcel Duchamp, Arnold Schönberg, John Cage and Samuel Beckett. Adorno defines this as art's 'dialectical negativity'.

Dialectical negativity, or 'negative dialectics', for Adorno means Hegel's principle of historical development driven by contradictions between concepts and their real referents; but without Hegel's conception of synthesis between theses and their anti-theses. Concepts are negated by their real referents, and these real referents are in turn negated as society strives to makes its world more adequate to its concepts. But this second negation is not a synthesis and is never necessarily a step forward (Adorno 1973).

Adorno locates the source of this false presumption of progress by synthesis in what he calls 'identity-thinking'. Identity-thinking has its roots in capitalism's logic of universal equivalence. It derives from money's power of abstraction from qualitative differences of experience. Art, however, has a potential for breaking this reifying thinking. It has a potential for redeeming reason from reason's instrumental relation to reality by showing the other of concepts, the other of words. By insisting on negation, on difficulty, enigma and labour of the spirit, art can redeem those dimensions of sensuous well-being which mass culture makes false. Art can rescue those qualities of feeling, sensation and emotion which mass culture reduces to sensationalism, cynicism and sentimentality.

However, Adorno adds that the destructiveness of capitalist modernity is such that art is already caught up in ambivalence in its very attempt to bear witness to this destruction. Adorno declares that there can be 'no art after Auschwitz'. The horrors of the Jewish holocaust are such that art's very attempt to represent suffering is already potentially violation. But art must bear witness to suffering. Art must speak for the silence of those deprived of voice. Art therefore lives under an infinite weight of responsibility. It cannot represent the horror; yet it must tell the truth. Art has a capacity and a responsibility to promote a different relationship of society to nature, rooted in peace, care and love, not mastery and possession. Art can impart intimations of the world in reconciliation with itself, in utopia; but it cannot represent utopia and it cannot deliver utopia.

Adorno and Horkheimer on the culture industry

In *Dialectic of Enlightenment*, Adorno and Horkheimer expound their concept of the 'culture industry'. They define the culture industry as the total invasion of creative life by money. The culture industry is the total colonization of creativity by economic reason. It rests on an equation between culture and capital. Under the rule of instrumental reason, capitalism comes to be viewed as the most natural satisfier of human needs, mental as well as material. Capitalism reduces culture to functional gratification of the self, like therapy or surgery administered to patients by doctors. The culture industry reduces qualitatively different sensuous experiences to a mass reproduction of the same. Pleasure is industrialized through a scientific parcelling up of structured contexts of experience into atomic units of sensory intensity. These units are then combined in standard formulae. Like processed food, aesthetic experience is broken down into basic elements, then treated with preservatives, sweeteners and chemical intensifiers for mass distribution.

Adorno and Horkheimer discern these processes in the structure of the products of Hollywood 'show business' (Adorno 1991). In various empirical studies of audience reactions to television, film and radio conducted in Los Angeles where they lived as emigrés in the 1940s, they point to some now familiar phenomena: reduced attention spans, boredom, passivity, impatience for titillation, voyeurism, prurience, hysteria. They argue that hit products corrode audiences' powers of imagination. Hit products have to put everything on display. They have to make everything explicit and immediate. Hit products absorb the audience without inviting the audience to involve itself reflexively in the object. They do not encourage audiences to exercise sensory-motor skills of subject–object distinction. They perform the spectator's work of imagining and schematizing *for* the spectator. They anaestheticize the spectator's perceptual capacities by reducing the spectator's readiness to respond to stimuli with cognitive reflexivity.

Adorno and Horkheimer (1979) show how hit films and songs attempt to address 'universal' themes. But they argue that this universality is hollow because it is not achieved through any labour of engagement with contradiction and complexity. Hit films and songs rest on morally black-and-white scenarios. There must be a happy ending. Contradictions in social realities must be smoothed over. Harmony, reconciliation and consonance of character relations must be engineered. Plot structure becomes a formal contrivance, not a dramatically necessary unfolding of developments, based on complex emotional dilemmas experienced by characters. Furthermore, where plot suspense is not enough to hold attention, stunts, special effects and hyperbolical self-promotion must take over. 'Stars' take on the guise of avatars. They are like latter-day saints. They appear to offer a transcendence from everyday routine. Yet they appear on earth only until fashion dictates that they are replaced by others. Their enchantment of what is disenchanted does not subvert routine. They resign people to the system of production and to perpetual repetition. Adorno and Horkheimer write:

Amusement under late capitalism is the prolongation of work.
... Pleasure hardens into boredom because, if it is to remain pleasure,
it must not demand any effort and therefore moves rigorously in
the worn grooves of association. No independent thinking must be
expected from the audience: the product prescribes every reaction:
not by its natural structure (which collapses under reflection), but by
signals.
[...]
Works of art are ascetic and unashamed; the culture industry is pornographic and prudish.
[...]
Fun is a medicinal bath. The pleasure industry never fails to pre-
scribe it. It makes laughter the instrument of the fraud practised on
happiness. ... In the false society laughter is a disease which has
attacked happiness and is drawing it into its worthless totality. ... Such
a laughing audience is a parody of humanity. Its members are monads,
all dedicated to the pleasure of being ready for anything at the expense
of everyone else. Their harmony is a caricature of solidarity.
[...]
The paradise offered by the culture industry is the same old drudgery.
Both escape and elopement are predesigned to lead back to the start-
ing point. Pleasure promotes the resignation which it ought to help to
forget.
[...]
We do not have the cap and bells of the jester but the bunch of keys
of capitalist reason. (1979: 137–42)

The Frankfurt School reassessed

In recent years the Frankfurt School has faced waves of criticism in
the wake of revaluations of popular culture and the rise of more
pluralistic conceptions of cultural value. These criticisms suggest
that Adorno and Horkheimer overstate their case in various respects.
They suggest that their empirical researches and conclusions are not
as well founded as they believed. They show the extent to which
Adorno and Horkheimer are compromised by an indiscriminating
attitude to what they term 'mass culture'. We will discuss these objections here. But first we must establish some points of clarification.

We must emphasize that Adorno, Horkheimer, Benjamin and
Kracauer all spoke of *Massenkultur* partly because no equivalent
term for 'popular culture' existed in German at the time of their
writing. In bourgeois intellectual circles of early twentieth-century
Germany, uses of the term *Massenkultur* tended to imply that only

high culture was worthy of the title of *Kultur* per se. But Adorno, Horkheimer, Benjamin and Kracauer consciously resisted this prejudice. Adorno's and Horkheimer's writings certainly exemplify a distinct genre of mandarin criticism from the interwar period; but they are not to be associated with more conservative variants of this genre, as Gans (1999) and some other writers have unfairly implied. Adorno's and Horkheimer's arguments are not comparable to the more decisively anti-democratic prejudices to be found in texts such as Ortega y Gasset's *The Revolt of the Masses*, in some of the writings of Thomas Mann, and among antediluvian English conservative writers such as F. R. Leavis and T. S. Eliot.

We must also repeat that Adorno and Horkheimer always saw capitalistic principles of commercial administration as threats to quality, diversity and freedom in *both* what is today called 'high culture' *and* what is today called 'popular culture'. Their concern was not, in its fundamental intention, with the preservation of the integrity of the 'high' from contamination by the 'low', as some critics have alleged. Their concern was with the preservation of freedom for *all* creative endeavour, with the defence of all cultural expression against its total colonization by profit motives and by state propaganda motives. In a letter to Benjamin, Adorno made clear that 'fine art' and 'light art' are to be seen as '*two halves of an integral freedom*' (Adorno 1977: 123). The 'high' and the 'low' are two complementary sides of a whole aesthetic life, which have become sundered from one another under rationalized capitalism. In *Dialectic of Enlightenment* Adorno and Horkheimer write:

> 'Light' art as such, distraction, is not a decadent form. Anyone who complains that it is a betrayal of the ideal of pure expression is under an illusion about society. The purity of bourgeois art, which hypostatised itself as a world of freedom in contrast to what was happening in the material world, was from the beginning bought with the exclusion of the lower classes . . . Serious art has been withheld from those for whom the hardship and oppression of life make a mockery of seriousness and who must be glad if they can use time not spent at the production line just to keep going. Light art has been the shadow of autonomous art. It is the social bad conscience of serious art. The truth which the latter necessarily lacked because of its social premises gives the other the semblance of legitimacy. The division itself is the truth. (1979: 135)

These considerations notwithstanding, we must now note at least four distinct problems with Adorno's and Horkheimer's work.

First, despite conducting extensive empirical research and claiming empirical warrant for their arguments, Adorno and Horkheimer did not go out of their way to inform themselves about varieties of entertainment forms. They tended to view mass culture as a monolithic bloc. They did not discriminate extensively between different genres of entertainment, nor between different social habits of consumption, in respect of gender, ethnicity, age and class.

Second, they underestimated audiences' capacities for reflexive self-distanciation from the contents of their consumption. They exaggerated audience passivity. Their evidence for direct causal influence over audience behaviour is not conclusive. Numerous researchers now demonstrate that meanings and functions attached to cultural objects by audiences may by no means correspond to those intended for them, or anticipated in them, by their producers and suppliers (Featherstone 1991). Audiences may react with scepticism and derision, irony and laughter, and they may often playfully recombine elements of their consumption in homespun ways. Watching TV and film is often a communicative process in which group members articulate and exchange views (Gans 1999).

Third, Adorno and Horkheimer compromised their empirical research by too many idiosyncratic value judgements. They did not make a sufficient effort to observe Max Weber's principle of distinction between factual components of discourse and normative components of discourse; and they made only a half-hearted attempt to abstain from value judgements in their empirical analyses. As a result, their work does not achieve an acceptable degree of analytical differentiation between value-distanciating sociological analysis and value-affirming aesthetic appraisal and political advocacy. They held many positive judgements in favour of classical European artists, writers and composers, and they neither (1) made a sufficient attempt to distanciate their empirical research from these judgements, nor (2) proffered sufficiently intersubjectively sustainable arguments for these judgements in the more normative parts of their writings.

In one of the most often cited objections to Adorno, Adorno condemned jazz music as unfocused, diffuse and repetitive. We may identify three problems with this. First, Adorno did not distinguish sufficiently between different varieties of jazz and different individual jazz musicians. He effectively associated all jazz with tin-pan alley jazz. Second, he did not make a sufficient attempt to distinguish his value judgement on jazz from his empirical research on jazz. And third, his arguments for this value judgement are not intersubjectively

172 Modernity and Modernism

sustainable. They have not proved to be persuasive. Adorno should have listened to jazz music more closely, with greater empathy and imagination. Similarly, although he did acknowledge the subversive artistry of entertainers such as Charlie Chaplin and the Marx Brothers in the 1930s and 1940s, he remained oblivious to strains of subversive artistry in 1960s rock music. He also praised Arnold Schönberg's modernist music as 'progressive' but unjustifiably condemned Igor Stravinsky's modernist music as 'regressive'.

Fourth, Adorno and Horkheimer took an unduly narrow view of the range of types of economic sponsorship of cultural production under which aesthetic enlightenment can be realistically fought for (Zuidervaart 1991). Although they saw not only low-cultural forms but also high-cultural forms of production as vulnerable to commercial colonization, they relatively overestimated the vulnerability of the former and relatively underestimated the vulnerability of the latter. Although they demonstrated the sociological falsity of nineteenth-century bourgeois claims to aesthetic autonomy in high culture, they underestimated the extent to which some low-cultural forms achieve degrees of freedom from commercial colonization, degrees of freedom of expression, and degrees of critical social self-consciousness. They wrongly tended to assume that high modernist art had an automatically better chance of fighting for freedom and truth than – for example – Pop Art, Beat writing, and rock music. They wrongly tended to assume that cultural forms that interact more closely with commercial environments than other cultural forms possess an automatically diminished chance of remaining critical of their social conditions of existence and acceding to truth.

In chapter 7 we discuss some further elaborations of these objections with reference to postmodernism. But we conclude our discussion now with some further points of assessment of a more positive character. We will argue that these more positive points demonstrate a degree of continuing relevance in the work of the Frankfurt School for contemporary analysis.

First, with regard to the objection about audience reflexivity, it is important not to be misled by the rhetoric of Adorno's and Horkheimer's statements. Although their chapter on the culture industry in *Dialectic of Enlightenment* is subtitled 'Enlightenment as Mass Deception', Adorno's and Horkheimer's view of audience responses to mass culture was not a simplistic conspiracy theory. Adorno and Horkheimer did not regard audiences as helpless victims of manipulation. Their view was that mass culture discourages audiences from exercising innate faculties of cognitive reflection.

Mass culture does not invite reflection, and does not usually stimulate reflection. It does not usually perform what Brecht and Benjamin see in experimental theatre and film: thought-provoking estrangement of the taken-for-granted. Adorno and Horkheimer therefore argued that audience attitudes to mass culture can be both active *and* passive, both disbelieving *and* believing, both ironizing *and* accepting (Bernstein 1991: 12). People can laugh at stereotypes on TV and at the same time reproduce them in their daily behaviour. People can chuckle at tabloid newspapers, soap operas and astrology columns and at the same time orient their lives around them every day. Adorno and Horkheimer wrote: 'The triumph of advertising in the culture industry is that consumers feel compelled to buy and use its products *even though they see through them*' (1979: 167) (italics added).

We must also stress that when Adorno and Horkheimer spoke of massification, they always meant a contingent process: not a state in which people essentially exist but a process that occurs under historically specific circumstances. They did not regard mass culture audiences as aggregates of atomized monads in any a priori sense. The mass was not what people *are* but what they potentially *become* under specific regimes – such as in the *particular* circumstances of economic collapse in Germany after the world stock market crisis of 1929 and the *particular* circumstances of postwar social conservatism and conformism during the Cold War. Hannah Arendt notably argued in her *Origins of Totalitarianism* that massification is a potential consequence of political and economic structures that break down both freedoms of self-expression of individuals and mediating bonds of normative association between individuals (Arendt 1973).

We must also stress that the Frankfurt School never opposed *democracy* in cultural life. The Frankfurt School theorists always opposed what they saw as a certain perversion of democracy into intolerant forms of *populism* in cultural life. The term 'populism' has several meanings in social and political theory, and it is arguable that not all forms of populism are intolerant. But the Frankfurt School gave serious reasons for arguing that the populism they had in mind was, and is, intolerant. If democracy in cultural life can be defined as a condition in which all members of society possess equal rights of determination over allocations of economic resources for cultural life, the Frankfurt School's view of populism was that it is a condition in which *not* all members of society but only a *majority* possess such equal rights of determination over resources. Their view was that populism becomes an intolerant influence over culture *both* when it is actively cultivated by nationalistic single-party states *and* when it is allowed to gain ground by ostensibly liberal-democratic states that permit unrestrained capitalist market-places to dictate that only majorities, not minorities, shall determine allocations of resources for cultural life in so far as only majorities, not minorities, return profits on investments.

It is true that Frankfurt School arguments are not generally sufficiently appreciative of the range of options open to cultural production companies that operate mainly, if not wholly, as private commercial businesses but mainly serve minority tastes and consequently do not make large profits; for example, some publishing houses, some dance and theatre companies, some film distributors and cinemas, some record labels, some TV channels. But we must note that contemporary capitalist structures place severe limits on the survival abilities of such companies. Under globalized capitalist structures, such companies face severe pressures either to move over to a systematic profit model, based on production contracts oriented to majority consumption; or to merge with other companies; or to be taken over by more powerful companies that have already moved over to the systematic profit model; or to dissolve. They are highly vulnerable to competitive assimilation by the largest multinational media and entertainment corporations which dominate market agencies and often feed resentment of minority arts activities when these corporations are simultaneously the owners of mass-selling cut-price tabloid newspapers.

These considerations suggest that Adorno's and Horkheimer's analysis of the culture industry in the 1940s bears certain affinities with what George Ritzer (1993) has recently called 'McDonaldization'. Ritzer and Adorno and Horkheimer each speak of a system that enables every component part of a corporation's holdings to promote every other part through franchising and merchandising deals. It is a system based on a fundamental principle of capital concentration. It arises from common capital ownership between the production companies that make films, records and shows, and the newspapers, magazines and radio stations that advertise and report on them, and the cinemas and TV channels that present them. Such capital concentration arises from an imperative to maximize shareholder value; and from the imperative to maximize shareholder value follows an imperative to win mass audiences; and from the imperative to win mass audiences follows a structural aversion to contracting artists whose projects might be expected to deviate from a calculated mean of greatest sales receipts.

Admittedly, some entertainment corporations occasionally contract projects not expected to be hits. But such decisions are primarily determined by financial risk calculations. They are based on a commercial principle that dictates that safe bets on tried-and-tested formulae have to be periodically offset against novelty deviations capable of replenishing the stock of future formulae. The decisions are not primarily based on judgements of the aesthetic value of the projects in question. Adorno and Horkheimer argue in this sense that the culture industry operates essentially by a logic of self-validation. By promoting its sales statistics in radio hit parades, bestseller lists and TV award ceremonies, the culture industry operates by a tautology that says 'X must be good because everyone is paying to get X; therefore, it is worth paying to get X.' The culture industry ensures that its products function as advertisements for themselves and as advertisements for each other.

We may conclude that Adorno and Horkheimer are not wrong to be sceptical of the notion of capitalist market-places as transparent mediators of cultural goods that are most appreciated in society. They are not wrong to suggest that those cultural products reported in mass media outlets as being most 'in demand' might have been hyped into demand by their suppliers through self-fulfilling prophecies that might not actually reflect what most people *would* find most rewarding to experience were they to have a chance to express their evaluations by some alternative collective means. Products that sell the most are not necessarily those that people value the most.

Conclusion

We have discussed five thinkers who elaborate themes of modernity, modernism and modernization in art and society. All five thinkers develop themes of time, urbanism and aesthetic redemption as they are evoked in the poetry of Charles Baudelaire and in numerous modern artists and writers. Weber identifies radical value conflict between autonomously differentiated spheres of society. Simmel observes more and more complex structures of formalization and aestheticization of social relations. Weber and Simmel both speak of processes of rationalization and secularization in modern aesthetic consciousness; and both draw 'tragic' conclusions about the fate of contemporary culture. Benjamin, Kracauer and Adorno espouse a more programmatic vision of the contribution of art to revolutionary social self-consciousness. However, they remain melancholy about the reality of reason in history. Benjamin and Kracauer search ardently for moments of hope in a technologically mediated world of mechanized production and mass consumption. Adorno is more severe about the prospects for substantive social enlightenment in a world administered under instrumental reason. Adorno turns only to autonomous modernist art for possible intimations of reconciliation between society and nature. In his writings on the culture industry with Horkheimer, Adorno takes an excessively condemnatory view of mass culture. He fails to discriminate possible degrees of resistance to domination within mass culture, and he clouds his empirical analyses with idiosyncratic value judgements. But Adorno and Horkheimer both point cogently to some fundamentally destructive tendencies of commercial penetration in cultural life. They show how this destruction is intrinsic to the contemporary capitalist system of economic organization.

We may describe the theorists discussed in this chapter and in chapter 5 not only as theorists of modernity in art. We may also describe most of them as modernist theorists of art. They are 'modernist' theorists in the sense that they think of history as moving in certain definite sequences of normative progression and regression. In the next chapter, we discuss several ways in which this specific modernist consciousness is questioned and qualified by theorists of a more recent generation whose writings have become associated in various respects with what is called postmodernism.

7

Postmodernism and After

'Postmodernity' may be defined as the thesis of the end of modernity's ideals, struggles, problems and 'grand narratives' of historical development. 'Postmodernism' may be defined as the articulation of this thesis in a diffuse body of motifs, images and discursive constructions in late twentieth-century culture.

In this chapter we discuss the origins, heyday and aftermath of postmodernist discourse in the work of several late twentieth-century social theorists of the arts. Some of these theorists still belong within the framework of modernist reflection, but many of them lay the seeds of ways of thinking that have since become associated with postmodernism, or have become partly assimilated into postmodernism. We first discuss a range of contributions by several postwar German thinkers, including Martin Heidegger, Hans-Georg Gadamer and Jürgen Habermas. We then discuss a range of contributions by several postwar French thinkers, each of whom pay tribute to the aesthetic thought of the eighteenth-century French writer, the Marquis de Sade. These are Georges Bataille, Michel Foucault, Jacques Derrida and Gilles Deleuze. Then we turn to the central constituents of the thesis of postmodernity in art as these are theorized in the commentaries of Arthur Danto, Jean-François Lyotard, Jean Baudrillard and other notable writers. We then discuss several normative critiques of postmodernism in the writing of Fredric Jameson and David Harvey, in reflexive modernization theory, and in several recent European aesthetic theorists. We also examine Niklas Luhmann's alternative systems theory of aesthetic modernity. We conclude with an assessment of the impact of capitalistic globalization on contemporary arts institutions and the future of artistic life.

German aesthetic thought since 1945:
from Heidegger to Habermas

Although Martin Heidegger and Hans-Georg Gadamer are not primarily social theorists but philosophers, and although they do not think
in distinctively social-theoretic terms, Heidegger and Gadamer have
both been very influential in developments in social theory since the
Second World War, as well as in literary and aesthetic theory.

In *Being and Time* (of 1927), Heidegger argues that scientific
thought can give only a limited account of the way of being of the
world because scientific thought reduces the world to an object
standing apart from a knowing subject of consciousness. Heidegger
argues that before human beings come to think scientifically about
the world, they already exist *in* the world as embodied agents
and already carry with them, in this being-in-the-world, a more
primordial understanding of their relationship to things in the
world that is more meaningful, practical and holistic than scientific
representations. Heidegger therefore sees the task of all thought
as being to recover this basic ontological understanding from its
concealment by science. This is the task he calls 'hermeneutics'
(from the Greek word for 'interpretation', *hermeneuein*).

In his essay 'On the Origin of the Work of Art' from 1936,
Heidegger (1993) proposes that art is one exemplary source of this
more revelatory mode of pre-scientific existential understanding.
He proposes that great works of art reveal the 'being of beings': they
reveal the way in which things exist as what they are, in their relations to each other and to human purposes. Great works of art open
up lived worlds of experience to meaningful insight. In this existential revealing, they impart truth or 'set truth to work'. Heidegger
speaks of truth not in the sense of propositional correspondence to
facts but in the sense of deep holistic relevance. He invokes the idea
of an 'unforgetting' of the everyday world from habitual perception.
He appeals to a link between the Greek word for truth, *aletheia*, and
the Greek myth of the waters of oblivion at Lethe.

Heidegger comments on Van Gogh's painting of a pair of peasants'
shoes beside a chair. The painting shows up the 'thingness' of the
shoes, their heavy materiality, their expressive relationship to the
daily labour of the peasant. The painting imparts truth in the way it
revisits an everyday world and transfigures that world in its total
existential interconnectedness. Similarly, Heidegger comments on
the position of the ancient Greek temple at the centre of the Greek

city. In its open structure and centred location, the temple sets up a relationship between 'earth' and 'world'. The temple bodies forth the social space and spiritual identity of the Greek people. In this sense ancient classical works of art and architecture crystallize the existential world-structure of historical peoples.

Heidegger contends that modernity has forgotten and suppressed this more authentic understanding of art. Modernity has either confined beauty mostly to matters of perception and subjectivity (as with Kant and eighteenth-century aesthetics) or it has subjugated it to rationalistic thought (as with Hegel and the idealists). Modernity has disfigured the channels through which experiences of truth can be communicated to us from ancient mythic sources. It has tried to make language a means of instrumental purposes at the expense of language's poetic plenitude. Seeking to control and enlighten all being, modernity loses the sense of the play between veiling and unveiling, between concealing and unconcealing, between speech and silence, enigma and revelation. According to Heidegger, only German romantic poets such as Friedrich Hölderlin understood this sense in which modern man takes leave of the gods and retreats into exile. According to Heidegger, modern man languishes in a para-doxical night of enlightened rationalism, and only emerges from this night in the rare moments when he recognizes his radical finitude in the face of death.

Gadamer shares Heidegger's opposition to scientific rationalism and takes a similar view of the historical dignity of classical tradition – though he does not endorse Heidegger's apocalyptic rejection of modernity. In *Truth and Method*, first published in 1960, Gadamer (1975) argues that classical works of art contain reserves of truth that can extend human beings' existential orientation in the world by bringing them into confrontation with different worldviews. These reserves of truth are not accessible when art is approached in a purely scientific methodical manner, when it is objectified and reduced to sociological functions of its time, or when it is read solely in terms of present-day interests. Works of art have truth for the present only when audiences involve themselves in their intrinsic aesthetic content and historical voice.

Gadamer (1986) proposes that art's existential significance con-sists in three universal features. First, art enables 'play': a work of art involves its viewers in free acts of imagination that contribute to the phenomenal existence of the work as an inexhaustible sensuous whole. Second, art involves 'symbol': a work of art releases mean-ings that resist discursive translation, meanings that remain elusive and veiled in Heidegger's sense, not translatable into univocal semantic references. Third, art embodies 'festival': each event of perception or performance of a work creates a community of involved members who are drawn into communication with one another, and each of these events articulates the structure of existential time in which the work is experienced. Gadamer compares this communal and temporal character of aesthetic experience to the way in which pagan and religious festivals do not only occur *within* time but *define* time: festivals define the time of the social community by their very regularity and repetition. However, Gadamer adds that modern commercial culture threatens to corrode this communicative time-structuring feature of aesthetic experience. Commercial culture tends to isolate members from one another. It breaks down the regularity and continuity of socially experienced time into disconnected instants.

Heidegger's and Gadamer's ideas pose notable problems for social theory. Both thinkers raise some intrinsically sociological claims, yet neither see any need to substantiate these claims empirically. Instead, both assert their claims as 'ontological facts'. Heidegger in particular advocates uncritical nostalgia for an archaic past, motivated by nihilistic disaffection with modernity. Heidegger's arguments about the civilization-founding significance of historic forms such as the Greek Parthenon tend to dissolve debate about aesthetic value into sheer assertions of existential folk authenticity in art. As several critics make clear, including most notably Habermas (1988) and Bourdieu (1996), neither Heidegger nor Gadamer grasp the degree to which acts of hermeneutic interpretation can occur under conditions of power and material privilege that can undermine open democratic debate about culture.

These problems notwithstanding, however, Heidegger's and Gadamer's ideas retain importance for social theory of the arts. Their importance remains in part for the very reason that they reject all possibility of strictly scientific accounts of social meaning in art, religion, myth and philosophy. Like Wittgenstein and Alfred Schütz, they show how scientific explanation is a derivative mode of cognition that itself depends on norms of communicative practice that are first learned in daily life and first expressed through the very things science tries to explain. They show how interpreters have to interpret not only the object of their investigations but also their own relationship to that object. Interpreters also have to interpret their way of constituting that object *as* an object of thought. This remains a valuable insight.

In Germany in the 1960s and 1970s, Heidegger's and Gadamer's thinking led to numerous scholarly reappraisals of the idealist tradition in German philosophy. This in turn fostered a rethinking of the work of Adorno and the Frankfurt School. We now consider three theorists who attest to this legacy: Hans-Robert Jauss, Peter Bürger and Habermas.

In the 1960s and 1970s Hans-Robert Jauss and Wolfgang Iser developed Gadamer's ideas about 'play' and 'effective history' (*Wirkungsgeschichte*) into a reception theory of aesthetic meanings in works of art. Jauss in particular developed these ideas into a critique of Adorno's aesthetics. Jauss (1982) argues that Adorno vitiates his own programme by suppressing dimensions of shared emotive involvement in art. Jauss comments on Adorno's austere assertion that 'aesthetic experience is not genuine experience unless it becomes philosophy' (Adorno 1997: 131). Jauss here argues that Adorno forecloses any possibility of revolutionary social effects for art by excluding any role for empathic catharsis in aesthetic experience. Jauss argues that Adorno closes down the very channels of audience communication that might have the power to convert a work of art's transfigurative effects into emancipatory social practices.

In *Theory of the Avant-Garde* Peter Bürger (1984) criticizes Adorno by a different route. Bürger contends that Adorno is not sufficiently aware of the construction of aesthetic autonomy as a specifically bourgeois institutional form. He argues that Adorno failed to appreciate adequately the sense in which twentieth-century avant-garde movements such as Dada, surrealism, futurism and constructivism not only revolutionized internal aesthetic norms of art but also attacked the very *raison d'être* of art as an institution. Twentieth-century avant-gardes sought to dissolve art's institutional alienation from life by drawing art back into contexts of material culture. Bürger accepts that many of these attacks on aesthetic autonomy subsequently became both recuperated by art worlds and commodified by fashion industries. But, like Jauss, Bürger maintains that Adorno stands for a rather restrictive vision of high modernism that cannot open out onto a wider communicative space of popular engagements with art.

The most influential social theorist to develop these ideas of communicative engagement with art is Jürgen Habermas. Habermas is usually regarded as the leading second-generation representative of Frankfurt School critical theory. However, one of the most striking aspects of Habermas's differences with his earlier colleagues is his relative downgrading of the importance of aesthetics as a dimension in the critique of instrumental reason. In all his writings since the 1960s, Habermas's leading concern has been to propound an alternative conception of critical theory that dispenses with Hegelian Marxism's framework of subject–object dialectics in favour of the more pluralistic, 'communicative' framework of intersubjective argumentation over linguistic validity-claims. In Habermas's vision, domination by instrumental reason is not an inevitable outcome of the dialectic of enlightenment. Modernity contains the potential for a more differentiated understanding of the scope of reason that goes beyond purely scientistic rationality to encompass broader competences of rational communication over moral, political and aesthetic values and norms.

In a Kantian manner, Habermas (1984) distinguishes three principal spheres of rational validity in the modern world: scientific validity, moral-practical validity and aesthetic validity. Habermas argues that modernity rationalizes art not only *from within*, in its aesthetic codes, genres, techniques and instruments of production, but also *from without*, in the way that art's claims to validity are both played off by actors against other validity spheres and discursively evaluated by actors in relation to these other spheres. Works of art come to be judged by criteria of expressive truthfulness. They come to be judged by the extent to which they truthfully articulate intersubjectively experienced needs, feelings and sensations – in distinction to scientific statements, which come to be judged by theoretical criteria of propositional truth, and in distinction to moral, political and legal norms, which come to be judged by practical criteria of rightness and justice.

In his account of aesthetic modernity since Baudelaire, Habermas (1987, 1996) argues that modern art dramatizes modernity's cultural idea of itself as a 'project'. Modern art is modernity's symbolic vanguard, its emblem and medium of self-understanding. Habermas shows how modern artists come to act as critics in the public sphere, championing the public good and exposing its deliquescence. However, Habermas emphasizes that modern art is still only one part of the meaning of modernity. Aesthetic modernity is neither identical to, nor exhaustive of, the scope of modernization per se. Habermas points out that precisely because art operates at a symbolic level, it gives an impression of moving much more swiftly through the course of modernization than any other sphere: it creates an illusion of racing ahead to the 'end' of modernity before all other dimensions of modernization have caught up with it. Art thus appears to pro-claim 'postmodernity' before most of modernity's underlying *societal* objectives have been secured: before democracy and social justice have been secured. Habermas acknowledges that cultural modernity stands for freedom of expression and imagination without fear of censure, repression or cooption by traditional authority. It is a space for transgression, subversion and irony. It means the winning of a prerogative to play with nonsense and excess, without the deadening restraint of immediate practical responsibility and utility. Its func-tion is to loosen up rigid forms of perception, dissolve dogmas, disrupt staid procedures of thought. But Habermas argues that postmodernism nihilistically aggrandizes this prerogative beyond all just proportion. Postmodernism idly proclaims the end of modern-ity on purely aesthetic grounds. It forgets that the precondition of aesthetic liberation is freedom from material necessity, which is not open to all because modernity has not been achieved for all.

Habermas (1984) also argues that Adorno and Horkheimer underestimated modernity's potential for broad-reaching substant-ive, non-destructive rationalization. Habermas asserts that Adorno and Horkheimer fall back on aesthetics because they can think of no structural alternative to instrumental reason that is not tainted by its own poison. They do not think of peace, love and solidarity in terms of concretely realizable social structures but only in terms of aesthetic mimesis. They rely on aesthetic utopianism because their subject–object model of dialectics remains trapped within the same philosophical metaphysics to which they impute the source of all violence. Thus they cannot find a way of transforming aesthetic utopianism into a more socially effective paradigm oriented to discursive redemption of validity-claims in everyday communicative action (see also Duvenage 2003).

There are certain problems with Habermas's view of art's place in modernity. Habermas has a habit of using the label 'aesthetic' too indiscriminately. He tends to describe anything as 'aestheticized' which does not neatly fit into his predefined system of communicat-ive rationality. He tends to refuse any sense in which the experiences he categorizes as 'aesthetic' might legitimately challenge the very construction of this system of communicative rationality, rather than simply constituting a sphere within it. This prejudice particularly affects his view of the French poststructuralist thinkers, to whom we now turn. We will return to further aspects of Habermas's critique of postmodernism shortly.

French aesthetic thought since 1945:
literary thinking after the Marquis de Sade

French writing on art and literature since the Second World War is informed by a variety of intellectual sources ranging from phenomenology, hermeneutics and psychoanalysis to semiotics and structural linguistics. Much of it is specifically literary in outlook, focusing on the distinctively literary problematics of signification, representation, narrative, authorship and textuality, rather than on more specifically sociological issues. However, there are several respects in which philosophical, anthropological and historical reflections come into productive dialogue with social-theoretic thinking about art in French writing. We begin here with a few remarks on some twentieth-century legacies of the eighteenth-century French writer, the Marquis de Sade. Then we discuss themes in the writing of Georges Bataille, Michel Foucault, Jacques Derrida and Gilles Deleuze, who each partly elaborate Sade's vision.

For a long time, Sade's outrageous novels about sexual debauchery, torture and rape have been viewed as deeply problematic pieces of writing that teeter on the brink of moral nihilism. However, at their core, they contain a set of rigorous reflections about the imbrication of reason and morality with power and terror and about the ambiguous interlacing of desire and pleasure with evil and transgression that cannot be dismissed as decadent fantasy. Sade inaugurates a line of thinking that runs throughout modern thinkers and writers such as Baudelaire, Huysmans, Poe, Wilde and Nietzsche.

Sade's inaugurating insight lies in his diagnosis of a number of striking paradoxes in both Catholic Christianity and secular humanism. On the one hand, Catholic Christianity officially proscribes the life of the senses and the flesh as sin, but unofficially exalts the life of the senses and the flesh in its rituals, its mysticism and its art. On the other hand, enlightened secular humanism openly legitimates the life of the senses and the flesh, but can find no metaphysically meaningful way of limiting and articulating the life of the senses and the flesh within a coherent balanced structure of restraint and excess. On the one hand, Catholic Christianity becomes constantly entangled in corruption, so that what it publicly calls virtue and purity effectively rests on despotism and hypocrisy, while what it publicly banishes as vice effectively means vitality and affirmation. On the other hand, the secular republican state claims to liberate its citizens from repression and to restore health to society. Yet its attendant lawyers, pedagogues, doctors and therapists effectively reduce pleasure and happiness to abstract utilitarian functions voided of vital meaning.

Sade concludes that in a rationalized secular world born of the demise of traditional religiosity, only crime, transgression and violation can restore meaning to ethical life. Sade's characters seek extremes of crime because they seek that sovereignty of self which alone can give meaning to moral restraints on the self. The self must transgress ethical limits in order first to *be* a self capable of ethical limitation. The self must transgress limits in order to set these limits for itself, for only then will the self truly be a self, rather than an automaton. Sade's fiction thus stands for a figure of aesthetic enlightenment. In the mirror of his imagination, Sade finds a world which has turned itself upside down, a world that betrays and perverts itself, first in religious hypocrisy and then in secular liberal humanism. This theme runs throughout numerous modern artists and theorists, from Adorno and Horkheimer's discussion of Sade's *Juliette* in *Dialectic of Enlightenment* to the theatre of Antonin Artaud, the cinema of Pier Paolo Pasolini and Luis Buñuel and the philosophical criticism of Pierre Klossowski.

Georges Bataille (2001) starts out from this Sadean thought of the limit and its transgression in a post-traditional world. Bataille begins from anthropological studies of prehistoric cave painting and tribal sacrifices, as well as from modern French poetry and surrealist painting. Central to Bataille's interests is his search for what he calls *expérience intérieure*. He searches beyond scientific positivism and behaviourism for what he calls the interior expressive self. He portrays the self as standing in a relationship of finitude to physical nature, to desire, and above all to death. He describes how primitive incest taboos and other boundaries between the sacred and profane marked out by feasting and sacrifice trigger energies of transgression and violation that are the creative fulfilment of interdictions. They are the excesses that first give meaning to moral law. In his writings on eroticism, Bataille describes how beauty is transgressed by soiling and denuding as purity and nobility are implicated in abasement through a fluid corrupting of borders between forms, substances and bodies, as well as between social classes. He sees beauty and the sublime as a dangerous involvement in terror and violence fuelled by a thirst for ecstatic self-annihilation. At the same time, this thirst for annihilation is sister to a stance of sovereign gratuity and generosity to others, of sovereign expenditure and play. Bataille sees art as protest against capitalism's demeaning rubric of thrift, economy and prudence. Art stands for hope in the possibility of an exceptional emotional communality, a defiance of the fragility and solitude of the self.

Michel Foucault (1998) also builds on Sade's, Nietzsche's and Bataille's thinking. In his writings on language and discursive practices, Foucault begins from Roland Barthes's theme of the 'death of the author' and from Maurice Blanchot's conception of authorial expropriation. Foucault's thinking has been described as 'post-structuralist' in so far as it takes its point of departure from Ferdinand de Saussure's semiotic theory of the differential character of textual meanings within bounded systems of signifying elements. Foucault radicalizes Saussure's conception, however, by asserting that even bounded systems of signifying elements acquire meanings only by their differential relationships to yet further bounded systems. This produces an endless deferral of sense which Foucault calls 'language to infinity'. Foucault writes that authors and originators are 'not an indefinite source of significations that fill a work' but 'a certain functional principle by which, in our culture, one limits, excludes and chooses . . . by which one impedes . . . the free composition, decomposition and recomposition of fiction' (1998: 221). Foucault argues that language cannot come into view as a stable object of reflection except in the degree to which both its speakers and its referents disappear from view – because language is not merely an instrument of communication. Language is rather the very medium of communication in which all identities of speaking subjects and all identities of represented objects are first constructed.

Foucault demonstrates this conception through numerous analyses of works of art and literature. He discusses René Magritte's famous painting of a pipe, *Ceci n'est pas une pipe*. Paradoxically, Magritte's painting only appears to succeed in its reference by failing in its reference: the painting is not a pipe – it is a painting of a pipe. Similarly, Foucault discusses the figure of Scheherazade in the tales of *The Thousand and One Nights*. In the Arabian tales, the bride Sheherazade tells a story each night to King Shariyar in order to stave off the day of her execution for her natural infidelity as a woman. Each story resumes the previous night's story and simultaneously defers its conclusion until the following night. Foucault here sees narration and fabulation as an endless warding off of silence, a desperate flight from the collapse of sense in the face of death. Speech is flight from what Foucault calls the 'thought of the outside' (*la pensée du dehors*). The 'thought of the outside' denotes the space vacated by the death of God, who once stood as a

7 **Diego Velázquez, *Las Meninas*, 1656.** Prado Museum, Madrid

transcendental guarantor of meaning but whose place has now been taken by stop-gap humanism and pragmatism.

In his meditation on the end of anthropocentric metaphysics, *The Order of Things*, Foucault famously opens with an interpretation of Diego Velázquez' *Las Meninas*, a seventeenth-century painting of a scene in the royal court of Philip IV of Spain from 1656–7 (see illustration 7). In the painting, Velázquez does not paint the King and Queen of Spain themselves. Instead he paints a painter painting the King and Queen, and their image is seen only in a mirror behind the royal maids (the *meninas*) who are bowing in greeting to the Infanta Margarita. Foucault here argues that 'man' and 'woman' – 'king and queen of nature' – appear only as coordinates within a scheme of representation. They do not appear within the scene of representation itself. 'Man' and 'woman' are absent to representation; they are empty signifiers.

In his late writings on 'care of the self' in *The History of Sexuality*, Foucault develops this anti-humanist thrust of his earlier thinking with reference to Greco-Roman stoic and epicurean ethics of the body. Foucault argues that modern subjects who search for the truth of themselves through scientized definitions of the self – through medicine and psychiatry – mistake the character of their existence. Personal enlightenment can occur only through a work of feeling, sensing, perceiving and thinking: through a work of *aisthesis*. Foucault argues that the self is a work of self-crafting and self-fashioning; the self is a work of art.

Jacques Derrida's reflections on art, writing and modernity share similar concerns to Foucault's with the ambivalence of sense and the elusiveness of ideas of authorship, intentionality and subjectivity. In *The Truth in Painting* (1987) – a title taken from a remark of Cézanne's to one of his patrons, '*je vous présente la verité – en peinture*' – Derrida deconstructs Heidegger's essay 'On Origin of the Work of Art'. Derrida questions how Heidegger can affirm art as a site of the presence of being, and hence of truth, while at the same time holding this truth to be 'concealed'. Heidegger appears not to see that his notion of the 'making present' of the world in the work implies just as much the possibility of *absence* of the world as of presence of the world. If marks of paint make the world present without resembling or 'representing' anything in the world, it is equally possible for the world to be absent from these marks, and hence for the work to slip out of the truth.

Derrida articulates this through some reflections on the symbolist poetry of Stephane Mallarmé. Mallarmé held that in the instant that a poem reaches its highest moment of self-subsistent being, when its words lose all determinate semantic sense and reverberate purely as sounds, worldhood is both absolutely present in the poem *and* absolutely absent from the poem. Derrida concludes that Heidegger's ontological hermeneutics does not 'overcome metaphysics'. Rather, Heidegger slips back into a 'metaphysics of presence'. Derrida writes that Heidegger evinces 'the most naively archaic regression into the element of ingenuous truth' (Derrida 1987: 354–5). Heidegger fails to come to terms with complexity and aporia in modernity. He is entangled in what Bernstein (1992) and Rose (1978) – both drawing on Benjamin – call modernity's condition of 'aesthetic alienation'. This condition affirms futurity and irreversibility of time even as it betrays a desire to return to the origin and the absolute. Modernity in this sense consists in an essential work of mourning; and the fate of modern art consists in an essential 'bereaving of beauty'.

Gilles Deleuze radicalizes Foucault's and Derrida's considerations on the crises of western metaphysics. Deleuze rejects all notion of an 'outside' realm of transcendence counterposed to an 'inside' realm of expressive interiority (Deleuze 1981; Deleuze and Guattari 1987). Deleuze abandons the idea of the artist as an expressive self suffering from a 'lack' of unfulfilled desire. He proposes that modern art comes to be less and less the expression of individual subjectivities set apart from 'external' physicality. Deleuze invokes the monistic worldview of the seventeenth-century Dutch philosopher Benedict de Spinoza. Spinoza held that God and nature are 'one substance', and therefore that everything that is ideal is identical to everything that is material. Following Spinoza, Deleuze argues that 'expression' and 'expressionism' today are little more than metaphors that try to let us come to terms with this identity of mind and matter. He does not interpret this postulate in the same manner as German idealist philosophy. No metaphysical distinctions are drawn between man and machine, soul and brain, spirit and computer. These for Deleuze are illusions of humanistic discourse. He argues that what is called art, poetry and philosophy are only different attributes of the modes of being and becoming of Spinoza's one physical substance. Thus Deleuze interprets writers, painters and film directors such as Kafka, Proust, Leopold von Sacher-Masoch, Francis Bacon, Robert Bresson and Jean-Luc Godard as exploring different relationships of aesthetic experience to the body, to corporeal trauma and desire, to dispersion and distention, to physical power, will, violence, technology and machine life. Deleuze (1986–9) interprets the cinematic image through Henri Bergson's conception of time-consciousness as pure experienced duration in moving forms on two-dimensional surfaces. He points to the salience of planes, plateaus, angles, movements and repetition as abstract sensory intensities devoid of any expressive closure or telos.

We may say that in their writings on art, Bataille, Foucault, Derrida and Deleuze each thematize different aspects of crisis in western philosophical metaphysics. These thinkers do not propound a sociology of art, nor a theory of art. However, their thinking is eminently concerned with the social and with the aesthetic. They treat literary and artistic forms as sources of normative insight into philosophical questions about religion, science, ethics and history. They show the extent to which all thought is shaped by aesthetic frameworks of perception. But they do not 'aestheticize' thought in any especially problematic sense. They do not 'collapse philosophy into literature and poetry', as Habermas (1987) contends. Their thinking is not 'postmodernist' in any sense of an outright abandonment of substantive modern values of rational conduct of life. However, their thinking certainly insists markedly on constitutive epistemological uncertainty and linguistic ambivalence. This has made it open to association with some of the thematic slogans of postmodernism. We will now need to see how elements of their thinking inform commentaries on postmodernism in late twentieth-century art and aesthetic culture.

Postmodernism

The term 'postmodernism' first became current in the early 1970s when it was used by the architects Charles Jencks and Robert Venturi to describe a new mode of pastiche and playful eclecticism in building aesthetics (Harvey 1990). The term soon took hold in art criticism to denote growing disaffection with high modernist assumptions of linear progress in art history. After the explosion of Pop Art in the 1960s, no particular art school or 'ism' could be said to follow in sequence as a spearhead movement. The 1960s and 1970s saw a plurality of more or less simultaneous movements ranging from minimalism and conceptualism to land art, body art, performance, installations and happenings. After the Second World War, New York had taken over from Paris as the centre of the art world, but by the 1970s no one city could claim a leading position. In this sense, postmodernism has been associated with spatial and temporal indeterminacy in art styles and movements, with 'decentring'. Postmodernism denotes a turning away from modernist principles of stylistic consistency and purity in favour of stylistic eclecticism. It suggests a mixing of genres and media. It suggests an embrace of the disparate and heterogeneous, the humorous and the vernacular, a celebration of surface, play, dispersal, combination and parataxis.

We will now review a number of contributions that relate postmodernist motifs in twentieth-century art and culture to more structural dynamics in the social conditions of late modernity.

Tracking the scent of the new disarray in aesthetic style, art critics of the 1970s began to rethink the meaning of modernism since the late nineteenth century. From the perspective of the cultural revolutions of the 1960s, modernism came to seem a rather exclusive affair, out of touch with popular life. Architects and designers such as Le Corbusier, Mies van der Rohe and Walter Gropius had stood for utopian social ideals. Yet their austere forms and urban plans did not seem made for human habitation. In some cases they looked uncannily close to the dreary high-rise tower blocks and mass housing projects of Soviet eastern Europe. A house, Le Corbusier once provocatively said, was 'a machine for living in'. Similarly, Adolf Loos declared that the goal of art was the 'union of form and function'. Modernist painters had once stood for revolutionary socialist ideas. Now their works appeared to have become sequestered away behind protective institutional doors.

The American critic Clement Greenberg has been seen as epitomizing this image of a cloistered modernist canon. Writing in the 1950s and 1960s, Greenberg deplored both surrealism and Pop Art as deviations from the true course of development of modern art. Greenberg asserted that innovation consisted 'in the use of the characteristic methods of a discipline to criticize the discipline itself, not in order to subvert it but in order to entrench it more firmly in its area of competence' (1993: 85). Greenberg championed abstract expressionism and hard-edge abstraction of the 1950s, arguing that they alone fulfilled authentic modernist principles of fidelity to the two-dimensional properties of the flat canvas. In a similar spirit to the Frankfurt School, Greenberg took a derogatory view of 'mass culture'. He spoke of 'kitsch' as trafficking in 'vicarious experience and faked sensations', in 'academicized simulacra of genuine culture' (1961: 10).

Greenberg's vision is repudiated by numerous critics of the 1970s and 1980s who point to constant interaction between modernist art and popular culture. Rosalind Krauss (1985) speaks of the 'modernist myth' of an irreversible canon, sacredly set apart from daily repetition, founded in 'depth', 'originality' and 'singularity'. Drawing on Roland Barthes (1972), Krauss shows how modernist artists combine and substitute elements from already circulating systems of signs in everyday urban life. Artists do not so much invent new signifiers as recombine them from matrices of forms, images, surfaces and myth structures in the social imaginary.

Similarly, Andreas Huyssen (1986) argues that modernism arose essentially out of a reaction to 'mass culture'. Huyssen argues that modernism's concern was to police a 'great divide' between itself and the 'mass'. Modernism 'constituted itself through a conscious strategy of exclusion, an anxiety of contamination by its other' (1986: vii). But modernism first emerged out of the streets, the cafés and the dance halls. 'High' and 'low' were always secretly interdependent. Huyssen describes mass culture as modernism's 'family ghost rumbling in the cellar'. Following Peter Bürger, Huyssen proposes a distinction between modernism and the avant-garde. While modernism eventually became an institutionalized formation, the avant-garde actively participated in mass cultural life. Huyssen associates the avant-garde in the 1920s and 1930s with Dada, with political cartoon satire, with factory workers' theatre and cabaret. Huyssen argues that Beat writers and Pop artists of the 1960s were the first to reinvigorate this spirit of a popular transgressive avant-garde. Huyssen sees 1960s pop culture as a first wave of postmodernist cultural contestation. This was then followed by a second wave of the 1970s and 1980s which saw a greater presence of the decorative and a diminution of the rebellious.

Huyssen's account is similar in some respects to Peter Sloterdijk's conception of postmodernism as sensual revolt, satirical laughter and bodily defiance. In his *Critique of Cynical Reason*, Sloterdijk links postmodernism to the ancient Greek figure of Diogenes, resister of Alexander the Great's imperialism, a 'kynic' in the ancient Greek sense of pleasure-seeking anarchist sceptic but not a 'cynic' in the modern sense of either dominator or defeatist (Sloterdijk 1988).

Arthur Danto (1997) speaks of a 'post-historical' condition of contemporary art. Revisiting his earlier writings on art worlds and his reconstruction of Hegel's thesis of the end of art, Danto argues that art no longer supports any 'master narrative' of sequences of development. He criticizes Greenberg by arguing that art's increasing self-referentiality in the later twentieth century is not a sign of any particular norm that works of art need to satisfy in order to count as Art. On the contrary, it is a sign of the exhaustion of any particular dominant norm, or set of norms, for art. Since the 1970s, art has followed 'after the end of Art'. Today there are no norms of appearance to which works of art need conform in order to be Art. 'There is no a priori constraint on how works of art must look – they can look like anything at all,' Danto writes (1997: 16). In this sense, art today returns to a condition of indeterminacy like that before the rise of the idea of Art in Renaissance Europe: before the rise of manifestos, programmes and 'isms' of Art.

We now consider two further theorizations that relate postmodernism in art to facets of late modern consumer culture and to philosophical self-images of modernity. These are the contributions of Jean Baudrillard and Jean-François Lyotard.

Baudrillard begins from Benjamin's essay on 'The Work of Art in the Age of Mechanical Reproduction'. Baudrillard (1985, 1997, 2001) argues that 'original' works of art no longer exist: only copies exist, and copies of copies – copies indistinguishable from their objects. Only 'simulacra' and 'simulations' exist: only photographic replications and filmic surfaces without real-world reference. A 'simulacrum' in Christian theology meant a false appearance of the divine that 'dissimulates' the presence of God. Today simulacra are neither false nor true. What is 'real' collapses into the imaginary. Social reality implodes into the system of the mass media whose images are 'more real than the real'. Baudrillard speaks in this sense of an 'ecstasy of communication' which substitutes circulations of information for real-world interaction. Baudrillard understands postmodern culture as a condition of positivity which, like cancer, recognizes no relationship to absence and negation, no 'symbolic exchange with death'. Spectacular architectural projects such as the Pompidou Centre and the Arc de la Défense in Paris do not integrate social space; they suck their surrounding urban environments into a vacuum, like black holes. Baudrillard judges that while such projects seek escape from the banal, they are fatefully seduced by the banal. He compares their attraction to the logic of 'fashion', which he defines as 'the beautiful that has absorbed all the energy of the ugly'. As 'simulation is the ecstasy of the real', so 'fashion is the ecstasy of the beautiful: the pure and empty form of a spiralling aesthetics' (2001: 190).

However, Baudrillard argues polemically that sociological analysis of culture has no purchase on its object unless it itself takes the risk of fateful seduction by the mediatized and banalized. According to Baudrillard, normative concepts of 'critique' and 'negation' do not challenge the system; they enable it to reproduce itself. Baudrillard wagers that thought is more critical when it risks abandoning 'critique'. In this sense he proposes a form of semiotics of evil where 'evil' (*le mal*) connotes specular vacuity. Baudelaire's *fleurs du mal* for Baudrillard are television, advertising and consumer culture. Where Benjamin's and Adorno's strategy is to negate evil dialectically, Baudrillard's strategy is to play with evil, 'fatally' and 'ironically'.

Lyotard's postmodernism is less nihilistic than Baudrillard's and is more concerned with normative philosophical discourses of modernity. Lyotard (1984a) particularly opposes Habermas's sub-ordination of aesthetic life to a component 'sphere' of reason. Lyotard views this as a legislative appropriation, potentially destructive of liberating antagonisms and 'differends' between language-games. He looks for a more subversive aesthetic sensibility, beyond what he sees as the implicitly controlling claims of Frankfurt School critical theory. He prosecutes this quest through a rereading of Kant's *Critique of Judgement*, pointing to Kant's account of the sublime as an experience of ideas of reason beyond all stable categories of representation. Lyotard argues that like Kant's sublime, postmodern art 'presents the unpresentable'. Postmodern art presents what cannot be presented under determinate categories. Postmodern art is the sensuous which creates the thought of the unpresentable.

Lyotard observes that modern art begins this passage away from realism and representation towards abstract presentation of the invisible, in the yearning for a presence which is absent. Postmodern art, however, goes further. The modern work is Proust's mourning for lost time. The postmodern work is Joyce's joyously transient signifiers. The postmodern work is in search of what already will have been done: the post-modo. Lyotard writes that 'a work can become modern only if it is first postmodern. Postmodernism thus understood is not modernism at its end but in the nascent state, and this state is constant' (1984a: 79). Works of art are not modern unless they anticipate their own transience, as having already become what they are. When modern art projects itself in the mode of the future perfect tense – as what will-have-been-done – it becomes postmodern and it repeats itself.

Both Baudrillard and Lyotard argue from the standpoint of a left radicalism that harbours doubts about classical enlightenment projects of universal critique. To understand these kinds of intervention in a more focused light, we need to broaden our discussion at this point and grasp some respects in which postmodern motifs articulate struc-tures of advanced capitalist production and consumption in late modern society. Two notable commentators in this regard are Fredric Jameson and David Harvey.

Jameson speaks of a postmodern aesthetic of 'random cannibaliza-tion of all the styles of the past', a 'play of random stylistic allusion' (1991: 18). This aesthetic is characterized by the disappearance of historicity behind pastiche, quotation and intertextuality. Jameson points to buildings such as the Bonaventure Hotel in Los Angeles, the Piazza Italia in New Orleans, and the vernacular popular architecture of Frank Gehry. These forms evince a flattening out of reference into pure surface. Jameson contrasts Van Gogh's peasant shoes and Edvard Munch's expressionist painting *The Scream* with Andy Warhol's *Diamond Dust Shoes*. Warhol's glitzy image ironizes its own absence of expressive memory and personal signature. Jameson argues that such forms attest to a 'waning of affect', a fracturing of subjectivity, a new 'depthlessness'. In the pop music video, the TV commercial and the advertising jingle, temporality is frozen into a schizophrenic present, into 'disconnected, discontinuous material signifiers which fail to link up into a coherent sequence' (1985: 119). Each isolated moment becomes more intense, present, vivid and immediate as signifiers collapse into the purely literal. The world 'threatens to become a glossy skin, a stereoscopic illusion, a rush of filmic images without density' (1984: 120). Harvey (1990) comments similarly on the highly spatialized, entropic character of late twentieth-century urban cityscapes, most archetypally in the city of Los Angeles. Historical contexts of social relations of production are here hollowed out behind specular surfaces. Films such as Ridley Scott's *Blade Runner* and Wim Wenders' *Wings of Desire* investigate this sense of spatiotemporal directionlessness, marked by a retreat of human singularity behind replication and repetition.

Jameson and Harvey both demonstrate postmodernism's symbolic erasure of real material relations of production. They highlight the significance of the nostalgia photograph, the factory warehouse turned café bar, the air-conditioned open-plan office, the super-smooth glass elevator. They deploy Ernest Mandel's concept of 'late capitalism' to show how postmodern cultural forms emanate from deregulated 'flexible' systems of capitalist production, distribution and consumption. They do not assert absolute causal determination of cultural superstructures by an economic base; they acknowledge relative autonomy and asynchrony of aesthetic and semiotic codes in relation to political and economic systems. But they show how postmodern cultural forms nonetheless articulate definite shifts in the structures of capitalist organization in the late twentieth century. They point to more and more ephemeral market trends and niches; to faster turnover rates, faster design variations and faster obsolescence calculations in consumer goods; to production systems driven more and more by information technology; and to consumption practices driven by mediated lifestyle images and signs.

Jameson's and Harvey's observations raise political issues about postmodernism which have prompted many recent contributors to move away from its governing assumptions. It is to these contributors that we now turn.

Beyond postmodernism: autonomy and reflexivity

Critical reflection on contemporary society would suggest that while modernism as a specific idiom of artistic representation now belongs to the past, modernity remains the only rationally defensible horizon for our present age and has not been definitively 'transcended' by postmodernism. As T. J. Clark has eloquently written,

> it is just because the 'modernity' which modernism prophesied has finally arrived that the forms of representation it originally gave rise to are now unreadable. (Or readable only under some dismissive fantasy rubric – of 'purism', opticality, formalism, elitism, etc.) The intervening (and interminable) holocaust was modernisation. Modernism is unintelligible now because it had truck with a modernity not yet fully in place. Post-modernism mistakes the ruins of those previous representations, or the fact that from where we stand they seem ruinous, for the ruin of modernity itself – not seeing that what we are living through is modernity's triumph. (1999: 2–3)

We now discuss some developments beyond postmodernism in recent social and aesthetic theory. We begin with the concept of 'reflexive modernity'.

Beck, Giddens and Lash (1994) propose conceptualizing postmodernism as a further dimension of 'reflexivity' within modernity itself. To apply Beck, Giddens and Lash's proposal to postmodernism in art is to see late twentieth-century art as not necessarily abrogating ideas of critique and enlightenment. It is to see it as framing these ideas in a more nuanced and distanced manner that tries to save them from dogmatism and from possible ossification within established institutions. In this sense we can say that art worlds in recent decades have become more institutionally self-aware, more responsive to public dialogue, less compromised by problematic discriminations in favour of particular provenances and canons of art at the expense of others. Compared with the 1950s, western art worlds are more inclusive of women and non-white majority artists, more egalitarian in their selection of exhibition themes and programmes; and public audiences for art have become more numerous and more diverse. Art has become a more socially participatory opportunity for broader sections of the public. Along these lines, Lash comments that late twentieth-century art gives explicit recognition both to cohabitation and co-originarity between 'high' and 'low' and to historically marginalized and occluded cultural identities in social life (Beck, Giddens and Lash 1994: 135–43).

These considerations suggest that even as the field of aesthetics undergoes manifold transformations at different stages of modernity, becoming fuzzier at its edges and more self-consciously involved in cultural identity contestation, it does not lose its basic aspect of relative autonomous validity. Art does not lose its ability to sustain practices of intersubjective communication about aesthetic value. Even as genres and taste cultures cut across one another and institutional 'great divides' dissolve away, possible argumentation about value in works of art is not jeopardized. We now discuss several recent European theorists who elaborate this continuing possibility of socially engaged aesthetic evaluation, turning first to the work of Albrecht Wellmer.

Originally an associate of the Frankfurt School in the 1960s, Wellmer (1992) argues that postmodernism throws out the baby of aesthetic enlightenment with the bathwater of modernist dogma. Postmodernism overlooks 'the dialectic of modernity and postmodernity'. Wellmer argues that Lyotard's discourse of the sublime is an inadequate account of how art can open up consciousness and transfigure social relations. It needs correcting by a stronger orientation to conceptual negativity. However, Wellmer argues that Lyotard does point to some respects in which Adorno's conception of truth in art requires greater thematization of feeling and affect in aesthetic experience. Wellmer argues that when Lyotard's emphasis on affectivity is combined with Habermas's insistence on communicability, Adorno's conception of truth can be reconstructively defended. Wellmer proposes understanding truth in art as a 'phenomenon of interference' between multiple dimensions of validity. Truth in art must be neither assimilated to cognitive representation, nor collapsed into affective intensity. Enlightening art can be shown to point to 'open structures of a no longer rigid type of individualization and socialization' and hence to a 'real utopia of non-violent communication'. But in so far as it does so, 'it is not the illusory presence of a condition that does not yet exist but the provocative latency of a process which begins with the transposition of aesthetic experience into symbolic or communicative action' (1992: 21).

Franz Koppe, Martin Seel and Christoph Menke each develop Wellmer's proposal in various ways (Harrington 2001). Koppe (1983) proposes that works of art enter into contexts of communication as objects that heighten our powers of communication by giving reflective expression to intersubjectively shared needs for sense-making in lived experience. The extent to which works of art articulate these needs truthfully and insightfully is the extent to which they are aesthetically impressive. The extent to which they betray these needs by making unfulfilled needs look fulfilled is the extent to which they are aesthetically poor. It is the extent to which they are 'illusory' and 'ideological'. It is the extent to which they obscure experience.

Martin Seel (1985) begins from John Dewey's (1934) philosophical pragmatist conception of 'art as experience'. Seel argues that value in art arises from the way works of art transfigure everyday experience. Works of art evoke ways of seeing, ways of 'making experience' (*Erfahrung machen*) out of the experience we already 'have' (*Erfahrung haben*). In Nelson Goodman's (1978) terms, works of art evoke 'ways of world-making': ways of exemplifying phenomena under semiotic systems that depart from stable discursive systems. Works of art thus impart experiential meanings that could not otherwise be conveyed through the propositional structure of theoretical discourse or through prescriptive moral-practical discourse. Those works which enlighten us about our world and our social relations to others elicit aesthetic approval. We thereby judge them 'successful'. Aesthetically successful works make use of their sensory media in a way that extends our horizons of perception and challenges our understanding. Aesthetically unsuccessful works only repeat or reproduce a perspective we already have (as in cliché), or refer to the world too literally (as in excessively realist art), or fail to mediate the aesthetic with the moral-practical (as in excessively moralistic, propagandist art). In each case, however, the successful work must always be shown to be successful through intersubjective argumentation supported by demonstrative reference to qualities of perceptual experience.

Christoph Menke (1998) argues that art in modernity achieves not only autonomy but also 'sovereignty'. By 'sovereignty', Menke means art's ability to raise claims against rationality at the same time as it is itself fostered by rationality. Art is sovereign in its ability to challenge, stretch and outbid rational thinking, even as it is itself a moment in reason's own criticism of itself. Art is both responsive to rational communication and sovereign in its aesthetic negativity. In its sovereign aesthetic negativity, art constantly annihilates itself and constantly reforms itself.

Similarly, the Belgian art theorist Thierry de Duve argues for a way of synthesizing Kantian aesthetics with relativizing historical consciousness. Duve (1996) argues that Kant can be read both 'after' and 'according to' (*d'après*) the legacy of Marcel Duchamp. On the one hand, institutional conferrals of art status on everyday objects are not merely classificatory acts; they are valuations responsive to intersubjectively shared experience. On the other hand, aesthetic experience of art depends on critical engagement with sociohistorical constructions of 'art'. In this sense Duve sees contemporary aesthetic understanding as at once modern and postmodern. Aesthetic understanding is postmodern in so far as art's institution is constantly being 'ended'. But it remains modern in so far as this very 'ending' constantly renews art's institution at another level. We can say that modernity modernizes itself. Modernity detraditionalizes tradition, but modernity lapses into its own traditionalism unless it continually modernizes its own process, reflexively and recursively.

We will now consider one final thematization of this reflexivity in the social systems theory of Niklas Luhmann.

In *Art as a Social System* (2000), Luhmann traces art's historical evolution towards an increasingly autonomous 'social system'. Luhmann's analysis is in this respect similar to Max Weber's and other classical narratives of modernization. However, Luhmann differs from classical sociology in his fundamental contention that social life cannot be conceived either exclusively in terms of intentional action (as with Weberian interpretive sociology) or exclusively in terms of structural functions of action (as with functionalist sociology in the school of Talcott Parsons). Rather, Luhmann argues that social life must be theorized in terms of 'communication' between social systems, where 'communication' refers not only to linguistic communication between human individuals but also to global information circulation between complex societal configurations, such as between the market and the state, civil law and public policy, and so on. Luhmann describes social systems as self-creating or 'autopoietic' in the sense that they come into existence by emergence from elements seceding from other systems that have ceased to be functional in relation to an environment. For example, we can say that in nineteenth-century England an urban industrial economic system replaced an agricultural economic system as land values in the countryside ceased to be competitive in relation to land in the cities.

Luhmann writes that art 'participates in society by differentiating itself as a system, which subjects art to a logic of operative closure – just like any other functional system' (2000: 134). Luhmann declares that he is 'not primarily concerned with problems of causality, of society's influence on art and of art on society', and that neither does he 'advocate the defensive attitude that the autonomy of art ought to be upheld and protected'. Modern art is autonomous purely in the sense that at a certain point in the functional differentiation of (western) society – around the time of the Renaissance and the first inroads against fixed status stratification in the Middle Ages – a type of societal communication emerged by splitting off from the surrounding environments of the church and the royal courts to form its own social system. Luhmann proposes that this new social system of art specialized in 'communicating the limits of communication'; that is, in communicating the breakdown of stable representation systems. Art in this sense is the specific integration of perception into communication in the medium of the binary code of beautiful/not-beautiful.

Luhmann argues that today 'the function of art is not (or no longer) to represent or idealize the world, nor does it consist in a "critique" of society':

> Once art becomes autonomous, the emphasis shifts from hetero-reference to self-reference – which is not the same as self-isolation, not *l'art pour l'art*.
>
> Art has no ambition to redeem society by exercising aesthetic control over an expanded realm of possibility. . . . The function of art . . . is to make the world appear within the world. (2000: 149)

Art's principal function is to assist in the construction of a distinction in social consciousness between 'reality' and 'imagination'. In the course of modernity, as art passes through the movements of realism, expressionism and abstraction, art performs this operation with ever sharper acts of self-reference. Art invents its own theoretical organon, which is called 'criticism' and 'aesthetics'. Luhmann says that in the twentieth-century avant-garde, art 're-includes what it excludes'. Art incorporates what is traditionally seen as opposed to art, namely ordinary objects, 'junk material', 'trash'. Thus even as art appears to dissolve into mass culture, the identity and functional autonomy of aesthetic communication remains. Aesthetic autonomy remains in so far as art remains a self-generating autopoietic system.

There are certain problems with Luhmann's systems theory of art. From an empirical point of view, Luhmann has strangely little to say about art institutions, such as galleries, dealers and publishers, and even less about important cross-penetrations of art by other social systems, such as by commerce, politics and the media (Sevänen

2001). From a normative point of view, Luhmann conveys little sense of the conditions of discursive power under which aesthetic discriminations come to be asserted and defended. He tends to take aesthetic valuations as social givens, frozen in historical process, so that acts of contestation over cultural hegemony appear as so many outcomes of functional relationships between social systems, not as flesh-and-blood disputes over worth and power. In this respect, his account suffers from some rather scientistic shortcomings. His assertion that art no longer consists in critique of society can be contested.

But Luhmann's account is, nonetheless, an important contribution which complements the arguments of other recent theorists about art's persisting claim to autonomy, even in times characterized for many people today by processes of fluidization, homogenization and 'globalization' in cultural life. We now turn to this problematic condition of 'globalization' and its significance for the future of artistic life.

Globalization and the arts

The concept of globalization has many contested definitions in contemporary discourse. However, a general consensus prevails that globalization refers primarily in an economic sense to the worldwide penetration and integration of capitalist markets through neoliberal state policies of free trade. Globalization in a political sense of universally binding structures of international law today lags far behind globalization in this economic sense. But globalization in a cultural sense of interconnecting worldwide networks of social communication is undoubtedly an advanced tendency of our age. In the following we review some of the most striking effects of economic globalization on contemporary artistic life. We concentrate on commercial intervention in arts funding; on new kinds of media involvement in the arts; on processes of 'de-differentiation' between cultural and economic fields; and on the nature and direction of artistic protest.

We have already discussed some aspects of the erosion of state arts funding since the 1980s (chapter 3). Although we stressed that public arts institutions have always been embedded in market environments, it is important to make a sober assessment of the current global intensity of commercial pressures on cultural policy and arts funding decisions.

In an important study of corporate involvement in arts institutions since the 1980s, Chin-tao Wu (2002) shows how commercial
sponsors have moved from being relatively low-profile financial
supporters of arts events to high-profile active promoters and
effective joint organizers of arts events. Contemporary commercial
arts sponsorship no longer consists of relatively simple agreements
between art galleries and companies according to which companies
donate funds in return for a conspicuous display of their name.
Today, commercial agents possess considerably enhanced power to
determine how arts events are themselves programmed, constructed
and organized. Many contemporary arts institutions possess insuffi-
cient capital resources fully to determine their own decisions about
programme contents prior to soliciting sponsors. Their financial
dependence on renewed sources of external sponsorship is such
that management decisions can be commercially determined in very
striking ways. Some typical consequences of this since the 1980s
have been policies aimed at boosting visitor numbers through blockbuster exhibitions; through shops, cafés, merchandising and media
publicity drives; through building extensions and renovations named
after corporate donors; as well as arts events staged on corporate
premises, and travelling corporate art collections.

In the case of corporate-funded art prizes, Wu shows how
commercial agents assume a role of public adjudicators of artistic
taste. They thereby graft themselves onto pre-existing structures of
the art world. Wu modifies Bourdieu's theory of elite habitus to
propose that the new 'Medici of the enterprise culture' (Wu alludes
to the Medici family of Renaissance Florence) accumulate cultural
capital for purposes of conversion into social capital, for business
networking, image refining and alliance building. This social capital
ultimately serves conversion into economic capital. Wu discusses
the case of the British advertising agent Charles Saatchi, collector
of works by 'young British artists'. Charles Saatchi's well-publicized
exhibitions of these works in the 1990s generated intense media
attention and ultimately profit for his own business.

Developing Wu's analysis, we can say that the elites who exercise
greatest real power over arts institutions today are no longer wealthy
industrialists or members of the landed gentry seeking to legitimate
their wealth through charitable donations. Nor are they traditional
middle-class elites educated at prestigious schools and universities
and employed by the state as civil servants. The new elites are
commercial elites, most often composed of executives in the media
and entertainment industries. In contrast to traditional gentlemanly

elites, the new commercial elites have a greater interest in the short-term reconvertibility of cultural capital back into economic capital.

Increased corporate intervention in arts funding has not come without a certain degree of active encouragement by national governments. Commercial arts sponsorship has increased in conjunction with government drives to boost tourist revenues through regional cultural development projects in alliance with local business. Discussing the policies of the French culture ministry under the presidency of François Mitterrand, including notably the renovation of the Louvre, Marc Fumaroli (1992) writes of the policies of governments aimed at marketing the treasures of their national histories on a competitive global stage. Fumaroli argues that the French model of apparently benign state protection that resists full-scale privatization of public goods is not less vulnerable in principle to 'theme park effects' than Anglo-Saxon models. In the French case, the state retains more of a monopoly over arts institutions, but the principles of this monopoly remain no less commercial.

Increased commercial involvement in tandem with increased media publicity for the arts certainly appears to have been accompanied by greater popular participation in arts events compared with earlier decades of the twentieth century. Convergence in 'taste cultures' and equalization of prestige between 'high' and 'low' have been facilitated by greater public promotion of arts events through increased television, radio, newspaper and magazine coverage. In some cases, these processes have become the subject of analysis by artists themselves. Numerous contemporary artists thematize new media and new social mediatization tendencies in their artistic statements and interventions. Today it is even possible to assert that the paradigmatic art media of modernity are no longer film and photography but TV, video, digital processing and the computer interface.

In a provocative study of mediatization tendencies in British art of the 1990s, Julian Stallabrass (1999) describes a condition of art in which artists pour ridicule on public media hysteria and media sensationalism while themselves simultaneously courting such sensationalism in their own performances. Stallabrass speaks of a condition of 'high art lite', where artists claim to subvert the stuffiness of traditional high culture in the name of accessible communication. The artists heap further media attention on themselves but do not necessarily challenge dominant distributions of power. Stallabrass's thesis is open to debate, but his general analysis raises trenchant questions about the prospects for genuine democracy and genuine social enlightenment in art in an age dominated by globalized mass media publicity for the arts.

Increased commercial media involvement in the arts is closely related to what several commentators have referred to as processes of structural 'de-differentiation' between cultural and economic fields. 'De-differentiation' here refers to a blurring of distinctions between money and art as bearers of value. Some commentators have argued that money and art are merging into one another in a zone of diffuseness characterized by 'lifestyle aesthetics' (Welsch 1997). Although there have been many classic statements of such theses reaching back to the work of Simmel, contemporary conditions appear to lend added weight to the proposal. One of the most interesting contemporary theorizations is Luc Boltanski's and Ève Chiapello's study of the sociology of neoliberal economic discourse. Boltanski and Chiapello (1999) speak of a 'new spirit of capitalism' founded on a certain idea of 'artistic critique'. They argue that since the shift towards policies of economic deregulation since the 1980s, new forms of convergence have been occurring between business management and a certain idea of 'art'. 'Artistic critique' has been co-opted into 'enterprise culture'. Post-1960s youth rebellion is now a part of the system of 'enterprise creativity'. Where artists might once have seen themselves as mortal enemies of managers, some artists today have become forms of 'managers', and some managers have become forms of 'artists' (Chiapello 1998). Contemporary business managers characteristically employ aestheticized vocabularies of 'vision', 'innovation', 'creativity' and 'inspiration' in their approaches to cost-saving, productivity and competitiveness and to product marketing and branding. Boltanski and Chiapello argue that this commercial aestheticism arises out of a drive to silence more fundamental forms of critique aimed at the system of erosions of employment rights on which such discourse is founded. The new spirit of capitalism is an aestheticizing subterfuge that attempts to buy into the politics of multiculturalism, environmentalism and youth culture.

These aestheticizing tendencies of business management are paralleled to a certain degree by changing economic fortunes and lifestyles among contemporary artists. In recent years, many western cities have seen the emergence of gentrified bohemian zones populated by relatively affluent arts workers and journalists rubbing shoulders with media stars, celebrity actors and corporate agents. This situation largely contrasts with the economic fortunes and social opportunities of most artists and writers in earlier decades of the twentieth century.

Thomas Mann, in an early novella from 1903, set in nineteenth-century Protestant Hamburg, tells a story about a young aspiring artist brought up by his parents to follow in the family business. In the story of *Tonio Kröger*, Mann's character defies his parents' expectations and dedicates himself to a life of art. Tonio Kröger's psychological predicament is that he cannot reconcile his idea of art as his own authentic 'calling', his vocation, with his family's assumption of the vocation of business. Max Weber's 'Protestant ethic' and the 'spirit of capitalism' are fundamentally antithetical to Tonio Kröger's understanding of the calling of art. Thus Tonio Kröger experiences an irreconcilable tension between business and art. We may say that today this tension between business and art appears to have been transcended in the ethos of enterprise culture.

From a normative point of view, however, we may assert that the tension exists more than ever before. From a normative point of view, we may suggest that there can be no 'profession of art'. Art is not business, and art cannot be reconciled with business. From a normative point of view, we may suggest that there can be no such thing as 'cultural capital'. Culture is not capital, and culture cannot be reconciled with capital. To speak with the Frankfurt School, the enterprise culture's attempt to reconcile culture and capital is reification. The enterprise culture pretends to a false transcendence of the antinomy of instrumental and expressive action. It pretends to resolve work into play, calculation into creativity, economy into generosity. What Adorno defined as resistance to instrumental reason the enterprise culture tries to appropriate as its own medium of domination. Modernity's normative idea of art as autonomous creativity implies that even as artists strive to make a living from their art, their artistic action is free, spontaneous and uncalculating. Art is not a means to an end; it is its own end; and in so far as it is its own end, it is a protest against the reduction of life purely to means and instruments of achieving ends. Art is protest against instrumentalization of experienced values. Art is protest against alienation, reification and commodification. It is the sensuous work of freedom.

We may therefore conclude that modernity's normative idea of artistic protest has not fundamentally changed since the rise of postmodernism. Artistic protest has only changed in some of its modes, strategies and sites of expression. Under contemporary conditions of capitalistic globalization, new media technologies make possible a certain global diffusion and global integration of sites of artistic protest against oppression and injustice. Today some of the very facilitating technologies of capitalist expansion are open to being turned against the system by artistic action. In the world today, artists have a role to play as witnesses to suffering and exploitation in forgotten corners of the globe; as catalysts and canalizers of non-violent anarchic energies from peripheries to centres; as champions of carnival, contestation and defiance against imperialism and militarism; as keepers of hope, imagination, courage and trust that 'another world is possible'.

Conclusion

We have considered a range of thinkers who broaden, diversify and qualify some of the ideas associated with modernism in art and social theory. Some of these thinkers introduce elements of thought that have become associated with postmodernism in contemporary cultural discourse. German thinkers such as Heidegger and Gadamer thematize cultural traditions beyond the horizons of enlightenment rationalism. Others such as Habermas, Jauss, Bürger and Wellmer argue for more 'communicative', more 'dialogical' understandings of the agendas of social and political enlightenment in art. French thinkers such Bataille, Foucault, Derrida and Deleuze reveal paradoxes and contradictions in the art and literature of modern western philosophical self-consciousness. Postmodernism refers to various motifs in the art, architecture, literature and popular culture of late twentieth-century society that articulate these questioning attitudes to modernity. It unties some of the governing metaphysical ruses of modernism that privilege originality above repetition, depth above surface, consistency above eclecticism. But postmodernism is not tenable as the normative assertion of a condition of 'postmodernity' after modernity. Postmodernism is best understood as a further dimension of reflexivity within modernity itself. Capitalistic globalization demonstrates the urgency of ways of thinking about cultural and aesthetic value that challenge simplistic proclamations of the end of orientations towards universal discursive determination of the most ethical goals of social life. If postmodernism is the beauty, capitalistic globalization is the beast.

Conclusion

We have sought to demonstrate a conception of the relevance of social theory to questions of art and aesthetics that shows how art objects and practices can figure at once as thematic subjects of sociological analysis and as normative sources of social understanding in their own right. We have argued that art objects and practices do not sustain treatment in strictly value-neutral scientific terms. If art objects and practices are to form subjects of sociological analysis at all, they should be understood as theoretical partners in the construction of statements about themselves and about the relations of social practices on which they throw light. We have therefore argued that social theory should seek to mediate between value-distanciating methods in social science and the value-affirming impulses of those disciplines of the humanities in which art objects and practices are recognized as imparting sources of existential insight for life and experience. Social theory should seek to foster an understanding of art in which art objects and practices are experienced as value-relevant sources of sensuous knowledge.

However, we have seen that social theory confronts many profound problems of conflicting epistemological standpoints in its various attempts to accomplish this task. We will summarize these problems here in terms of five constitutive antinomies of social-theoretic thinking about the arts.

A first antinomy obtains between what Norbert Elias (1987) has called 'involvement and detachment'. Social theory of the arts moves between engagement for values and detached self-distanciation from values. On the one hand, it considers art from the standpoint of aesthetic values of beauty and grace and from the standpoint of moral and political values of goodness and rightness. On the other hand, it stands back from these values and tries to widen the range of knowable social states of affairs in relation to which they can be affirmed. Involvement without detachment leads to dogmatism, moralism and prescriptivism. Detachment without involvement leads to scientific irrelevancy, positivism and descriptivism.

A second antinomy obtains between transcendentalism and relativism. Many traditional metaphysical ideas of art assert conceptions of art that claim transcendental validity. These include Platonic ideas of essences of beauty, as well as many neo-Platonic conceptions of art in western culture. In contrast, many sociological and sociohistorical approaches to art emphasize the relativity of all conceptions of art to historically specific frameworks of social perception, to social institutions and social power relations. The metaphysical conceptions invariably turn out to be culturally shortsighted and exclusionary. But the relativizing approaches run a risk of reducing questions of value in art to questions of social group convention and behaviour. They run a risk of relinquishing any attempt to demonstrate rational grounds for general agreements about aesthetic value. Aesthetic value therefore has to be presumed to be more than relative to social group situations. It has to be assumed to be capable of universalization. But it cannot be asserted as universal by reference to any a priori authority.

A third antinomy obtains between objectivism and subjectivism. On the one hand, aesthetic judgements are capable of being argued about; and to the extent that they are capable of being argued about, they are capable of objectivity. However, aesthetic judgements are not capable of objectivity in the same sense in which scientific statements are capable of objectivity. Aesthetic judgements are essentially rooted in subjective responses of sensuous pleasure and displeasure to lived experiences. Approaches in social studies of the arts that deny these subjective roots of aesthetic experience are guilty of objectivism. They effectively assimilate aesthetic experience to putatively objective facts of history, or to classificatory declarations by institutional authorities, or to structural 'social functions'. On the other hand, aesthetic judgements are not reducible to pure sense reactions in individual subjects. Aesthetic judgements are more than sensate consumption. They are an attempt to discern intersubjective value in perceptual experience through critical communication. Approaches that fail to recognize this discursive dimension in aesthetic appraisal are guilty of subjectivism. They effectively reduce aesthetic valuation to consuming behaviour.

A fourth antinomy obtains between autonomy and heteronomy. In the eighteenth century, Kant and several other writers affirmed that art objects were to be appreciated under states of 'disinterested contemplation'. These writers affirmed the autonomy of aesthetic judgement in relation to considerations of practical utility and scientific veracity. But ideas of the autonomy of aesthetics are open to question on both empirical grounds and some normative grounds. From a historical-sociological point of view, art objects are not autonomous: they serve a wide range of social functions, interests and purposes, from decoration and entertainment to group status-marking; and they are consumed by different social classes and groups in different practices of cultural 'habitus'. In addition, from a normative point of view, art objects are not absolutely exempt from moral and political criticism. The doctrine of 'art for art's sake' is an indefensible ideological conception. But aesthetic experience nonetheless remains distinct from scientific analysis of the world and from moral criticism of the world. It composes its own sphere of normative validity. Art objects are the embodiments of this relatively autonomous sphere in society. They are therefore at once heteronomous in their empirical existence and relatively autonomous in their normative principle. They are at once their 'own law' and not their 'own law'.

A fifth and final antinomy obtains between modernism and postmodernism. Modernism as a definite stylistic idiom in art, architecture and literature of the nineteenth and twentieth centuries appears to have come to an end. Artistic practices today no longer follow any one predominant creed, ethos or movement of invention. An artistic work or performance may take any form, any medium, any genre, and it may combine them in any number of permutations. Further, all categories of cultural production today enjoy more or less equal social prestige, 'high' as well as 'low'. However, value pluralism and value equality across forms and categories of cultural production do not imply that all projects of intersubjective discrimination of value in individual cultural objects are futile or undesirable. Modernity remains the life horizon of all contemporary social life; and in so far as modernity remains this life horizon, it implies possibilities of universally shareable critical determinations of value in objects of experience. Modernity implies that communication about value in art and the public good is possible and desirable. Although there can be multiple competing conceptions of this public good, value pluralism does not preclude possibilities of transcultural critical dialogue about the ends of art and about the ends of social and political life in general.

We may conclude that the task of social-theoretic thinking about the arts is to seek ways of resolving these five antinomies. It is to seek ways of generating intersubjectively defensible conceptions of the relation of value-distanciating sociological analysis to value-affirming aesthetic appraisal and value-affirming social and political philosophy and practice.

Further Reading

The following titles are a small selection of further guides to topics and theorists, including some classic texts. The full list of cited texts follows under 'References'.

CHAPTER 1: CONCEPTIONS AND APPROACHES

H. Becker, *Art Worlds* (Berkeley: University of California Press, 1982).
I. Edwards (ed.), *Art and its Histories* (Buckingham: Open University Press, 1999).
O. Hanfling (ed.), *Philosophical Aesthetics: An Introduction* (Oxford: Blackwell, 1992).
C. Harrison and P. Wood (eds), *Art in Theory, 1900–1990: An Anthology of Changing Ideas* (Oxford: Blackwell, 1992).
W. Lepenies, *Between Literature and Science: The Rise of Sociology*, trans. R. J. Hollingdale (Cambridge: Cambridge University Press, 1988).
J. Tanner (ed.), *The Sociology of Art: A Reader* (London: Routledge, 2003).
V. Zolberg, *Constructing a Sociology of the Arts* (Cambridge: Cambridge University Press, 1990).

CHAPTER 2: AESTHETIC VALUE AND POLITICAL VALUE

J. Berger, *Ways of Seeing* (London: Penguin, 1972).
W. Chadwick, *Women, Art, and Society* (London: Thames and Hudson, 1990).
T. Eagleton, *Literary Theory: An Introduction* (Oxford: Blackwell, 1983).
S. Hiller (ed.), *The Myth of Primitivism: Perspectives on Art* (London: Routledge, 1991).
L. Nochlin, *Women, Art, and Power and Other Essays* (London: Thames and Hudson, 1989).

G. Pollock, *Differencing the Canon: Feminist Desire and the Writing of Art's Histories* (London: Routledge, 1999).

J. Wolff, *Aesthetics and the Sociology of Art*, 2nd edition, (London: Allen and Unwin, 1993).

CHAPTER 3: PRODUCTION AND SOCIOECONOMIC STRUCTURE

M. Baxandall, *Painting and Experience in Fifteenth-Century Italy* (Oxford: Oxford University Press, 1972).

A. Hauser, *The Social History of Art* (4 vols, London: Routledge, 1951).

A. Rifkin, 'Sociology of Art', in T. Bottomore and W. Outhwaite (eds), *The Blackwell Dictionary of Twentieth Century Social Thought* (Oxford : Blackwell, 1992).

A. Swingewood, *Sociological Poetics and Aesthetic Theory* (London: Macmillan, 1986).

H. White and C. White, *Canvases and Careers* (New York: John Wiley, 1965).

R. Witkin, *Art and Social Structure* (Cambridge: Polity, 1995).

J. Wolff, *The Social Production of Art* (London: Macmillan, 1981).

CHAPTER 4: CONSUMPTION AND AESTHETIC AUTONOMY

M. H. Abrams, *How to Do Things with Texts: Essays in Criticism and Critical Theory* (New York: Norton, 1989).

P. Bourdieu, *Distinction: A Social Critique of the Judgement of Taste*, trans. R. Nice (London: Routledge, 1984).

P. Bourdieu, *The Rules of Art*, trans. R. Nice (Cambridge: Polity, 1996).

P. Bourdieu, *The Field of Cultural Produciton*, ed. R. Johnson (Cambridge: Polity, 1993).

H. Gans, *Popular Culture and High Culture: An Analysis and Evaluation of Taste*, 2nd edn (New York: Basic Books, 1999).

C. Harrison, P. Wood and J. Gaiger (eds), *Art in Theory, 1648–1815: An Anthology of Changing Ideas* (Oxford: Blackwell, 2000).

M. Lamont and M. Fournier (eds), *Cultivating Differences: Symbolic Boundaries and the Making of Inequality* (Chicago: Chicago University Press, 1992).

CHAPTER 5: IDEOLOGY AND UTOPIA

E. Bloch et al. (eds), *Aesthetics and Politics: The Classic Texts of German Marxism* (London: Verso, 1977).

H. Broch, *Hugo von Hofmannsthal and his Time: The European Imagination, 1860–1920*, trans. M. P. Steinberg (Chicago: Chicago University Press, 1984).

S. Bungay, *Beauty and Truth: A Study of Hegel's Aesthetics* (Oxford: Oxford University Press, 1987).
T. Eagleton, *The Ideology of the Aesthetic* (Oxford: Blackwell, 1990).
C. Harrison, P. Wood and J. Gaiger (eds), *Art in Theory, 1815–1900: An Anthology of Changing Ideas* (Oxford: Blackwell, 1998).
M. Jay, *The Dialectical Imagination: A History of the Frankfurt School and the Institute for Social Research, 1923–1950* (Berkeley: University of California Press, 1973).
H. Marcuse, *Eros and Civilization: A Philosophical Inquiry into Freud* (London: Routledge, 1956).

CHAPTER 6: MODERNITY AND MODERNISM

J. M. Bernstein (ed.), *The Frankfurt School: Critical Assessments* (4 vols, London: Routledge, 1994).
D. Frisby, *Sociological Impressionism: A Reassessment of Georg Simmel's Social Theory* (London: Heinemann, 1981).
D. Frisby, *Fragments of Modernity: Theories of Modernity in the Work of Simmel, Kracauer and Benjamin* (Cambridge: Polity, 1985).
W. Haftmann, *Painting in the Twentieth Century*, trans. R. Mannheim and J. Seligman (2 vols, London: Lund Humphries, 1965).
R. Hughes, *The Shock of the New: Art and the Century of Change*, 2nd edn (London: Thames and Hudson, 1991).
R. Wolin, *Walter Benjamin: An Aesthetic of Redemption* (New York: Columbia University Press, 1982).
L. Zuidervaart, *Adorno's Aesthetic Theory: The Redemption of Illusion* (Cambridge, Mass.: MIT Press, 1991).

CHAPTER 7: POSTMODERNISM AND AFTER

G. Delanty, *Modernity and Postmodernity* (Sage: London, 2000).
H. Foster (ed.), *The Anti-Aesthetic: Essays on Postmodern Culture* (London: Pluto, 1985).
D. Harvey, *The Condition of Postmodernity* (Oxford: Blackwell, 1990).
A. Huyssen, *After the Great Divide: Modernism, Mass Culture, Postmodernism* (Bloomington: Indiana University Press, 1986).
F. Jameson, *Postmodernism, or, The Cultural Logic of Late Capitalism* (London: Verso, 1991).
R. Krauss, *The Orginality of the Avant-Garde and Other Modernist Myths* (Cambridge, Mass.: MIT Press, 1985).
C.-T. Wu, *Privatizing Culture: Corporate Intervention in the Arts since the 1980s* (London: Verso, 2002).

References

Abrams, M. H. (1989) 'Art-As-Such: The Sociology of Modern Aesthetics', in Abrams, *How to Do Things with Texts: Essays in Criticism and Critical Theory*. New York: Norton.

Adorno, T. W. (1973) *Negative Dialectics*, trans. F. Ashton. London: Routledge.

—— (1974) *Minima Moralia*, trans. E. Jephcott. London: Verso.

—— (1977) 'Letters to Walter Benjamin', in F. Jameson (ed.), *Aesthetics and Politics: The Key Texts of the Classic Debate within German Marxism*. London: Verso.

—— (1981) *In Search of Wagner*, trans. R. Livingstone. London: Verso.

—— (1991) *The Culture Industry*, ed. J. M. Bernstein. London: Routledge.

—— (1992) 'The Essay as Form', in Adorno, *Notes to Literature*, vol. 1, trans. S. W. Nicholsen. New York: Columbia University Press.

—— (1997) *Aesthetic Theory*, trans. R. Hullot-Kentor. Minneapolis: University of Minnesota Press.

Adorno, T. W. and Horkheimer, M. (1979) *Dialectic of Enlightenment*, trans. J. Cumming. London: Verso.

Adorno, T. W., Aron, B., Levinson, M. H. and Morrow, W. (1950) *The Authoritarian Personality*. New York: Harper and Row.

Antal, F. (1948) *Florentine Painting and its Social Background*. London: Routledge.

Arendt, H. (1973) *The Origins of Totalitarianism*. New York: Harcourt Brace.

Aristotle (1982) *The Poetics*, trans. J. Hutton. New York: Norton.

Bakhtin, M. (1968) *Rabelais and his World*, trans. H. Iswolsky. Cambridge, Mass.: MIT Press.

—— (1981) *The Dialogic Imagination*, ed. M. Holquist. Austin: University of Texas Press.

—— (1996) *Speech Genres and Other Late Essays*, trans. V. McGee. Austin: University of Texas Press.

Barthes, R. (1972) *Mythologies*, trans. A. Lavers. London: Cape.

Bataille, G. (2001) *Eroticism*, trans. M. Dalwood. London: Penguin.

Baudelaire, C. (1995) *The Painter of Modern Life and Other Essays*, trans. J. Mayne. London: Phaidon.

Baudrillard, J. (1985) 'The Ecstasy of Communication', in H. Foster (ed.), *The Anti-Aesthetic*. London: Pluto Press.

—— (1997) *Art and Artefact*, ed. N. Zurbrugg. London: Sage.

—— (2001) *Selected Writings*, 2nd edn, ed. M. Poster. Cambridge: Polity.

Baxandall, M. (1972) *Painting and Experience in Fifteenth-Century Italy*. Oxford: Oxford University Press.

Beck, U., Giddens, A. and Lash, S. (1994) *Reflexive Modernization*. Cambridge: Polity.

Becker, H. (1982) *Art Worlds*. Berkeley: University of California Press.

Bell, D. (1976) *The Cultural Contradictions of Capitalism*. New York: Basic Books.

Benjamin, W. (1973a) 'The Task of the Translator', in Benjamin, *Illuminations*, ed. H. Arendt, trans. H. Zohn. London: Fontana.

—— (1973b) 'Theses on the Philosophy of History', in Benjamin, *Illuminations*, ed. H. Arendt, trans. H. Zohn. London: Fontana.

—— (1973c) 'The Work of Art in the Age of Mechanical Reproduction', in Benjamin, *Illuminations*, ed. H. Arendt, trans. H. Zohn. London: Fontana.

—— (1977) *The Origin of German Tragic Drama*, trans. J. Osborne. London: Verso.

—— (1999) *The Arcades Project*, trans. H. Eiland and K. McLaughlin. Cambridge, Mass.: Harvard University Press.

Berger, J. (1972) *Ways of Seeing*. London: Penguin.

Berman, M. (1982) *All That is Solid Melts into Air*. London: Simon and Shuster.

Bernstein, J. M. (1991) 'Editor's Introduction', in Theodor Adorno, *The Culture Industry*, ed. J. M. Bernstein. London: Routledge.

—— (1992) *The Fate of Art: Aesthetic Alienation from Kant to Derrida and Adorno*. Cambridge: Polity.

Blau, J. (1989) *The Shape of Culture*. Cambridge: Cambridge University Press.

Bloch, E. (1986) *The Principle of Hope*, trans. N. Plaice, S. Plaice and P. Knight. 3 vols, Oxford: Blackwell.

Boas, F. (1955) *Primitive Art*. New York: Dover.

Boltanski, L. and Chiapello, E. (1999) *Le Nouvel Esprit du capitalisme*. Paris: Gallimard.

Boltanski, L. and Thévenot, L. (1991) *De la justification*. Paris: Gallimard.

Borzello, F. and Rees, A. L. (1986) *The New Art History*. London: Camden Press.

Boudon, R. (1999) *Le Sens des valeurs*. Paris: Presses Universitaires de France.

Bourdieu, P. (1980) *Questions de sociologie*. Paris: Minuit.

—— (1984) *Distinction: A Social Critique of the Judgement of Taste*, trans. R. Nice. London: Routledge.

—— (1990) *The Logic of Practice*, trans. R. Nice. Cambridge: Polity.
—— (1993) *The Field of Cultural Production*, ed. R. Johnson. Cambridge: Polity.
—— (1996) *The Rules of Art*, trans. R. Nice. Cambridge: Polity.
Bourdieu, P. and Darbel, A. (1991) *The Love of Art*, trans. C. Beattie and N. Merriman. Cambridge: Polity.
Bourdieu, P. and Passeron, J.-C. (1979) *The Inheritors: French Students and their Relation to Culture*, trans. R. Nice. Chicago: Chicago University Press.
Bourdieu, P., Boltanski, L., Castel, R. and Chamboredon, J-C. (1990) *Photography: A Middle-Brow Art*. Cambridge: Polity.
Brecht, B. (1967) *Schriften zur Kunst und Literatur*. Frankfurt am Main: Suhrkamp.
Buci-Glucksmann, C. (1994) *Baroque Reason: The Aesthetics of Modernity*, trans. P. Camiller. London: Sage.
Bungay, S. (1987) *Beauty and Truth: A Study of Hegel's Aesthetics*. Oxford: Oxford University Press.
Bürger, P. (1984) *Theory of the Avant-Garde*, trans. M. Shaw. Minneapolis: University of Minnesota Press.
Canetti, E. (1984) *Crowds and Power*, trans. C. Stewart. New York: Farrar Strauss Giroux.
Cassirer, E. (1953) *The Philosophy of Symbolic Forms*, trans. R. Mannheim. 3 vols, New Haven: Yale University Press.
Castoriadis, C. (1987) *The Imaginary Institution of Society*, trans. K. Blamey. Cambridge: Polity.
Certeau, M. de (1984) *The Practice of Everyday Life*, trans. S. Rendall. Berkeley: University of California Press.
Chadwick, W. (1990) *Women, Art, and Society*. London: Thames and Hudson.
Chiapello, E. (1998) *Artistes versus managers*. Paris: Métaillé.
Clark, P. P. (1987) *Literary France: The Making of a Culture*. Berkeley: University of California Press.
Clark, T. J. (1973) *The Image of the People: Gustave Courbet and the 1848 Revolution*. London: Thames and Hudson.
—— (1985) *The Painting of Modern Life: Paris in the Art of Manet and his Followers*. London: Thames and Hudson.
—— (1999) *Farewell to an Idea: Episodes from a History of Modernism*. New Haven: Yale University Press.
Coote, J. and Shelton, A. (eds) (1992) *Anthropology, Art and Aesthetics*. Oxford: Oxford University Press.
Crane, D. (1987) *The Transformation of the Avant-Garde: The New York Art World 1940–85*. Chicago: University of Chicago Press.
Danto, A. (1964) 'The Artworld', *Journal of Philosophy* 61(19): 571–84.
—— (1987) 'Approaching the End of Art', in Danto, *The State of the Art*. New York: Prentice Hall.
—— (1991) 'Narratives of the End of Art', in Danto, *Encounters and Reflections: Art in the Historical Present*. New York: Noonday Press.

—— (1997) *After the End of Art: Contemporary Art and the Pale of History.* Princeton: Princeton University Press.

Deleuze, G. (1981) *Francis Bacon. Logique de la sensation.* Paris: Éditions de la Différence.

—— (1986–9) *Cinema 1: The Movement-Image* and *Cinema 2: The Time-Image,* trans. H. Tomlinson and B. Habberjam. 2 vols, Minneapolis: University of Minnesota Press.

Deleuze, G. and Guattari, F. (1987) *A Thousand Plateaus: Capitalism and Schizophrenia,* trans. B. Massumi. Minneapolis: University of Minnesota Press.

DeNora, T. (1995) *Beethoven and the Construction of Genius: Musical Politics in Vienna, 1792–1803.* Berkeley: University of California Press.

Derrida, J. (1987) *The Truth in Painting,* trans. G. Bennington and I. McLeod. Chicago: Chicago University Press.

Dewey, J. (1934) *Art as Experience.* London: Allen and Unwin.

Dickie, G. (1974) *Art and the Aesthetic.* New York: Cornell University Press.

DiMaggio, P. (1982) 'Cultural Entrepreneurship in 19th Century Boston', *Media, Culture and Society* 4: 33–50.

—— (1987) 'Classification in Art', *American Sociological Review* 52: 440–55.

DiMaggio, P. and Useem, M. (1978) 'Social Class and Arts Consumption', *Theory and Society* 5: 141–62.

Dollimore, M. and Sinfield, A. (eds) (1985) *Political Shakespeare: Essays in Cultural Materialism.* Manchester: Manchester University Press.

Dubin, S. (1987) *Bureaucratizing the Muse: Public Funds and the Cultural Worker.* Chicago: Chicago University Press.

Durkheim, É. (1995) *The Elementary Forms of Religious Life,* trans. K. Fields. New York: Free Press.

Duve, T. de (1996) *Kant after Duchamp.* Cambridge, Mass.: MIT Press.

Duvenage, P. (2003) *Habermas and Aesthetics: The Limits of Communicative Reason.* Cambridge: Polity.

Duvignaud, J. (1972) *The Sociology of Art.* London: Paladin.

Eagleton, T. (1983) *Literary Theory: An Introduction.* Oxford: Blackwell.

—— (1990) *The Ideology of the Aesthetic.* Oxford: Blackwell.

Elias, N. (1987) *Involvement and Detachment,* trans. E. Jephcott. Oxford: Blackwell.

—— (1993) *Mozart: Portrait of a Genius,* trans. E. Jephcott. Berkeley: University of California Press.

—— (1996) *The Germans,* trans. E. Dunning and S. Mennell. Cambridge: Polity.

Featherstone, M. (1991) *Consumer Culture and Postmodernism.* London: Sage.

Foster, H. (ed.) (1985) *The Anti-Aesthetic: Essays on Postmodern Culture.* London: Pluto.

Foucault, M. (1998) *The Essential Works of Michel Foucault 1954–84*, vol. 2: *Aesthetics*, ed. J. Faubion. London: Penguin.

Francastel, P. (1956) *Art et technique aux XIX et XX siècles*. Paris: Gallimard.

—— (1970) *Études de sociologie de l'art*. Paris: Denoël.

Freud, S. (1985) *Art and Literature*, vol. 14 of *The Penguin Freud Library*, ed. J. Strachey. London: Penguin.

Fumaroli, M. (1992) *L'État culturel. Essai sur une religion moderne*. Paris: Fallois.

Gadamer, H.-G. (1975) *Truth and Method*, trans. G. Barden and J. Cumming. London: Sheed and Ward.

—— (1986) *The Relevance of the Beautiful and Other Essays*, trans. N. Walker. Cambridge: Cambridge University Press.

Gans, H. (1999) *Popular Culture and High Culture: An Analysis and Evaluation of Taste*, 2nd edn. New York: Basic Books.

Geertz, C. (1973) *The Interpretation of Cultures*. New York: Basic Books.

—— (1983) 'Art as a Cultural System', in Geertz, *Local Knowledge*. New York: Basic Books.

Gell, A. (1998) *Art and Agency: An Anthropological Theory*. Oxford: Oxford University Press.

Giddens, A. (1984) *The Constitution of Society: Outline of the Theory of Structuration*. Cambridge: Polity.

Ginsburg, C. (1985) *The Enigma of Piero: Piero della Francesca*, trans. M. Ryle and K. Soper. London: Verso.

Goldmann, L. (1964) *The Hidden God: A Study of Tragic Vision in the Pensées of Pascal and the Tragedies of Racine*, trans. P. Thody. London: Routledge.

—— (1970) 'The Sociology of Literature: Status and Problems of Method', in M. C. Albrecht, J. H. Barnett and M. Griff (eds), *The Sociology of Art and Literature: A Reader*. New York: Praeger.

Gombrich, E. (1960) *Art and Illusion: A Study in the Psychology of Pictorial Representation*. London: Phaidon.

Goodman, N. (1976) *Languages of Art: An Approach to a Theory of Symbols*. Indianapolis: Hackett.

—— (1978) *Ways of Worldmaking*. Hassocks: Harvester.

Greenberg, C. (1961) *Art and Culture: Critical Essays*. Boston: Beacon.

—— (1993) 'Modernist Painting', in *Clement Greenberg: Collected Essays and Criticism*, vol. 4: *Modernism with a Vengeance*, ed. J. O'Brian. Chicago: Chicago University Press.

Greenblatt, S. and Gallagher, C. (eds) (2000) *Practicing New Historicism*. Chicago: Chicago University Press.

Griswold, W. (1986) *Renaissance Revivals: City Comedy and Revenge Tragedy in the London Theatre, 1576–1980*. Chicago: Chicago University Press.

Habermas, J. (1984) *The Theory of Communicative Action*, vol. 1: *Reason and the Rationalization of Society*, trans. T. McCarthy. Cambridge: Polity.

—— (1987) *The Philosophical Discourse of Modernity*, trans. F. Lawrence. Cambridge: Polity.

—— (1988) *On the Logic of the Social Sciences*, trans. S. Weber Nicholsen and J. Stark. Cambridge, Mass.: MIT Press.

—— (1996) 'The Unfinished Project of Modernity', in M. Passerin d'Entrèves and S. Benhabib (eds), *Habermas and the Unfinished Project of Modernity*. Cambridge: Polity.

Hall, S. (ed.) (1980) *Culture, Media, Language: Working Papers in Cultural Studies, 1972–79*. London: Hutchinson.

Halle, D. (1993) *Inside Culture: Art and Class in the American Home*. Chicago: Chicago University Press.

Hanfling, O. (1992) 'The Problem of Definition', in Hanfling (ed.), *Philosophical Aesthetics: An Introduction*. Oxford: Blackwell.

Harrington, A. (2001) 'New German Aesthetic Theory', *Radical Philosophy* 109: 6–13.

Harvey, D. (1990) *The Condition of Postmodernity*. Oxford: Blackwell.

Hauser, A. (1951) *The Social History of Art*. 4 vols, London: Routledge.

Hegel, G. W. F. (1991) *Elements of the Philosophy of Right*, trans. H. B. Nisbet. Cambridge: Cambridge University Press.

—— (1993) *Introductory Lectures on Aesthetics*, ed. M. Inwood. London: Penguin.

Hegel, G. W. F., Hölderlin, F. and Schelling, F. W. J. (1996) 'The Oldest Systematic Programme of German Idealism', in F. Beiser (ed.), *The Early Political Writings of the German Romantics*. Cambridge: Cambridge University Press.

Heidegger, M. (1993) 'The Origin of the Work of Art', in *Martin Heidegger: Basic Writings*, ed. D. Farrell Krell. London: Routledge.

Heinrich, N. (1998) *Ce que l'art fait à la sociologie*. Paris: Minuit.

Hennion, A. (1993) *La Passion musicale. Une Sociologie de la mediation*. Paris: Métaillé.

Henrich, D. (1966) 'Kunst und Kunstphilosophie der Gegenwart', in W. Iser (ed.), *Immanente Ästhetik: Ästhetische Reflexion*. Munich: Fink.

—— (2001) *Versuch über Kunst und Leben. Subjectivität, Weltverstehen, Kunst*. Munich: Carl Hanser.

Heywood, I. (1997) *Social Theories of Art: A Critique*. Basingstoke: Macmillan.

Hiller, S. (ed.) (1991) *The Myth of Primitivism: Perspectives on Art*. London: Routledge.

Hobsbawm, E. and Ranger, T. (eds) (1983) *The Invention of Tradition*. Cambridge: Cambridge University Press.

Horkheimer, M. (1972) *Critical Theory: Selected Essays*, trans. M. J. O'Connell. New York: Herder and Herder.

Huyssen, A. (1986) *After the Great Divide: Modernism, Mass Culture, Postmodernism*. Bloomington: Indiana University Press.

Jameson, F. (1984) 'Postmodernism, or, The Cultural Logic of Late Capitalism', *New Left Review* 146: 53–92.

—— (1985) 'Postmodernism and Consumer Society', in H. Foster (ed.), *Postmodern Culture*. London: Pluto.

—— (1991) *Postmodernism, or, The Cultural Logic of Late Capitalism.* London: Verso.

Jauss, H.-R. (1982) *Aesthetic Experience and Literary Hermeneutics,* trans. M. Shaw. Minneapolis: University of Minnesota Press.

Joas, H. (1996) *The Creativity of Action,* trans. J. Gaines and P. Keast. Cambridge: Polity.

Kant, I. (1928) *The Critique of Judgement,* trans. J. C. Meredith. Oxford: Oxford University Press.

Kierkegaard, S. (1944) *Either-Or: A Fragment of Life,* trans. D. F. Swenson, L. Swenson and W. Lowrie. 2 vols, Princeton: Princeton University Press.

Klingender, F. (1968) *Art and the Industrial Revolution.* London: Evelyn, Adams and Mackay.

Koppe, F. (1983) *Grundbegriffe der Ästhetik.* Frankfurt am Main: Suhrkamp.

Koselleck, R. (1985) *Futures Past: On the Semantics of Historical Time,* trans. K. Tribe. Cambridge, Mass.: MIT Press.

Kracauer, S. (1937) *Jacques Offenbach and the Paris of his Time,* trans. G. David and E. Mosbacher. London: Constable.

—— (1947) *From Caligari to Hitler: A Psychological History of the German Film.* London: Denis Dobson.

—— (1960) *Theory of Film: The Redemption of Physical Reality.* Oxford: Oxford University Press.

—— (1971) 'Der Detektivroman. Ein philosophischer Traktat', in Kracauer, *Schriften,* vol. 1. Frankfurt am Main: Suhrkamp.

—— (1995) *The Mass Ornament: Weimar Essays,* trans. T. Y. Levin. Cambridge, Mass.: Harvard University Press.

Krauss, R. (1985) *The Originality of the Avant-Garde and Other Modernist Myths.* Cambridge, Mass.: MIT Press.

Kristeller, P. (1970) 'The Modern System of the Arts', in M. Weitz (ed.), *Problems of Aesthetics.* London: Macmillan.

Kroeber, A. L. (1957) *Style and Civilizations.* New York: Cornell University Press.

Lamont, M. (1992) *Money, Morals, and Manners: The Culture of the French and American Upper-Middle Classes.* Chicago: University of Chicago Press.

Lamont, M. and Fournier, M. (eds) (1992) *Cultivating Differences: Symbolic Boundaries and the Making of Inequality.* Chicago: Chicago University Press.

Larson, M. (1993) *Behind the Postmodern Facade: Architectural Change in Late Twentieth-Century America.* Berkeley: University of California Press.

Lepenies, W. (1988) *Between Literature and Science: The Rise of Sociology,* trans. R. J. Hollingdale. Cambridge: Cambridge University Press.

Levine, L. W. (1988) *Highbrow/Lowbrow: The Emergence of Cultural Hierarchy in America.* Cambridge, Mass.: Harvard University Press.

Löwenthal, L. (1957) *Literature and the Image of Man: Sociological Studies of the European Drama and Novel, 1600–1900.* Boston: Beacon.

Luhmann, N. (2000) *Art as a Social System*, trans. E. Knodt. Stanford: Stanford University Press.

Lukács, G. (1971) *The Theory of the Novel*, trans. A. Bostock. London: Merlin.

Lyotard, J.-F. (1984a) 'An Answer to the Question: What is Postmodernism?' in Lyotard, *The Postmodern Condition*, trans. G. Bennington and B. Massumi. Manchester: Manchester University Press.

—— (1984b) *The Postmodern Condition*, trans. G. Bennington and B. Massumi. Manchester: Manchester University Press.

McGuigan, J. (1996) *Culture and the Public Sphere*. London: Routledge.

Malraux, A. (1967) *Museum Without Walls*, trans. S. Gilbert and F. Price. London: Secker and Warburg.

Mannheim, K. (1991) *Ideology and Utopia*, trans. L. Wirth and E. Shils. London: Routledge.

Marcuse, H. (1956) *Eros and Civilization: A Philosophical Inquiry into Freud*. London: Routledge.

—— (1964) *One-Dimensional Man*. London: Routledge.

—— (1972) *Counter-Revolution and Revolt*. Boston: Beacon.

—— (1978) *The Aesthetic Dimension: Towards a Critique of Marxist Aesthetics*. Boston: Beacon.

Marx, K. (1972) *The Eighteenth Brumaire of Louis Bonaparte*. New York: International Publishers.

—— (1975a) 'A Contribution to the Critique of Hegel's Philosophy of Right', in Marx, *Early Writings*, trans. R. Livingstone and G. Benton. London: Penguin.

—— (1975b) 'Economic and Philosophic Manuscripts', in Marx, *Early Writings*, trans. R. Livingstone and G. Benton. London: Penguin.

Marx, K. and Engels, F. (1965) *The German Ideology*, ed. C. J. Arthur. London: Lawrence and Wishart.

—— (1976) *On Literature and Art*. London: Lawrence and Wishart.

Menger, P.-M. (1983) *Le Paradoxe du musicien. Le Compositeur, le mélomane et l'état dans la société contemporaine*. Paris: Flammarion.

Menger, P.-M. and Ginsburgh, V. A. (eds) (1996) *Economics of the Arts: Selected Essays*. Amsterdam: Elsevier.

Menke, C. (1998) *The Sovereignty of Art: Aesthetic Negativity after Adorno and Derrida*, trans. N. Solomon. Cambridge, Mass.: MIT Press.

Moulin, R. (ed.) (1986) *La Sociologie de l'art*. Paris: Documentation Française.

—— (1987) *The French Art Market*, trans. A. Goldhammer. New Brunswick: Rutgers University Press.

Mulvey, L. (1989) *Visual and Other Pleasures*. London: Macmillan.

Musil, R. (1953–60) *The Man without Qualities*, trans. E. Wilkins and E. Kaiser. 3 vols, London: Secker and Warburg.

Nietzsche, F. (1968) *The Will to Power*, trans. W. Kaufman and R. J. Hollingdale. London: Weidenfeld and Nicolson.

—— (1993) *The Birth of Tragedy out of the Spirit of Music*, trans. S. Whiteside. London: Penguin.

Nisbet, R. (1976) *Sociology as an Art Form*. London: Heinemann.

Nochlin, L. (1989) 'Why Have There Been No Great Women Artists?', in Nochlin, *Women, Art, and Power and Other Essays*. London: Thames and Hudson.

Panofsky, E. (1955) *Meaning in the Visual Arts*. London: Penguin.

Peterson, R. A. (1986) 'The Role of Formal Accountability in the Shift from Impressario to Arts Administrator', in R. Moulin (ed.), *La Sociologie de l'art*. Paris: Documentation Française.

—— (1997) *Creating Country Music: Fabricating Authenticity*. Chicago: Chicago University Press.

Peterson, R. A. and Kern, R. M. (1996) 'Changing Highbrow Taste: From Snob to Omnivore', *American Sociological Review* 61: 900–7.

Peterson, R. A. and Simkus, A. (1992) 'How Musical Tastes Mark Occupational Status Groups', in M. Lamont and M. Fournier (eds). *Cultivating Differences: Symbolic Boundaries and the Making of Inequality*. Chicago: Chicago University Press.

Plekhanov, G. (1953) *Art and Social Life*, trans. A. Rothstein. London: Lawrence and Wishart.

Pollock, G. (1988) *Vision and Difference: Femininity, Feminism and the Histories of Art*. London: Routledge.

—— (1999) *Differencing the Canon: Feminist Desire and the Writing of Art's Histories*. London: Routledge.

Price, S. (1989) *Primitive Art in Civilized Places*. Chicago: Chicago University Press.

Rancières, J. (2001) *La Fable cinématographique*. Paris: Seuil.

Raphael, M. (1968) *The Demands of Art: An Empirical Theory of Art*. London: Routledge.

Rees, A. L. and Borzello, F. (eds) (1986) *The New Art History*. London: Camden Press.

Ricoeur, P. (1970) *Freud and Philosophy: An Essay on Interpretation*, trans. D. Savage. New Haven: Yale University Press.

—— (1985–8) *Time and Narrative*, trans. K. Blamey, K. McLaughlin and D. Pellauer. 3 vols, Chicago: Chicago University Press.

Rifkin, A. (1992) 'Sociology of Art', in T. Bottomore and W. Outhwaite (eds), *The Blackwell Dictionary of Twentieth Century Social Thought*. Oxford: Blackwell.

Ritzer, G. (1993) *The McDonaldization of Society*. Thousand Oaks: Pine Forge.

Rose, G. (1978) *The Melancholy Science: An Introduction to the Thought of Theodor W. Adorno*. London: Macmillan.

Rose, J. (1986) *Sexuality and the Field of Vision*. London: Verso.

Ruskin, J. (1991) *Selected Writings*, ed. K. Clarke. London: Penguin.

Said, E. (1978) *Orientalism*. London: Routledge.

Schama, S. (1987) *The Embarrassment of Riches: An Interpretation of Dutch Culture in the Golden Age*. London: Collins.

Schapiro, M. (1973) 'The Social Bases of Art', in Schapiro, *Words and Pictures: On the Literal and the Symbolic in the Illustration of a Text*. The Hague: Mouton.

Seel, M. (1985) *Die Kunst der Entzweiung. Zum Begriff der ästhetischen Rationalität*. Frankfurt am Main: Suhrkamp.

Sevänen, E. (2001) 'Art as an Autopoietic Sub-system of Modern Society: A Critical Analysis of the Concepts of Art and Autopoietic Systems in Luhmann's Late Production', *Theory, Culture and Society* 18(1): 75–103.

Simmel, G. (1978) *The Philosophy of Money*, trans. T. Bottomore, D. Frisby and K. Mengelberg. London: Routledge.

—— (1997) *Simmel on Culture*, ed. D. Frisby and M. Featherstone. London: Sage.

—— (2000) 'Gesetzmässigkeit im Kunstwerk', in *Georg Simmel Gesamtausgabe*, vol. 13. Frankfurt am Main: Suhrkamp.

Sloterdijk, P. (1988) *Critique of Cynical Reason*, trans. M. Eldred. Minneapolis: University of Minnesota Press.

Sorokin, P. (1985) *Social and Cultural Dynamics*. New Brunswick: Transaction.

Stallabrass, J. (1999) *High Art Lite: British Art in the 1990s*. London: Verso.

Stendhal (1975) *Love*, trans. G. Sale and S. Sale. London: Penguin.

Swingewood, A. (1986) *Sociological Poetics and Aesthetic Theory*. London: Macmillan.

Tolstoy, L. (1995) *What Is Art?* trans. R. Pevear and L. Volokhansky. London: Penguin.

Veblen, T. (1994) *Theory of the Leisure Class*. New York: Dover.

Wagner, P. (1994) *A Sociology of Modernity: Liberty and Discipline*. London: Routledge.

Watt, I. (1957) *The Rise of the Novel*. Cambridge: Cambridge University Press.

—— (1996) *Myths of Modern Individualism*. Cambridge: Cambridge University Press.

Weber, M. (1930) *The Protestant Ethic and the Spirit of Capitalism*, trans. T. Parsons. London: Routledge.

—— (1948a) 'Religious Rejections of the World and their Directions' (otherwise known as 'Intermediate Reflections'), in Weber, *From Max Weber*, ed. H. Gerth and C. Wright Mills. London: Routledge.

—— (1948b) 'Science as a Vocation', in Weber, *From Max Weber*, ed. H. Gerth and C. Wright Mills. London: Routledge.

—— (1949) *Max Weber: The Methodology of the Social Sciences*, ed. E. Shils and H. Finch. Glencoe: Free Press.

—— (1958) *The Rational and Social Foundations of Music*, trans. D. Martindale, J. Riedel and G. Neuwirth. Carbondale: Southern Illinois University Press.

—— (1978) *Economy and Society: An Outline of Interpretive Sociology*, ed. G. Roth and C. Wittich. Berkeley: University of California Press.

Wellmer, A. (1992) *The Persistence of Modernity*, trans. D. Midgeley. Cambridge: Polity.

Welsch, W. (1997) *Undoing Aesthetics*, trans. A. Inkpin. London: Sage.

White, H. (1975) *Metahistory: The Historical Imagination in Nineteenth Century Europe*. Baltimore: Johns Hopkins University Press.

White, H. and White, C. (1965) *Canvases and Careers*. New York: John Wiley.

Williams, R. (1981) *Culture*. London: Fontana.

Witkin, R. (1995) *Art and Social Structure*. Cambridge: Polity.

Wittgenstein, L. (1953) *Philosophical Investigations*, trans. E. Anscombe. Oxford: Blackwell.

Wolff, J. (1981) *The Social Production of Art*. London: Macmillan.

—— (1993) *Aesthetics and the Sociology of Art*, 2nd edn. London: Allen and Unwin.

Wölfflin, H. (1950) *The Principles of Art History*, trans. M. D. Hottinger. New York: Dover.

Wollheim, R. (1970) 'Sociological Explanations of the Arts', in M. C. Albrecht, J. H. Barnett and M. Griff (eds), *The Sociology of Art and Literature: A Reader*. New York: Praeger.

—— (1980) 'The Institutional Theory of Art', in Wollheim, *Art and its Objects*, 2nd edn. Cambridge: Cambridge University Press.

Worringer, W. (1953) *Abstraction and Empathy: A Contribution to the Psychology of Style*, trans. M. Bullock. London: Routledge.

Wu, C.-T. (2002) *Privatising Culture: Corporate Intervention in the Arts since the 1980s*. London: Verso.

Zolberg, V. (1990) *Constructing a Sociology of the Arts*. Cambridge: Cambridge University Press.

Zuidervaart, L. (1991) *Adorno's Aesthetic Theory: The Redemption of Illusion*. Cambridge, Mass.: MIT Press.

Index

Index

fascism 131, 133

feminism: art criticism 44–9, 52; male gaze 45; sexual stereotypes 45; traditional categories and 47–8

Feuerbach, Ludwig 126

Fielding, Henry: *Tom Jones* 77

film: culture industry of 167–9; Kracauer's critical study of 162–4

The Flagellation (Piero della Francesca) 66, 67, 74

Flaubert, Gustave: *Sentimental Education* 98, 127

Les fleurs du mal (Baudelaire) 144

Florence 62

formalism 79

Foucault, Michel: *The History of Sexuality* 188; representation and language 186–8

Fountain (Duchamp) 23–4, *24*, 37

France: *Annales* school 30–1; art market 80; *l'art pour l'art* 91

Frankfurt School 197; critique of *Massenkultur* 169–75; democracy versus populism 173–4; founding members of 164; Habermas and 181–2

freedom: German idealism and 118–19

Freud, Sigmund: *Civilisation and its Discontents* 138, 139; on creativity and art 138–9; *The Future of an Illusion* 138; 'hermeneutics of suspicion' 137–8; *The Interpretation of Dreams* 138; *Jokes and their Relation to the Unconscious* 138; *Moses and Monotheism* 138–9

From Caligari to Hitler: A Psychological History of German film (Kracauer) 159, 162–3

Fromm, Erich 139

Fumaroli, Marc 203

The Future of an Illusion (Freud) 138

Gadamer, Hans-Georg 123; Heidegger and 179–81; *Truth and Method* 179

Gainsborough, Thomas: *Mr and Mrs Andrews* 42

Gans, H. 100, 170

Gauguin, Paul 50

Geertz, Clifford 6; 'Art as a Cultural System' 26–7

Gehry, Frank 194

Gell, Alfred: *Art and Agency* 27–8

The Genealogy of Morals (Nietzsche) 136

German idealism 112; freedom and art 117–19; Hegel and 121–4; reappraisals of 181; Schelling's mind and matter 120; Schiller on aesthetic education 119–20

The German Ideology (Marx and Engels) 124

Germany 162–3

Gershwin, George: *Rhapsody in Blue* 95–6

Giddens, Anthony 62, 196–7

globalization: corporate funding 201–3; cultural 201; neoliberal discourse 204; social protest of art 205–6

Goethe, Johann Wolfgang von: *Elective Affinities* 156; *Faust* 149

Goldmann, Lucien 59

Gombrich, Ernst: *Art and Illusion* 12; *The Story of Art* 40

Goodman, Nelson 12, 198

Gramsci, Antonio 20

The Great Tradition (Leavis) 40

Greek culture: freedom and 122; mimesis 11; myth and 123, 138; Plato on beauty 10; *technē* 10; Witkin on art of 69–70

Greenberg, Clement 191, 192

Gropius, Walter 92

Malraux, André: *museé imaginaire* 50–1
Mandel, Ernest 195
Mann, Thomas 170; *Tonio Kröger* 205
Mannheim, Karl: *Ideology and Utopia* 117
Marcuse, Herbert 164, 166; *Eros and Civilisation* 139–40; *One-Dimensional Man* 139–40
Marx, Karl: all that is solid 146; on art 124–6; 'Contribution to the Critique of Hegel's Philosophy of Right' 125; *Economic and Philosophic Manuscripts of 1844* 125; on Feuerbach 126; *The German Ideology* (with Engels) 124; 'hermeneutics of suspicion' 137–8; materialist critique 112
Marxism 6; class and art production 18–19; class structure and 58–63; critical theorists and 141; dialectical 113; diversity of expression 60–1; ideology of the aesthetic 93–4; individual agency and 61–3; social history of art 17–19, 28; Soviet bloc arts support 78–9; use value and exchange value 151 see also socialist criticism
mass media: artists' relationship with 203–4; culture industry 168; Kracauer on 161
'The Mass Ornament' (Kracauer) 161
The Mastersingers of Nuremberg (Wagner) 134
materialism, cultural 6
Mauss, Marcel 30
Mayer, Carl: *Dr Caligari's Cabinet* 162
The Meaning of Contemporary Realism (Lukács) 128
Memling, Hans: *Vanity* 46

Las Meninas (Velázquez) *187*, 187–8
Menke, Christoph 197, 198
metaphysics 31; beauty 9–10; German idealism 70–1; imitation of nature 10–12
'The Metropolis and Mental Life' (Simmel) 151
Michelangelo 72
mimesis: imitation of nature 10–12
Mitterrand, François 203
modernism 175–6, 206; antinomy with postmodernism 209; defined 142, 143; reaction against 191; reaction to mass culture 191–2
modernity 175–6; Baudelaire and 142–6; change and complexity 152–3; communication and 209; defined 142, 144; Habermas on 181–3; Heidegger on 179; postmodernism and 143; reflexivity 196–7; time and complexity 144–6; triumph of 196
money: creation and destruction of value and 151–2
Montesquieu, Charles Louis de Secondat 14
Morris, William 92
Moses and Monotheism (Freud) 138–9
Moulin, R. 80
Mozart, Wolfgang Amadeus 74
Mr and Mrs Andrews (Gainsborough) 42
Munch, Edvard: *The Scream* 195
Museum of Modern Art 80
music: Adorno on jazz 171–2; German *Lieder* 88; opera 75; patronage 72; Weber on rationalization of 146–7
Musil, Robert 145
The Mysteries of Paris (Sue) 18
mysticism 131